D0778441

Rufus Robbins. Courtesy of Richard Robbins.

THROUGH ORDINARY EYES

THE CIVIL WAR CORRESPONDENCE OF RUFUS ROBBINS, PRIVATE, 7TH REGIMENT, MASSACHUSETTS VOLUNTEERS

EDITED WITH AN INTRODUCTION BY
ELLA JANE BRUEN
BRIAN M. FITZGIBBONS

JON WAKELYN, ADVISORY EDITOR

University of Nebraska Press
Lincoln and London

Through Ordinary Eyes: The Civil War Correspondence of Rufus Robbins, Private, 7th Regiment, Massachusetts Volunteers by Ella Jane Bruen and Brian M. Fitzgibbons, originally published by Praeger, an imprint of Greenwood Publishing Group, Inc., Westport CT, USA. Copyright © 2000 by Ella Jane Bruen and Brian M. Fitzgibbons. Published in paperback by arrangement with Greenwood Publishing Group, Inc. All rights reserved. Manufactured in the United States of America

∞

First Nebraska paperback printing: 2005

The editors gratefully acknowledge permission for the use of the following material: The letters written during the years 1861–1863 to and by Rufus Robbins Jr. and members of his family are reprinted by permission of Richard Robbins.

Library of Congress Cataloging-in-Publication Data
Robbins, Rufus, 1828–1863.
Through ordinary eyes: the Civil War correspondence of Rufus Robbins, private, 7th Regiment, Massachusetts Volunteers / edited and with an introduction by Ella Jane Bruen and Brian M. Fitzgibbons; John Wakelyn, advisory editor.
p.   cm.
Originally published: Westport, CT: Praeger, 2000.
Includes bibliographical references and index.
ISBN 0-8032-9006-3 (pbk.: alk. paper)
1. Robbins, Rufus, 1828–1863—Correspondence.   2. United States. Army. Massachusetts Infantry Regiment, 7th (1861–1864)   3. Massachusetts—History—Civil War, 1861–1865—Personal narratives.   4. United States—History—Civil War, 1861–1865—Personal narratives.   5. Robbins family—Correspondence.   6. Soldiers—Massachusetts—Whitman—Correspondence.   7. Whitman (Mass.)—Biography.   I. Bruen, Ella Jane. II. Fitzgibbons, Brian M.   III. Title.
E513.57th .R63   2005
973.7'444—dc22   2004025468

To
Daniel J. Reagan
First Sergeant, Company I
Twenty-second Massachusetts Volunteer Infantry
A Comrade in Arms

CONTENTS

Illustrations follow page 104.

PREFACE

Rufus Robbins was a native of South Abington (now Whitman), Massachusetts. He was a soldier in the Seventh Massachusetts Volunteer Infantry Regiment and was among the first to answer President Lincoln's call for volunteers to suppress the rebellion.

The correspondence of Rufus Robbins and his family members provides important insights into the lives of an ordinary Union soldier and those left behind. This collection is highly unusual in that we have an extensive, two-way exchange of letters. Articulate, often graphic and witty, the letters provide a highly personalized view of what life was like for a Union soldier as well as what civilian life was like back home.

Although more has been written on the military aspects of the American Civil War than on any other war in history, both professional researchers and amateur enthusiasts never have had enough material. And now, there is a growing interest in the more ordinary aspects of those times and events to supplement our understanding of the political and military leaders and of the strategies and tactics of battles. These letters contribute significantly toward that end.

On the personal side, Rufus' letters demonstrate the depth of his character. Showing through quite clearly are the maturity, confidence, and likableness of the man. As the war progresses, we see

Rufus' belief in the righteousness of the Union's cause, his confidence in God, and his somewhat naive simplicity gradually replaced with a more realistic idealism. Yet perhaps what stands out above all other qualities is Rufus' resiliency—through the early months of training, through the boredom of winter camp, through the later months in battle, and through his struggle with disease. His observations as a soldier and his remembrances of home are especially noteworthy.

The letters from Rufus' family members provide important insights into life on the home front. The ever-present worry and concern for his well-being; his brothers' discussions of sewing army boots, including a detailed description of one of Edwin's inventions; his sister's reports about her farm in Maine, her husband's intentions to enlist, and the activities of her young children; his parents' and others' comments about life in the village of South Abington and on the farms; his cousin's humorous account of a trip to the beaches at Marshfield—these all contribute to a more complete understanding of the lives of those left behind by an ordinary Massachusetts soldier.

Rufus also reports on matters distinctly military: picket and fatigue duty; Provo guard; life in winter quarters; building barracks, forts, entrenchments, breastworks, and corduroy roads; drills; target practice; camp games, including football; camp visits by "Old Abe"; the soldier's food; the peninsula campaign and other battles; military equipment and clothing; military hospitals; his perceptions of the "rebs"; his encounters with Negroes; parades; relations with sutlers; Thanksgiving festivities; the needs of "Uncle Sam"; and how he came to view the uniform George Washington had worn when he resigned his Revolutionary War commission at Annapolis.

For readers especially interested in the military aspects of Rufus' career, we have provided maps and a chronology of the Seventh Massachusetts Regiment. In addition, we have added a letter from George Reed, captain of Rufus' company, that details a major engagement during the Seven Days' Battle.

We need to note some conventions we have adopted in presenting these letters to facilitate reading by the modern reader. Often the writers omit punctuation, such as a comma or a period at the end of a sentence. Where this is the case, we have added the appropriate punctuation without indicating this to the reader. Sometimes there are grammatical errors other than those of punctuation; we have not corrected those. Where a writer uses abbreviations, we usually have spelled the words. Where a writer uses a numeral, we often have spelled the word. Although we generally have used modern spellings where appropriate (e.g., *stopped* for *stopt*) we have retained original spellings where such might be of historical interest.

We are each about 50 percent responsible for the editing of the letters and the Introduction, with Sister Ella Jane concentrating on Rufus' family and religion, Brian focusing on the introductory section and the war years, and both involved in the section on Rufus' hometown of Abington. Brian drew the maps, compiled the Chronology of the Seventh Regiment presented in Appendix I, researched the background information presented in the endnote references to the letters, and located the pictures—except for those of Rufus, Henry, Edwin and his wife, and Ruth and her husband, which Richard Robbins kindly offered for inclusion.

ACKNOWLEDGMENTS

I am indebted to many people who have assisted me along the way as the Rufus letters and manuscript gradually developed into a book. My dear friends, Sister Dolores Kohout, C.D.P. and Dr. Prudence Steiner, Mr. John Enos, Michele Ford, and of course, my sister Virginia (Ginger) M. Bruen—for all of them, I say *Deo Gratias*.

Ella Jane Bruen, C.D.P.

I wish to express my thanks to the members of the Civil War reenactment groups—my own Twenty-second Massachusetts Regiment and Twelfth Massachusetts Regiment, my friends in the Seventh Massachusetts Regiment and those in the Pequot Mess—who have helped me acquire a firsthand understanding of what the life of a Civil War soldier was like and to my father, Robert E. Fitzgibbons, who patiently listened to many hours of my reading from Rufus' letters as they were being transcribed, who helped from time to time with the typing, and who was always willing to assist me in my attempts to decipher particularly difficult aspects of Rufus' handwriting.

Brian M. Fitzgibbons

Special thanks from both of us to Richard Robbins for his kindness in offering the pictures of Rufus and his family for inclusion in this book.

INTRODUCTION

Scarcely eighty-six years after the first shots of the American Revolution were fired on the Lexington green, a renewed patriotism coursed through the towns and villages of Massachusetts. Founded "in Order to form a more perfect Union, establish Justice, insure domestic Tranquillity, provide for the common defense, promote the general Welfare, and secure the Blessings of Liberty to ourselves and our Posterity," the United States of America faced the most profound challenge in its brief existence—incipient dissolution.

In the early morning hours of April 12, 1861, secessionist Confederate troops under the command of General P.G.T. Beauregard launched an artillery attack on the Union garrison at Fort Sumter located in the harbor of Charleston, South Carolina. For thirty-four hours, almost 4,000 shells were exchanged, yet incredibly neither side lost a man. Nevertheless, because his food supplies were almost exhausted and resupply was out of the question, the commanding Union officer, Major Robert Anderson, felt compelled to surrender the fort and its sixty-eight man contingent to the insurgent Confederates—and the great American Civil War had begun.

In the North, news of the surrender was electrifying. The smoldering fires of the "irrepressible conflict" could no longer be held in check. Business came to a halt, party lines were obliterated or forgotten, and all talk was of preserving the Union with a stern and relentless war.[1] James McPherson offers a sense of the spirit in the North.

On April 15 Lincoln issued a proclamation calling 75,000 militiamen into national service for ninety days to put down an insurrection "too power- ful to be suppressed by the ordinary course of judicial proceedings." The response from free states was overwhelming. War meetings in every city and village cheered the flag and vowed vengeance on traitors. "The heather is on fire," wrote a Harvard professor who had been born during George Washington's presidency. "I never knew what a popular excite- ment can be. . . . The whole population, men, women, and children, seem to be in the streets with Union favors and flags."[2]

In Massachusetts, the war fervor was perhaps even more intense than in other northern states. On April 19, four days after Lincoln's proclamation—which coincidentally was the anniversary of the minutemen's battle with the British troops on Lexington green— the Massachusetts Sixth Regiment of Volunteers was rushing south to aid in the defense of Washington. Passing through Baltimore, the militia was attacked by secessionist sympathizers and in the ensuing bloody skirmish lost several men. As in the Revolutionary War, Massachusetts men were the first to be killed in action.

Throughout the North, the response to President Lincoln's call was immediate and overwhelming. In Massachusetts, by early May 1861 "almost two hundred companies had been formed, and thousands of young men volunteered to begin active duty. . . . In their eagerness to serve, three thousand men from Massachusetts enlisted in other states (six companies in New York state alone!), but still the supply of men who desired to enlist was greater than the demand in the spring of 1861."[3] One of the enlistees was Rufus Robbins, Jr., thirty-one years old and unmarried, a shoemaker and part-time farmer, from South Abington, Massachusetts.

HOMETOWN

The small community of Abington, Massachusetts, is located midway between Plymouth to the south and Boston to the north, approximately twenty miles from each. During the Civil War years, the town was divided into four sections: Centre Abington, North

Abington, East Abington, and South Abington—the section in which Rufus Robbins lived. Not many years after the war, South Abington was incorporated as the separate town of Whitman, and East Abington became the present town of Rockland, leaving only Centre Abington and North Abington in today's Abington.

Rufus' Abington was a generally peaceful, mixed rural and industrial community that by 1860 could boast of a growing population of 8,527.[4] Because the land was exceptionally rocky and difficult to plow, farming had been much more difficult there than in most of the other towns of the original Plymouth Colony. Consequently, from the time of its settlement in the late seventeenth century, Abington farmers typically raised animals in preference to cultivating crops. Most common were cows, sheep, pigs, chickens, and geese. "Geese were kept in great numbers: scarcely a farmer was without his flock; and many, who had no farms, kept them."[5] Geese were easy to raise and could be slaughtered and later sold at the markets in Boston and the surrounding towns. Yet even more important were their feathers, which were valuable for use in the manufacture of bed mattresses, pillows, and quilts. A mature goose would have its feathers picked at least twice a year.

Geese picking was quite a merry scene with children; the pickers were all covered with down and feathers. The geese, especially the old ones, were very spiteful: They would bite and strike with their wings. To prevent their biting, a stocking was pulled over their heads; and to prevent their striking with their wings, the wings were locked over their backs. From such picking arose the name, "live geese feathers."[6]

As with geese, sheep were raised not only as a source of food and as a marketable commodity, but also for the wool they produced. Many of Abington's women used this wool, and the cotton and flax grown on their farms, to make cloth. By the turn of the century in 1800, "these operations were greatly facilitated by machines to card the wool into rolls; and afterwards, cotton yarn, or factory yarn, as it was called, came into use for wraps for cotton and wool cloth, and for all cotton cloth."[7]

As the nineteenth century began, invention, mechanization, and steam power were conspiring to gradually transform the Abington in which Rufus Robbins, Jr. would come to live from a farming community into a manufacturing town. Yet manufacturing was not completely new to Abington; it had always existed alongside farming. Not only had the production of cloth been an occupation since the earliest days of the settlement, but the first bells and cannon in this country were cast there beginning about 1769, when "a deserter from the British Army, by the name of Gallimore, a bell founder, came to Abington and was employed by Col. Aaron Hobart."[8] In fact, it was to Abington that Paul Revere and others traveled to learn the art of casting meeting house bells. When the Revolutionary War began in 1775, this same Colonel Hobart began manufacturing cannons and cannon balls, "and was the first person in the country who introduced and carried on this branch of business."[9] In addition to these industries, Abington was also well known for tanning, along with the associated making of leather saddles and harnesses, brick manufacture, and cabinetmaking.

Yet perhaps most important to the development of Abington's industry throughout the eighteenth century was the fact that the town had been blessed with timber—tall, sturdy oaks and pines—and with rivers along which were built several sawmills. In South Abington, the first sawmill was built in 1698. Many of the huge oaks from which were produced the white oak planks (known as "wale planks") of many ships, including the famed frigate, *Constitution*, had grown on its hillsides as did the exceptionally tall pine trees that provided the raw material for the masts of many ships built both in Boston and on the old North River. Wood, sawed at the mills, was sold for use in building houses, barns, and later factories. And significantly, the mills provided wood for one of the fastest growing local businesses: box-making. The most important of those early Abington industries "to which chief attention has been paid, and which have over-shadowed all the rest, are box-making, tack-making and shoemaking."[10]

By the early 1800s, the importance of the lumber business gradually decreased because of the depletion of raw materials, and the significance of tack-making and shoemaking increased. Tacks were a major commodity in the early days of the young republic.

The manufacture of cut nails and tacks originated in Abington over sixty years ago [i.e., prior to 1780]. The first attempts, as is common with all great improvements, were very imperfect. Old iron hoops and afterwards rolled iron plates were cut into angular points, with lever shears. The points were then taken up one by one, by hand, put into a common vice and headed with a hammer. Mr. Ezekiel Reed, a native of the town, made an important improvement. Instead of putting the points into a vice, he put them into dies set in the two upper and inner sides of an iron frame, somewhat in the shape of an oxbow. The dies were brought together so as to gripe the points, by a lever, moved by the foot. In the former mode, one person could make about 1,000 nails or tacks in a day and about 8,000 in the latter.[11]

Other tack-making inventions rapidly followed so that by 1837 one person could produce between 100,000 and 150,000 tacks per day and "the number of these articles manufactured in one year ending 1st of April, 1837, was 1832 millions, valued at 82,000 dollars."[12]

The economic world into which Rufus Robbins, Jr. was born had begun to change significantly from its earlier colonial orientation. And the major contributor to this process—of far greater significance than either the box-making or tack-making industry—was the growth of the shoe trade. The Abington shoe industry had developed from the many tanners who had worked there as early as the 1700s. The shoe business had begun on a small scale with each shoemaker traveling to the homes of those local families who were his regular customers. He measured and took orders to each person's specifications and then returned to his workshop where he made up the stock and finished the shoes. This was known as "Whipping the Cat."[13]

During the 1700s, shoemaking was primarily an occupation carried on by individual shoemakers. By the beginning of the 1800s, however, this had begun to change dramatically with the introduction of "sale-shoes." No longer made to the personal specifications of a shoemaker's local customers, sale-shoes were mass produced for sale in shoe stores. And with mass production came the division of labor. Usually women stitched the thin leather of the "uppers" (i.e., the top parts of the shoe) and made the eyelets and buckles. The shoe was "made" by tacking the insole to a wooden last, stretching the stitched upper over the last and tacking it to the insole, attaching the upper and insole to the outer sole, and finally tacking on the heel. Men typically "made" the shoe.

Prior to the beginning of the nineteenth century, the upper and insole were fastened to the outer sole by hand sewing. Then, around 1810, "pegging" was introduced. Two rows of sharply pointed wooden pegs, as long as the thickness of the outer sole and insole, were hammered through the outer sole and into the insole over which the sewn upper had been stretched. "Pegging diffused rapidly in the 1840s and 1850s, so that in 1860 their manufacture 'constituted at least three-fourths of the general business' according to the census of that year."[14]

In Abington, the sale-shoe industry was initiated around 1793 by Captain Thomas Hunt who was later joined by David Gloyd.

In the absence of railroad accommodation for transportation, they used the more primitive way of packing the shoes in large saddle-bags, and placing them on the old family horse, mounting the nag, and trudging off to Boston,—returning thence in due time with two or three sides of sole leather in one side of the bags, and, in the other, upper stock, and perhaps some small articles for family use. So things went on increasing as fast as the young men [their workmen] could be instructed, till from these small beginnings, the shoe trade of the town amounts to millions of dollars annually.[15]

By 1850, the Old Colony railroad line had been extended from Boston through the town allowing shoe manufacturers easily to transport their finished products to the city and beyond. Abington came to have over 100 shoe factories, many of which developed major markets not only throughout the Northeast but also in New Orleans and Cuba. The shoe industry in Massachusetts grew so rapidly that by the 1850s the state held a 95 percent share of all interstate markets.[16] As a result of the increase in shoemaking and related jobs, Abington's population burgeoned, and by the 1860s—counting men, women, and children—85–90 percent of the population was employed in one way or another in the shoe trade.[17]

Of the many shoe factories that sprang up in different sections of the town, some of the larger and wealthier ones began to employ steam power for driving the machinery used in cutting and otherwise preparing the stock. Yet whether steam powered or not, most of the Abington shoe factories operated in the same manner. The factory would receive the basic stock, prepare and sort it by quality, cut it into various sizes and designs, and pack the pieces. Some of the larger factories employed as many as fifty to sixty people directly in this process. In his *History of the Town of Abington*, Benjamin Hobart provides a description of the factory of Jenkins Lane and Sons, a company for whom the Robbins family pegged and sewed shoes.

The main building is forty by eighty, built in 1859; three stories and basement, heated by steam; machinery propelled by an engine of ten horse-power. The basement is used for storing and cutting sole leather.
   On the first floor are the receiving, drying, scouring, finishing, packing rooms, and room for storing lasts. The second floor contains counting room, two stitching, vamp, and wash rooms. Third floor, cutting room. The attic, for storing leather, boxes, &c.
   Dimensions of smaller building, thirty by sixty-five; three stories and basement; basement used for grocery store; a part of the first floor used for machine shop; the rest of the building for making shoes. The machinery is propelled by an engine, in a large building, and consists of a pegging machine, two of McKay sewing machines, leveling machine, &c. the whole value of shoes manufactured annually, $650,000.[18]

From these factories, individual contractors, such as members of the Robbins family,[19] would pick up the pre-cut materials and take them to their homes or places of business to peg (and later stitch) and in other ways finish the shoes or boots. The products of their labors, in turn, were returned to the factory where the individual contractor was paid for his or her services. The factory workers would pack and ship the finished shoes or boots to those retail customers who had contracted for them in the first instance.
   By the middle of the 1800s, a second revolution that would significantly affect the Robbins family and other individual contractors emerged. Mr. D. Edmund Shaw had begun selling Singer sewing machines door-to-door in Abington as a new mechanized way to attach the outer sole to the shoe. To enhance his sales, he had added a gooseneck to the machine to facilitate sewing on the soles. His sales increased and he drew the attention of Seth Bryant, who improved the machine to effect even greater production. Bryant took his idea to Washington and demonstrated it to Secretary of War Stanton. Stanton was so impressed that Bryant returned to Abington with a contract to make boots for the Union army, which had the effect of increasing the opportunities for more contract work for individuals such as the Robbinses.
   While many Abington families were attempting to come to grips with these and other life-altering economic changes, a major social and moral upheaval had been gradually approaching: the growing

movement to abolish slavery in the United States. In various and complex ways the lives of people living in every Massachusetts town would be profoundly affected by the abolitionist movement, and Abington was no exception. By the middle of the nineteenth century, the town had acquired a reputation for supporting the sentiment to eradicate slavery in the nation and abolitionists met regularly at Abington's Island Grove, a pleasant, large open area and pond. Since the Old Colony Railroad ran nearby, Island Grove was quite convenient for these meetings.

In 1846, William Lloyd Garrison traveled to Island Grove for the first of his many meetings there. By 1850, Island Grove had become a favorite meeting place for abolitionists, and, at least once a year until 1865, they held meetings there with Garrison and other notable abolitionist speakers such as Wendell Phillips, Theodore Parker, and Lucy Stone. On a tablet that marks the spot today it states, "The abolitionists stood steadfast until the slave was made free" and "they suffered all sorts of abuse." Once during an abolitionist meeting at Island Grove, William Lloyd Garrison was forced to seek refuge from anti-abolitionists. According to legend, anti-abolitionists from some surrounding towns had infiltrated the meeting by hiding under a load of hay. At the appropriate time, they sprang from the wagon and assaulted those gathered to hear Garrison. On another occasion in 1851, some Webster Whigs hired a cannon, mounted it on the opposite side of the pond, and fired all day long in a vain effort to break up an abolitionist meeting.[20]

These and similar incidents undoubtedly made a strong impression and fortified the abolitionist convictions of the anti-slavery people of Abington and, in particular, of the members of the Robbins family. Yet, as exciting as such events surely were, they were the exception, not the rule. Although increasingly concerned about the developing local and national discord over the abolition issue, the typical Abington family was primarily occupied with the more mundane affairs of family life: earning a living, providing adequate shelter and food, and caring for children.

THE ROBBINS FAMILY

The Robbins family included Rufus Robbins, Sr., his wife, Alice Soule Robbins, and their children:

Rufus, Jr., the eldest son;

Henry, two years younger than Rufus;

Ruth, five years younger than Rufus[21];

a brother, seven years younger than Rufus, who died at the age of two;

Edwin, ten years younger than Rufus.[22]

We have no record of why, or under what circumstances, the Robbins family moved to Abington. Rufus, Sr. had been born in Plymouth in 1805 and later married Alice Soule, a native of Duxbury. The young couple lived in Duxbury before purchasing their farm on High Street in Abington. The farm was not a large one, as the 1855 tax list for the town shows. Rufus Robbins, Sr. is listed as paying $11.48 for his house, barn, animals, and seven acres. Young Rufus and his brother, Henry, owned one additional acre each. Rufus paid $3.96 for his acre, and Henry paid $4.34 for his.

The life of the small Massachusetts farmer in the mid-1800s was difficult at best. With good farmland, which Abington did not have, a farm the size of the Robbins' would barely support the family, producing very little, if any, surplus for market. Compounding the farmer's economic difficulties was the growing agricultural competition from the much larger farms that were being developed in the Midwest.[23] Consequently, for most small farmers in Massachusetts a second occupation was required. And so as with many others in Abington, members of the Robbins family, while engaged in farming, also had been involved for some time in making shoes. At first, they made the older pegged shoes. Then later, with the introduction of the sewing machine, they learned how to produce the newer machine-sewn shoes and boots.

Along with the evolution of such developing forms of industry, a new concept of family life had begun to emerge in New England by the early 1800s. Men, as husbands and providers, came to link the family with the wider world. They acted for the family in public affairs and provided for its economic welfare. Women, as wives and mothers, managed the household and provided a nurturing atmosphere.

While the eighteenth-century family was patriarchal, with the father having a determining voice in the apprenticeship of his sons and in choosing the spouses for his children, the nineteenth century shattered his dominant role.[24] There was a revolution of choice. Many sons struck out on their own and many daughters, instead of marrying and raising families in the local setting, often moved away. There was a new meaning inherent in adulthood with each young man or woman assuming personal responsibility in a more extensive manner. The maternal role was seen as a stimulant and pattern for her children's lifetime choices, and the mother became more active in her children's development to adulthood.[25] In his children's late adolescent years the father's function as symbol of the hard outside world would convert to instructor in worldly affairs with encouragement to take some risks in future choices. The need for disciplined moderation and inner orderliness was stressed, so that the young adult would maintain a steady middle-of-the-road course.

The Robbins family was in most respects quite ordinary, not much different in structure, occupation, or values from many other Massachusetts families. And like the majority of the townspeople in Abington, they were and remained middle class. The tax lists for 1862 indicate that the value of their holdings had not changed appreciably since 1855. The father paid taxes of $10.52, Henry paid $2.00, and Henry and Rufus jointly paid $4.20.[26] Yet what is of particular interest are the strong family bonds of love, support, and unity that are evident in the correspondence between Rufus, Jr. and members of his family.

Rufus' father was the dominant personality within the family. Generally reserved and constrained in his letters, it is nevertheless clear that a mutually strong bond existed between him and Rufus. Their love and support of each other is reflected in their correspondence, despite the fact that Rufus' absence had placed an emotional and financial strain on the family. And there is, in his father's letters, a clear and ever-present expression of fear—fear for his son's safety and well-being, fear that his son might lose his religious faith, and fear that his son might dishonor himself and his family through a lack of courage.

Like so many others across the country, Mr. Robbins had been caught in the turmoil of war. There had been comfort and security with the old familiar ways of making pegged shoes, in taking care of his farm, and generally with the pattern and work of his life. Then suddenly, with the outbreak of the war, everything was turned upside down. Maintaining a farm with less help became difficult. The recent changes in the shoe industry meant giving up manufacturing pegged shoes and learning how to produce the new sewn boots. His son, Edwin, already was becoming successful with the new technique.

Although he did not emphasize his worries in his letters to Rufus, the war years were troublesome ones for Mr. Robbins. He was concerned about the economic difficulties associated with his farm and his family's lack of money. He was concerned with the rapidity with which changes were being made in the shoe manufacturing business and with his ability to keep pace with them. Most especially, he was concerned with his son, Rufus, being at danger in the Union army and with his daughter, Ruth, being so far away in Maine with her husband and young children. All of these contributed to Mr. Robbins' worry and confusion about his changing situation and his ability to cope with the many new developments stemming from the nascent Civil War.

Alice Soule Robbins was a loving, concerned mother who like Mr. Robbins worried about the entire family. Apparently, she was not as well educated as her husband, but told her son, Rufus, that she was always comfortable writing to him because she knew he would accept everything she wrote, even when she had difficulty in expressing her thoughts. Although Mrs. Robbins was often unwell, she never mentioned her illness to which other family members referred. And even though they do not state clearly the precise nature of her infirmity, there are some suggestions that she may have suffered from an emotional or mental condition. Her entire life seems to have revolved around the family and farm, and her relationship with Rufus was clearly a very loving one. She was always happy to make things for him—shirts, a little cloth case to hold his needles, a little silk bag for his Bible.

Mrs. Robbins enjoyed writing to Rufus in her bedroom, standing at the nightstand. Their neighbor, Josiah, often brought Rufus' letters from the village out to the farm. And sometimes Mrs. Robbins did not know whether to listen for the hoofbeats of Josiah's horse. She could not make up her mind "whether it was best to look for a letter or not." The emotional excitement, anticipation, and disappointment appear to have been difficult for her. The worry and fear that a mother has for her son's safety are always obvious in her letters. And Rufus remembered his mother lovingly. In many of the envelopes that were sent back home, he would include a flower, a pretty leaf, or seeds that he hoped she could plant in her garden.

On one occasion, Mrs. Robbins sent food in a barrel, or tub. This tub gave Rufus a tremendous sense of having a part of his home with him, and he often used it as a table on which to write his letters and as a storage place for his "stockings, needle book, papers and various other things." He kept this old tub with him while he was stationed in Washington, D.C., and it even followed him on the wagons when later he went to battle. For Rufus, the tub from home "was a source of great happiness."

The unselfishness and love that were prized in the Robbins family found expression in Rufus' interaction with his tentmates at their various encampments. When a barrel or package from home would arrive for him at camp, Rufus would take it to his tent and share the food with his companions. One of these was Rufus' good friend, Luke Noyes, who lived near the Robbins family on High Street in Abington. Both men would discuss what type of food they would want sent to them, and instead of burdening both families, they would divide their lists and share the results. Some of the money that Rufus sent home helped to pay the expenses of sending a barrel.

Sometimes Rufus used the supplies his family had sent him for barter. Instead of paying someone for a haircut or some other necessity, he was able to give him a pie or cake. This was much more agreeable to Rufus than paying the inflated prices charged by the sutlers, or peddlers, who surrounded the camp. These sutlers sold almost any item that a small city of soldiers might need or want. But their prices were usually very high, a fact of the soldier's life about which Rufus sometimes complained.

With the passage of time, the distance that separated Rufus from the members of his family became increasingly apparent. As many of their letters indicate, the family's concern for Rufus' needs and well-being gradually began to grow, as did his concern for theirs. Yet even though the war had moved him far from his loving family in Abington, Rufus found a strong emotional extension of home in the letters, clothes, and food he received. These brought him great comfort and joy. And even though Rufus very much missed his home and family, he regularly and sincerely assured his parents that he was not homesick and was proud to be a soldier in the Union army.

By the time that Rufus left his home state for the seat of war on July 12, 1861, his sister, Ruth, was married and lived in West Sumner, Maine, with her husband, Hiram, and their three children. By the beginning of September 1861, Hiram was thinking of enlisting in the Union army, and Ruth was torn between his sense of duty, which she supported, and her concern of being alone and running the farm all by herself with small children to care for. Hiram did enlist in the Ninth Maine Regiment and by October 1861 was stationed in Washington, D.C., barely two miles from Rufus' encampment. But Rufus was frustrated in his attempts to secure a pass to visit his brother-in-law and it appears that he never did get to see him.

Although Ruth was busy taking care of the children and doing the hard manual labor required by the farm, she continued to maintain close links with her family. Letters were sent back and forth from her parents to Rufus and to Hiram, so that the entire family could share in the news. In one of her letters to Rufus, Ruth tells of how she was aching to be with her family in Massachusetts, but the three older children were in school, and she was trying to wean the baby, who was being "very cross." However, the main reason Ruth did not return to Massachusetts was that she could not go back to her family without Rufus and Hiram[27] being there.

Rufus' brother Henry stayed at home to help take care of the farm and his parents along with trying to earn a living for himself. Henry was meticulous in his work and took seriously his new role as eldest son at home. In his correspondence, he showed some envy of Rufus' new life as a soldier, as he was seeing the countryside and having new adventures. The two brothers corresponded often and the strong bond that existed between them is apparent. Rufus depended on Henry for many of the things he needed. Henry took care of any money that Rufus sent home, money that Rufus wanted to save or money that the family might need. It is interesting to note that whenever Rufus needed money, he would always ask Henry, not his father. Rufus was also grateful that Henry stayed home to take care of his parents and the farm.

Like the others in his family, Rufus' youngest brother, Edwin, was involved in shoemaking and did some contract work. He was proud of his success in earning more money with the new techniques of making sewn shoes. In one letter, he notes that he made $5.25 for seventeen pair. The youngest brother, who did not write often, seemed to have more of a sense of humor than either Henry or his father. His wife, Sophie, said that "Edwin trembles likes a leaf" when they receive a letter from Rufus.

UNIVERSALISM

The members of the Robbins family were Universalists. In the United States, Universalism arose during the late 1700s out of a protest against Calvinism with its insistence on predestination and its publicly supported Puritan Congregational churches.[28] The Congregationalists believed that before a person's birth God determined whether he or she would go to heaven or hell and that nothing one did on this earth could alter this "predetermined" fate. Universalism thoroughly disavowed this and insisted on the eventual universal salvation of all humankind. Contrary to the Calvinist doctrine that there is nothing a person can do to affect his or her eternal salvation (or damnation), the young Universalist religion affirmed a much more liberal, positive faith in humanity and the natural, rational human personality. Universalists believed that through the revelations contained in the Bible one could understand both the deity in terms of the unipersonality (i.e., Unity) of God, as contrasted with the doctrine of the Trinity, and the normal humanity of Jesus, as contrasted with the eternal deity of Christ.

Although the Universalists had no highly defined, dogmatic set of beliefs and were not hindered by ecclesiastical authority, most subscribed to what came to be known as the Winchester Profession of 1803. As with most Universalist positions, this statement was purposely ambiguous so as to accommodate the many different opinions held at that time by the diverse members of the loosely formed religion. The Profession consisted of three simple articles of faith.

Article I. We believe that the Holy Scriptures of the Old and New Testament contain a revelation of the character of God, and of the duty, interest and final destination of mankind.

Article II. We believe that there is one God, whose nature is Love, revealed in one Lord Jesus Christ, by one Holy Spirit of Grace, who will finally restore the whole family of mankind to holiness and happiness.

Article III. We believe that holiness and true happiness are inseparably connected, and that believers ought to be careful to maintain order and practice good works; for these things are good and profitable unto men.[29]

To this was added a stipulation that any Universalist congregation was allowed to adopt additional articles of faith as long as they were consistent with this Profession.

Universalism's particular social interests were the moral and ethical issues of living and the requirements for conduct that these issues inspired. Universalists were "universal" in their goal of building finer human beings and uniting people in service to one another. They felt that people were capable of achieving a more ideal life through their own efforts to strengthen and sensitize themselves to the belief in the supreme worth of every human personality. Each individual man and woman was both the purpose and the instrument in the struggle for a better world.[30]

In the beginning, Universalist congregations typically organized themselves into *societies* rather than *churches*—although the distinction between a society and a church was not an especially clear one. A society was a fairly loose-knit collection of individuals who shared the basic tenets of Universalism and agreed to meet together to worship God. A society could be formed by as few as two or three individuals coming together, and in Massachusetts the only legal requirement was that a justice of the peace issue a warrant for the organization of the new society. Usually organized from within a society, a "church was said to exist when a group of believers adopted a set of rules for religious discipline or a profession of faith and when the ordinances of Baptism and the Lord's Supper were administered."[31]

The first Universalist society in Abington was formed in 1836 by forty-six individuals. At first its meetings were held in a local school house. Two years later they were moved to the Abington Town House, and in 1841 the Abington Universalists erected their own building in which to hold their services. When the Abington Universalist society was formed,

[n]o special declaration of faith was made, or statement of belief adopted, but the purpose of the society as set forth in the Second Article of the

Constitution was "the promotion of truth and morality among its members, and also in the world at large, by maintaining the preaching of the Gospel of the Lord Jesus Christ, and aiding in any other practicable way in spreading a knowledge of it."[32]

In 1862, twenty-eight members of the society's congregation joined together in organizing a formal church structure for the purpose of participating in the sacrament of the Lord's Supper.

Its "Declaration of Faith" [was] that adopted by the Universalist Churches generally, viz.:—that "God is one, a Being infinite in wisdom, power and goodness, and in every possible perfection. That Jesus Christ is the Son of God, the promised Messiah. That the Scriptures of the Old and New Testaments are a revelation from God, communicating teachings and principles for the direction of human conduct in all the relations and circumstances of life—showing the character and government of God, the rewards of virtue, the punishments of vice, and revealing the final purpose of Infinite Wisdom in the reconciliation of all things to God, so that He at last shall be All in All."[33]

In Abington, the Universalists met with strong resistance from the Congregationalists in the area, particularly over their denial of the existence of hell. Yet the derogatory epithets hurled at them— "liars," "blasphemers," and "heretics"—only strengthened the little congregation, and they were extremely loyal to each other and steadfast in their faith.

Since the Abington Universalists were neither as wealthy nor as numerous as many of the members of the predominant faiths in the area, they were obliged to share a minister and his salary with surrounding congregations. The minister would often hold another job to supplement his income. During the 1860s, the Robbins' Universalist minister was Brother Joseph Crehore, who had churches in Mattapoisset and Abington. Even with his travels back and forth between these small congregations, Brother Crehore held down a second job.

As a child Rufus attended, and as a young adult he taught in, the Universalists' Sunday School in Abington. He went to services with his family, read his Bible, and knew Scripture. Universalists applied a liberal interpretation to the Bible, finding it to be a book rich in human episodes. It offered great lessons, which gave Rufus much comfort. The Universalists believed that one did not have to rely on supernatural intervention. Man, with his potential for growth, and possessing some evidence of the divine, was little less than the angels. Man was too good for God to damn him. But because God is a good and rational being, there were some people who might have to be corrected. Hell was rejected as being unworthy of God. Universalists believed that all souls would be restored by God's grace, thus increasing the worth of each person.

In his letters, Mr. Robbins stressed the need for Rufus to set a good example for his fellow soldiers. He was concerned about Rufus' maintaining his religion because he was far from the support of the faith-filled environment of his home. Rufus regularly reassured his father that his commitment to his faith remained strong.

When stationed in Washington, D.C., Rufus regularly went to Sunday services and was often called upon to read the lesson of the day. He openly discussed his faith with his fellow soldiers, but never actively tried to convert anyone. He held to the belief that Universalists should be strongly anti-missionary, and thus did not seek out new converts. A Universalist did not want to close out anyone's options, although it troubled Rufus that many of his fellow soldiers had little or no faith.

It was typical of the Robbins family that someone would refer to scripture or a recent sermon. Mr. Robbins would often send Rufus an issue of *The Trumpet*, a religious periodical, published weekly by the Universalists. Like many other families who suffered during the war years, the Robbinses were devout, honest, and committed to their faith. Even in the stressful circumstances of war, with its disappointments, discouragements, and fears, Rufus lived his faith. His spiritual life supported him and furthered his belief to trust in God as a mature, unselfish, and committed Christian fighting for what he believed to be the just cause of the Union.

THE WAR YEARS

The Seventh Massachusetts Volunteer Infantry was mustered into service on June 15, 1861, at Camp Old Colony in Taunton, Massachusetts. The majority of the regiment was recruited from Bristol County through the efforts of its first colonel, Darius N. Couch, a West Point graduate who later rose to the rank of major general and assumed command of the Second Corps of the Army of the Potomac. Two of the regiment's companies—approximately 100 men each—were, however, not from Bristol County. The men of Company E came primarily from Dorchester in Suffolk County, and those of Company K were mainly from Abington in Plymouth County. Rufus Robbins was a member of Company K, commanded by Captain Franklin P. Harlow.

The first few months of the war were chaotic for the Union army. The overwhelming response of enlistees strained its organizational abilities. It lacked supplies and expertise in managing such a large number of new recruits. Rufus' first experience with the army's lack of planning was his army physical—the whole company of over 100 men was examined in half an hour, and the physician seemed more concerned with whether the men would be loyal to their captain than with conducting a serious physical examination. Despite the chaotic atmosphere, the difficulties of living with strangers, learning how to become a soldier, and suffering the shortages of supplies, Rufus was still pleasantly surprised with many of his adventures at Camp Old Colony and on the whole found "things generally better than I expected."

And he was still close to home. Abington was only a short ride— barely twenty miles—from Camp Old Colony. It was easy and quick to send messages home with friendly neighbors who passed through the camp, and because Camp Old Colony was so close, Rufus' father and brother Henry were able visit him. During the first weeks of his enlistment, life was still fairly uncomplicated for Rufus and for his family. Here in the "school of the soldier" the new enlistee began to learn the military skills he soon would need.

Rufus left Taunton on July 12, 1861, for Washington, D.C. His regiment traveled by train to Groton, Connecticut, where all boarded the steamer, *Commonwealth*, on which they sailed up the Long Island Sound to New York City. Rufus wrote to Henry recounting his trip and expressing his excitement at seeing the marvelous sights along the way and of the wharves and the three-masted boats there. While waiting onboard their ship in New York harbor, one of the men in Rufus' company "received a severe bayonet wound in the arm, the first serious casualty of the campaign thus far."[34] The regiment then boarded the ship, *Kill von Kull*, and proceeded to Elizabethport, New Jersey, where they disembarked and began a railroad trip through New Jersey and Pennsylvania. In his letter describing this part of his journey, Rufus carefully noted the various towns through which his regiment passed as well as its time schedule. He commented on the agriculture of the areas through which he traveled, the appearance of the fields, the types of crops planted, and the richness of the soil.

All the while the Seventh Regiment was approaching nearer and nearer to the seat of war, and when the troop train was about five miles outside Baltimore,

we filed out of the cars, and loaded our rifles; Col. Couch having no idea of being caught napping, as was the "Old Sixth" when they passed through Baltimore in the April preceding. And well do we remember how the old regiment looked as we marched through Baltimore, one thousand and ten strong, led by our gallant commander, Col. (now Major-Gen.) Couch. Company K was the leading company, its captain being the senior captain of the regiment.[35]

The march through the city, however, was uneventful and in time the soldiers climbed aboard a train and slowly progressed to Washington, D.C.

On July 15, 1861, Rufus and the Seventh Massachusetts Volunteer Infantry arrived in Washington and were quartered for the night in the still unfinished Capitol building. The next morning they marched to their first encampment on Kalorama Heights, located within the District of Columbia about one-quarter of a mile from Georgetown. In his letters, Rufus refers to the camp by the Taunton name of "Camp Old Colony." The camp was located on a high open plain on the east side of Rock Creek. Where it bordered the camp, the stream was at the foot of a very steep hill. About forty feet wide, it provided the soldiers with a place to bathe and, at least during their times of rest, with the agreeable background sounds of a murmuring brook. Everything about the camp contributed to Rufus' feeling that it was a "beautiful place."

The initial peacefulness of the place was shattered when on Sunday, July 21, just five days after establishing Camp Old Colony, the men of the Seventh Regiment had their religious observances disturbed by the booming sound of artillery fire coming from across the Potomac River. The first Battle of Bull Run was raging barely twenty-four miles away at Manassas, Virginia, and the Seventh Regiment was ordered to fall in. Quite suddenly, Rufus and his regiment had come face-to-face with the reality of war. But after "standing in line an hour or more, we were dismissed, and sent to quarters under orders to be ready to fall in again at a moment's notice."[36] The anxiety of the moment gradually dissipated as the order to reform and move to the battle never came.

The first Battle of Bull Run was a complete disaster for the Union forces that were engaged, yet it had little direct effect on the Seventh Massachusetts Regiment. Some of the regiment's ambulances were dispatched to assist with transporting casualties back to the Washington area, and, to protect against a Confederate attack on the city, Rufus' company was ordered to guard the Virginia side of Long Bridge that led across the Potomac River directly into Washington. The company no sooner arrived at the bridge, however, than they were ordered back to Camp Old Colony. Apparently, in the confusion someone had mistakenly ordered them to that post.

During the following days and weeks, the men of the regiment occasionally heard gunfire, but they saw no action. Instead, they drilled, and drilled, and drilled some more. In fact, during those summer days of 1861, drilling had become very important for the whole Army of the Potomac. It had become apparent that the loss at Bull Run was due in large measure to the fact that most of the men and their officers had little—and more often than not no—significant military knowledge or discipline.

There was no rout here [at Bull Run]. The Union attack had failed and the men were withdrawing, but there was no panic. One trouble apparently lay in the fact that the tactical maneuver by which troops fighting in line would form column and go to the rear was very complicated, and most of these green Union troops did not have it down pat; a withdrawal under fire was bound to become disordered and finally uncontrollable, not because the men had lost their courage but simply because they had not had enough drill.[37]

So, drill they did, and the Massachusetts men gradually became more skillful in the art of nineteenth-century warfare in preparation for that day when they would directly engage the Confederate troops.

On August 6, 1861, the regiment moved five miles from Kalorama Heights to Camp Brightwood. This new camp, still in Washington, D.C., was located at the junction of Seventh and Fourteenth Streets. At this time there were about 3,000 soldiers camped in the immediate environs of Camp Brightwood, and the civilian population had mixed feeling toward the army. Some were friendly and trusted the soldiers, while others regarded them with suspicion. The soldiers were neither clearly friend nor enemy. Rufus wrote that military orders forbade soldiers from filling their canteens from civilian wells, or, worse yet, to destroy civilian property. In his letters Rufus recounted for his family some of the interesting experiences he had with local inhabitants.

At Camp Brightwood, the men of the Seventh Massachusetts continued to drill. And, although most did not appreciate it at the time, it was later recognized that to "this thorough training was due much of the steadiness of the men in action, and the regiment felt the benefit of [this] early discipline in its later hours of need and trial."[38] Drilling, however, was not all that the men did. In that first summer of the war, Washington was quite vulnerable to a Confederate attack. Located between the border state of Maryland and secessionist Virginia, the city needed a strong defense. So, the soldiers were put to work building a series of forts that eventually would ring the city. The Seventh Massachusetts was involved in building Fort Massachusetts (renamed Fort Stevens in 1863) and Fort Slocum, along with many attendant guard booths. This is how the regiment passed the summer and fall, and the battle cry was "All quiet on the Potomac."[39]

In time, winter quarters were constructed at Camp Brightwood and the men of the Seventh Regiment settled in with no real expectation of facing the enemy until spring. The long days spent in waiting were frustrating for Rufus, since, like many of his fellow soldiers, he yearned to be in actual battle. For the time being, however, he had to content himself with the ordinary soldier's life, digging fortifications, learning how to drill, standing on picket duty, and cleaning up the campgrounds. Rufus spent a peaceful winter at Camp Brightwood. But in the early spring things began to change.

On March 11, 1862, the Seventh Massachusetts crossed the Potomac into Virginia and marched twelve miles to Prospect Hill, Virginia, as part of what was being called "the Manassas campaign." It seemed as if the regiment was finally to join the fight. Yet, when the lead elements of the Army of the Potomac arrived at the Confederate earthworks outside Manassas, they found them completely abandoned. The "campaign" had turned out to be nothing other than a long march, and three days later the regiment returned to Camp Brightwood.

They remained there until March 14, when they marched to Fort Marcy in Washington. From there the regiment boarded the steamer, *Daniel Webster*, and on March 25 sailed for Fort Monroe at the tip of the Virginia peninsula. Four days later, they disembarked at the fort, marched eight miles, and camped at Camp W. F. Smith near Newport News, Virginia. Finally, Rufus was coming closer to the battlefront and his days of anxious waiting were over. The Seventh Massachusetts Volunteer Infantry was now a part of a massive Union force that was preparing to launch what came to be known as the "Peninsula Campaign." Under the leadership of General George McClellan, the plan was for the Union army to march up the Virginia peninsula through Yorktown and Williamsburg to the gates of Richmond itself. The final objective was the capture of Richmond, the capital of the Confederacy. Rufus was full of enthusiasm for the Union cause and was convinced that it was just and right. Pleased with the progress of Company K, Rufus knew that they were fit and ready for combat and "could face the enemy." He was now so close to the rebels that he could hear their guns. The Peninsula Campaign had begun and the Seventh Regiment was to play a significant role.

By early April 1862, the Seventh was actively involved in McClellan's push up the peninsula toward the Confederate capital. The regiment supported the siege at Yorktown and later was fully engaged in its first full-fledged battle at Williamsburg. Rufus, along with the other members of the regiment

marched on to the field of Williamsburg at half-past two o'clock P.M., much exhausted and fatigued, after floundering through seas of mud and thousands of troops. The regiment was subjected to a very severe artillery fire: but . . . they stood their first baptism of fire like veterans, and marched with steady ranks and proud bearing to the support of Gen. Peck's exhausted troops. At nightfall . . . Company K, having been detailed as skirmishers, advanced under Capt. Reed, with a detachment of Gen. Davidson's Brigade, and occupied Fort Magruder at daylight.[40]

During this battle, the Seventh Massachusetts suffered its first battle death—"Andrew S. Lawton, a private of Company A, killed by a projectile from Fort Magruder."[41] Yet it was not until the next major engagement at the Battle of Nine Mile Road[42] that the true nature of warfare would become apparent to Rufus and his fellow soldiers. In this battle, the regiment lost sixteen killed or wounded. In a letter to his brother, Henry, Rufus described some of the horrors he witnessed. The rebels pushed forward "seemingly regardless of consequences." In fact, "[s]o fierce was the contest for eight days commencing with Wednesday, June 25, that both armies were obliged to leave many of their dead unburied."

The Peninsula Campaign was an especially difficult one, not only because many men were killed and wounded, but also because the soldiers had to operate under severe conditions of weather and terrain. It was the spring, and this spring of 1862 it rained heavily on the red clay soil of the Virginia peninsula. The feet of more than 100,000 Union soldiers, the hooves of their animals, and the wheels of their artillery and wagons all conspired to make the rain-sodden Virginia roads almost impassable. Many reported sinking in the mud up to their knees as their units tried to forge ahead. "How the mud sucks in those 'little gunboat' brogans! It is a question of time whether the mud will take off the 'brogans,' or the 'brogans' will take off the mud. The brogan usually takes the mud, and our pedal extremities are assuming gigantic proportions under the adhesive qualities of the sacred soil of Old Virginia."[43]

The conditions under which he had to proceed to the fighting, rather than the fighting itself, were Rufus' greatest concern and his most immediate source of danger. His confidence in himself, in his comrades, in his cause, and in his God remained strong. He affirmed, "we believe in God and believe that He has raised up men equal to the work which is to be done." His major problem at this time was the lack of good water. Indeed, one of the greatest dangers to the Union soldier was not rebel bullets or shells but sickness. According to James McPherson, at the conclusion of the Peninsula Campaign,

The health of McClellan's army, already affected by the heavy rains and humid heat among the Chickahominy swamps in May and June, deteriorated further after the army's arrival at Harrison's Landing in July. Nearly a fourth of the unwounded men were sick. Scores of new cases of malaria, dysentery, and typhoid were reported every day. [And] . . . the sickliest season of the year (August–September) [was] coming on.[44]

During the first year of his enlistment, Rufus was active in the normal duties of soldiering and for the most part was in good health. He did have some problems, but none were as serious or as troublesome as those of many of his fellow soldiers who had gotten sick soon after arrival in Washington. ("Diarrhea is the most common complaint.") Nevertheless, as early as November 1861, Rufus reported that his eyes were bothering him. He attempted to treat his condition with a "pith of sassafrass wood soaked in cold water." When it had dissolved into a "gummy substance," he applied it to his eyes. He thought that these applications would cure his eyes in a short time. But the problem was a recurring one.

In a letter of February 2, 1862, just prior to the Peninsula Campaign Rufus reported his first episode of diarrhea. Typically, he came to attribute such bouts to something he had eaten—hard bread, apples, pears, and so on—or had drunk. Water, in particular, was always a major concern for the soldier. Rufus often wrote about how happy he was to find good water in which to bathe and wash his clothes, and most important for drinking and cooking. As with his eye problem, the diarrhea came and went, and Rufus relied more on home remedies than on army doctors. As did so many of his fellow soldiers, Rufus fought two wars—one against the rebels and the other against sickness.

Through bullets and sickness the Seventh Massachusetts pushed forward—from the Peninsula Campaign, through the major battles of Antietam, Fredericksburg, Gettysburg, Rappahannock Station, the Wilderness, Spotsylvania, Cold Harbor, and many lesser engagements. Originally, the Seventh Regiment was a member of the Fourth Corps, First Division, Third Brigade. But after the failed Peninsula Campaign, the Army of the Potomac was reorganized several times and, by the Battle of Fredericksburg in December 1862, the regiment had been reassigned officially and finally to the Sixth Corps, Third Division, Second Brigade.

The Seventh Massachusetts Regiment was a three-year volunteer infantry unit and, its time of service having expired, the regiment was mustered out on June 27, 1864, at Taunton, Massachusetts. Although probably not exact, the reported numbers[45] for the regiment were:

1,140	**Total mustered into the regiment**
32	Killed in action
52	Died of wounds on field or in rear
68	Died of disease in general hospital
152	**Total dead**
254	Discharged due to wounds or illness
10	Absent at muster-out due to wounds
416	**Total casualties**
7	Prisoners
160	Deserters
39	Mustered out for promotion
148	Transferred to other organizations
370	**Total present at muster-out**

Rufus Robbins was a proud member of Company K of the Seventh Regiment of Massachusetts Volunteer Infantry. The following are his letters and those of members of his family. During a time of trial through which so many suffered, this is his story, a small piece of the American Civil War seen through ordinary eyes.

NOTES

1. Samuel Livingston French, *The Army of the Potomac from 1861 to 1863* (New York: Publishing Society of New York, 1906), Chapter 1.

2. James M. McPherson, *Battle Cry of Freedom* (New York: Ballantine Books, 1989), p. 274.

3. Jordan D. Fiore, *Massachusetts in the Civil War, Volume II, "The Year of Trial and Testing" 1861–1862* (Boston: Massachusetts Civil War Centennial Commission, 1961), pp. 10–11.

4. *Celebration of the One Hundred and Fiftieth Anniversary of the Incorporation of Abington, Massachusetts, June 10, 1862; Including the Oration, Poem, and Other Exercises* (Boston: Wright & Porter, Printers, 1862), p. 114.

5. Benjamin Hobart, *History of the Town of Abington, Plymouth County, Massachusetts, From Its First Settlement* (Boston: T. H. Carter and Son, 1866), p. 72.

6. Ibid.

7. Ibid., pp. 72–73

8. Aaron Hobart, *An Historical Sketch of Abington* (Boston: Samuel N. Dickinson, 1839), p. 90.

9. Ibid.

10. *Celebration of the One Hundred And Fiftieth Anniversary of the Incorporation of Abington*, pp. 33–34.

11. Aaron Hobart, *An Historical Sketch of Abington*, pp. 90–91.

12. Ibid.

13. Benjamin Hobart, *History of the Town of Abington*, p. 151.

14. Ross Thomson, *The Path to Mechanized Shoe Production in the United States* (Chapel Hill: The University of North Carolina Press, 1989), p. 34.

15. Benjamin Hobart, *History of the Town of Abington*, pp. 151–152.

16. Ross Thomson, *The Path to Mechanized Shoe Production in the United States*, p. 19.

17. William Allan, *History of East Bridgewater Massachusetts* (Bridgewater, Massachusetts: East Bridgewater Historical Commission, 1980), p. 3.

18. Benjamin Hobart, *History of the Town of Abington*, pp. 290–291.

19. The 1855 Massachusetts census lists shoemaker as the primary occupation of Rufus Robbins, Sr. and his sons, Rufus, Jr. and Henry. It seems to be the case that young Rufus' mother, Alice, also worked at making shoes in her home.

20. William D. Coughlan, "Island Grove—A Shrine or a Swimming Pool," unpublished paper read to the Historical Society of Old Abington, December 8, 1971. Copy in archives of the Society at the Dyer Memorial Building, Centre Avenue, Abington, Massachusetts.

21. By 1861 Ruth was married to Thomas Hiram Barrows, known as Hiram, and they lived together in West Sumner, Maine, with their children.

22. On May 1, 1861, Edwin married Sophie E. Abbott, cf. *Annual Report of the Town of Abington for the Year Ending Feb. 1 1861*, p. 33.

23. Daniel Vickers, *Farmers & Fishermen: Two Centuries of Work in Essex County, Massachusetts, 1630–1850* (Chapel Hill: University of North Carolina Press, 1994), pp. 294–295.

24. Robert H. Wiebe, *Opening American Society* (New York: Random House, 1985), p. 267.

25. Nancy Woloch, *Women and the American Experience* (New York: Alfred A. Knopf, 1985), pp. 118–120.

26. Ibid.

27. Hiram was killed in 1864 in Virginia, thirty miles below Richmond, in the Battle of the Bermuda Hundred.

28. Alan Heimert and Andrew Delbanco, *The Puritan in America* (Cambridge: Harvard University Press, 1985), p. 196.

29. Russell E. Miller, *The Larger Hope* (Boston: Unitarian Universalist Association, 1979), pp. 45–46.

30. Ibid., p. 725.

31. Russell E. Miller, *The Larger Hope*, p. 64.

32. Benjamin Hobart, *History of the Town of Abington*, p. 222.

33. Ibid., p. 225.

34. Nelson V. Hutchinson, *History of the Seventh Massachusetts Volunteer Infantry in the War of the Rebellion of the Southern States Against Constitutional Authority 1861—1865* (Taunton, Massachusetts: The Regimental Association, 1890), pp. 8–9.

35. Ibid., pp. 9–10.

36. Ibid., p. 12.

37. Bruce Catton, *The American Heritage New History of the Civil War* (New York: Viking, 1996), pp. 85–86.

38. Nelson V. Hutchinson, *History of the Seventh Massachusetts Volunteer Infantry*, p. 18.

39. Ibid., p. 20.

40. Ibid., pp. 24–25.

41. Ibid., p. 25.

42. Cf. Appendix II: Letter from Captain George Reed, commander of Company K, originally published in *The Abington Standard*, September 6, 1862.

43. Nelson V. Hutchinson, *History of the Seventh Massachusetts Volunteer Infantry*, pp. 28–29.

44. James M. McPherson, *Battle Cry of Freedom* p. 488.

45. Nelson V. Hutchinson, *History of the Seventh Massachusetts Volunteer Infantry*, pp. 252–253.

LETTERS FROM 1861

First letter home from Taunton[1]

I know a few lines will be acceptable to you even tomorrow. It is almost dark now but I can send this by J. West tomorrow. I will give you a few of the most important items. We arrived here about noon. Were marched into a building about 40 ft. wide and as long as Faneuil Hall[2] market made of rough boards. Six of our company cooked the dinner for the rest. They did not get it ready until three o'clock. Salt beef and pork baked in bread and cold water was our fare, good meat but not cooked enough.

It is too dark to write any more tonight————

I now take my pencil to finish my letter. Our company was examined soon after supper. The examination was a short one. Not more than half an hour for the whole company. He wanted to know if I was a well hearty man and would stand by my Captain. "Yes Sir!" was my answer.

I have not more than fifteen minutes to write this morning. I have just got up, washed my face, and combed my hair. Had a good night's rest, feel as bright as a new cent this morning. I must stop now. I cannot write another word.

Rufus

June 14, 1861
Camp Old Colony
Taunton, Massachusetts

Dear Father,

I can hardly tell what I wrote you in my last [letter] which I sent to you by John West. I had but little time to write then and that little was well mixed with other duties. But I trust you have received a good report of me.

Our fare was not very good the first day because it was not well cooked, otherwise it would have been very good. Our company is divided into four sections. Each section mess together. I am in the second section where I have always been trained. Frank Hutchinson[3] is in the same mess with me. Frank Erskin[4] and myself were detailed to cook for our mess yesterday and I think we gave them good satisfaction. For breakfast, we had bread, beef, pork and coffee, though the meat was only a remnant of the day before. About ten o'clock our rations for the remainder of the day and breakfast this morning were brought in. The meat was good, the beef was fresh, and the pork salted. Washed it clean, scraped the pork clean with a knife, then put it on to boil together. Each man in the mess had a potato. When the meat was cooked, we cut it into 18 pieces each kind for as many men. One-third of a loaf of bread to a man such as you usually buy at the baker.

So you see we have enough to eat, though I came a little short last night, or should, had it not been for the cakes I took with me. The order said we were not to eat our supper until after drill. So after we had prepared the supper (white bread and coffee, we saved the meat left at noon for this morning) Thomas Sherman[5] and I went down to the brook to wash. When we got back, we then found them eating and two more added to our mess. So all that one of the cooks could do was to get a little riley coffee and a small crust. But I had saved my cakes against time of need.

Well, now I have just finished my dinner. Frank Hutchinson and——[6] cook for our mess today. We had halibut chowder and a small piece of pickle. Our company has its full compliment of men now 101. I have received a good woolen shirt, blanket and knapsack, a mattress pillow with good clean English hay. I keep warm and comfortable and find things generally better than I expected.

I shall expect to see you the first of next week. You must bring your dinner with you or buy it off the baker when you get here. If you conclude to write to me before you come, you will follow directions which I will give you on another paper.
Rufus

It will be sufficient if you write:

Camp Old Colony care of Captain Harlow,[7] Taunton, Mass.

I want one more towel, razor and strap, a cheap one and those needle books. I can send to the store at the village and get anything that I may need.

June 18, 1861
Camp Old Colony
Taunton, Massachusetts

THIS IS OUTLAWED

It is a very fine morning and I enjoy it very much for my health is good and I am comfortable in every respect. It is now just nine o'clock. I have been through with all the morning exercise and have nothing to do this hour but write to you.

I arose this morning at half past four. The roll is always called at five and every man must answer to his name. We breakfast at half past six, then drill from seven to eight, then another drill from ten to half past eleven, then from two to three o'clock, then again from four to half past five, then dress parade at half past seven in the evening. These are the order of our exercises. Dinner at half past twelve. Supper at half past six.

[The letter continues.[8]]

July 8, 1861
Taunton

Dear Father,

I have seen Mr. Bouldra and Mrs. Howland. I am much obliged for the portfolio. It is about the right size. I sent my shoes home last night in a band box by Mr. Tolman French. You will find them at Mr. Ransom's store. I am going to send my two cotton shirts and my cup home today by Mr. Bouldra. I do not think I shall need them. The whole company are sending their clothing home except what they have received from the state.

Our teamers are going to Boston after the teams this afternoon, two four horse teams. They will be here tomorrow night and we shall probably leave here Wednesday night or Thursday morning.

My health is very good. I think often of the privilege that I have of going to the river to bathe. I like my woolen shirt next to me better than I expected. Captain Harlow offered me the chance to go to Boston with the teamers after the teams. I told him I should like to go, but did not feel confidence in myself to undertake it.

I do not suppose I shall hear from you again whilst I remain here but I think I shall write you once more.
Rufus

June 20, 1861
Abington, Massachusetts

Rufus,

Having an opportunity to send a line to you by Charles Shaw and understanding that you're coming home next week, I thought that it might be well for you to book yourself as to the running of the cars so that you would not get bothered. I inquired of John West in regard to the way he came home and should suppose that you would have to be careful or you will get to New Bedford instead of Abington. So be careful to inquire that you are right.

It seems that C. Shaw has enlisted in the Fall River company. He was here today dressed in full overcoat and all.

We are all well here. Mother about as usual. Henry is going to pick some strawberries tomorrow. I think there will be two boxes by that time. We have been hoeing the orchard piece today, expect to finish it tomorrow.

I know of nothing particular to write more and Charles is waiting for this. He has come in since I commenced to write.
Yours affectionately,
R. Robbins

July 11, 1861
Thursday
Taunton, Massachusetts

Dear Father,

We are not to leave camp today as we expected yesterday. For some reason the regiment was not in readiness to move. But, according to orders read last night at dress parade, we shall be on the move tomorrow sometime in the course of the day. We have not drilled so much as usual for the last two or three days, but have spent most of the time in getting ready to leave.

The teams arrived here yesterday morning. There are now on the ground fifteen wagons and sixty-four horses. Each company is entitled to one to four horse teams and the regiment to two hospital teams so called. These are not here yet but will be soon with a few more horses.

The men are all anxious to be on the move. We have got all our equipment now. When I first got them all on, I felt as though I was in a strange harness. The first thing is to put on the cartridge box with the strap over the left shoulder, and the box is a little behind the right side. Next a belt, to which is attached a cap box and bayonet sheath, the latter hangs a little behind the left side. The cap box on the right in front. Next goes on the knapsack, then haversack to hold the bread and meat, then canteen. They are all easily carried but the knapsack. And that is not bad unless you load it too heavily.

I believe I have sent home every thing now that I shall not need excepting my blue jacket. If it was not for the heft, I should not care much to keep it. One is enough to care of. My government clothes are all that I have got now except trousers and I think they will be sufficient until I get more. I have got my washing all done, have got three pairs clean stockings in my knapsack and clean shirt and drawers.

My health is good and I don't have to work very hard. I wish I could share some of my leisure time with you. I am not homesick nor discontented. I am willing to stay [away] from you and do my duty as long as my services are required, but it will be a happy day when I can return to you again. I hope to hear from you again as soon as I make my place of destination known to you.

It is now about seven o'clock. I have just come off dress parade. We are to go tomorrow. I feel sure the cooks will be at work all night to cook rations for four days. I am one of the advance guard. We, the advance guard, will probably leave the ground at half past ten tomorrow morning to take possession of the cars which are to carry us as the order read tonight. There are six detailed from each company: Frank Hutchins[on], T. Sherman, E. M. Bane,[9] Willard Brown,[10] Joshua Winslow,[11] Corporal.

I shall write again soon.
Rufus

July 16, 1861
Camp Old Colony
Washington, D.C.

Brother Henry,

I do not think you are more anxious to hear from me than I am to write you. I want to tell you of all that I have seen but I do not suppose I can one half.

We left Taunton enroute for Washington at 1 P.M. I will try to give you the names of the some of the places which we passed through which are as follows. Mansfield, Attleboro, Pawtucket, Providence, Greenwich, Wickford, Kingston, Westerly, Stonington, Conn., Mystic, and Groton.

Went aboard the boat about 6 P.M. We had a very pleasant night and enjoyed the trip very much. Went to bed about 10 o'clock, arose next morning about half past three. And now commenced a sight more beautiful than I can express. We passed in full view of Jersey City, Brooklyn and several beautiful islands. Had a pretty good view of New York, until we arrived at the wharf and then such a forest of masts as I have never imagined prevented my seeing much more of it.

We got into New York Saturday morning about 6 o'clock. Stopped there about 15 hours, were not permitted to go ashore. Saw Mr. Meers, but could not speak with him. Left New York about 11 A.M. in the boat, *Kill von Kull* for Elizabethport, New York. Left there about 2 P.M., came through West Field, Plain Field, Bound Brook, Somerville, Lebanon, Clinton, High Bridge, and Hampton. These are all towns in New York.

Arrived in Harrisburg, Pennsylvania about 3 o'clock Sunday morning. Stopped there about four hours, did not see much of the place, as it rained quite hard. Left there about 7 A.M. through York and Glen Rock. Reached Baltimore about 3 P.M. Our company and [the] Fall River company were ordered to load our guns just before we arrived in Baltimore but we had no occasion to use them. It was a cry quiet there. Marched through the city and took cars for Washington. Passed the Belay House. It is not remarkable for size or beauty. It is about ten miles out of Baltimore.

Arrived at Washington about 8 A.M. Slept in the Capitol and next morning took an early leave for the campground. So I have not seen anything of the city yet, but the Capitol. We are encamped within a quarter of a mile of Georgetown. I went there yesterday afternoon. Saw the Potomac River.

I must close now just where I am. My health is good.

I shall write again soon and tell you how to address your letters.

I have time to tell you now.

R. Robbins

Camp Old Colony

Washington, D.C.

7th Reg. Mass V

Co. K Captain Harlow

Write as soon as you can.

Rufus

July 18, 1861
Camp Old Colony
Washington, D.C.

Henry,

This is the fourth day that I have been here and I am going to give you a little memorandum of each day. I am on guard duty today, am on the second relief. It is now about half past three P.M. and our squad will have to relieve the first in one and a half hours.

It is a nice day and I feel first rate. I am seated at the foot of a large white oak tree, my knapsack resting upon the roots upon which I am writing. The same root also furnishes me with a good seat, it being raised some 2½ ft. above the ground. I think the diameter of this tree must be near four feet. I wish I could continue to describe to you this beautiful place, but time is short and I want to begin with the first day here, Monday.

It was rather a busy day as we had the ground to clear and tents to pitch. But I managed to get a little leisure in the afternoon which I improved to good advantage. I had just taken my pencil and paper to write you a few lines when someone proposed that we should go over to Georgetown. A stream[12] of water about 40 ft. wide on the west side of our campground forms the boundary between us and Georgetown. We have to go down a steep, but short hill, before we come to the stream, then follow a well beaten path for a short distance until we come to a road, then turn to the left and cross the bridge and we are in Georgetown. Georgetown Heights are but a short distance from the bridge. From this place, we had a pretty good view of the city of Washington. I only went through a few streets of the town as I could stop there but a short time. They are not very pretty but quite thickly settled.

I saw about as many blacks as whites. The little darkie children are very pretty. Mostly free pigs, big and little, run in the streets. I counted 10 with one old sow.

I did not have to go far to see the Potomac River. I went within ¼ of a mile of it. It is a very pretty stream.

Now I must say a few words of Tuesday. Went down to the stream before breakfast and had a good bath. Was on police duty that day, helped remove the tents again to a more convenient place. Did not rest well the night before. Slipped out of bed 3 or 4 times but not a very serious fall as we sleep quite near the ground. We pitched them at first on the side of a hill. We do not have our sacks now, as we did at Taunton, nothing but the bare ground. Make your bed with such as you have. So I find my rubber blanket very convenient. I spread it upon the ground first, then ½ my woolen blanket under me and the other over. My overcoat, I use for a pillow. Rather a hard bed, but I don't know but I rest as well as I ever did.

Wednesday, went off of the ground before breakfast about ¼ of a mile for a regimental drill. Took breakfast about seven, then went out for a target shoot. Shot twice apiece. I hit it both times, distance 75 yards. Went to bathe in the afternoon. Picked a few ripe blackberries.

Of today, Thursday, I have but little to say, except I am on guard duty. I have to keep myself near the guard house all the time when I am off duty. I do not object to it. As you will see from what I have already written that I am very pleasantly located. I have to stand 4 watches out of the 24. Each 2 hours, 2 on and 4 off as there are 3 reliefs. This keeps one on all the time. Each consists of about 33 men. My duty commenced today at 11 A.M. I was relieved at 1 and now as it is nearly 5. I will take my leave of you until another convenient time for I shall soon hear the call.

Well, now it is Saturday and I have taken longer leave of you than I intended, but duty, pleasure and convenience are the only reasons. So I will go back to where I left off.

My duty Thursday night was not a very pleasant one as it rained some. But I got through with it, without taking any cold and have rested well since. So I feel quite well now.

Whilst I was on guard from 5 to 7, the President, Old Abe, visited our camp. I could not see him. I was very much disappointed. Frank's post was near mine. He had just a look at him.

Andrew Hinckley[13] was taken prisoner whilst sleeping on his post between 11 and 1 A.M. He is a member of our company, a South Abington boy. His post was not far from mine. He would not have slept, if he had not sat down. I don't know what his sentence will be. I hope not very severe. I would rather a ball would pierce my heart than to be found sleeping on my post. I would not make mention of this for the present.

Friday morning after the new guard was mounted, we the old guard, went out to discharge our guns. The target was placed at the distance of 125 yards. Of the 100 guards that shot, I was the last and but 8 shot better than mine and some of those but very little. After that a few of us with Lieut. M.[14] went to bathe.

Charles Sumner made us a visit in the afternoon. Was here at dress parade today. Saturday, a short drill before breakfast. After breakfast, went out to shoot blank cartridges by company. After that we went out with the Capt. H.[15] to bathe, picked quite a lot of blackberries. Had a first rate dinner, fried steak and bakers bread.

We have not fared so well here as we did at Taunton. The men are getting cross and there are signs of better things. My health continues very good. I do not see a great difference in the weather here from the

weather at home. I have many things in mind that I want to write, but I must close now. You must ask questions if you want information. Luke[16] is well, is seated beside me writing. Tell Edwin that I have not forgotten him. Will write to him soon. (To be continued.)
Rufus

July 24, 1861
Camp Old Colony
Washington, D.C.

Henry,

I have sat down to write you a few lines beneath the shade of some of these noble trees which surround our campground. I am waiting as patiently as I can for the mail to arrive for I have hopes of hearing from you this morning.

I am going to give you a little description of our campground. In the first place, I will say we are located upon a hill which contains somewhere from ten to fifteen acres which is entirely surrounded by a forest of large trees. We have an uneven plain upon the top of the hill from five to seven acres which does very well for a parade ground.

I am seated on the west side of the ground about thirty paces down from the plain where we drill. Fifty paces more, down a very steep pitch, would bring me to the edge of the stream which I mentioned in my last. I can see it from where I am seated and up a steep hill which is covered with corn on the opposite side.

I can see two houses, one of brick, the other of wood. The whole campground is surrounded by a public road outside of the forest.

I am very anxious that you should know how it looks here but I don't suppose that it will be possible for me to describe it so that you will.

I mailed a letter for you last Sunday morning. Saturday night I was on guard again, though I was not detailed, but took N. A. Reed's[17] place, as he was not well. It was a very pleasant night. I was stationed on the East side of the ground, near the colonel's quarters. The moon shone out so brightly among the trees that I could not help enjoying my situation although I was alone and had no one to speak to in the still hours from two til four. But I could think of the pleasant home that I had left, of you all as you were quietly sleeping in your beds, and not a spot did I neglect to visit. Now the orderly is coming with the mail. I will go and see if he has one for me.

Well, there were many names called before mine and I had begun to despair. But I am satisfied now, for I have received two very interesting letters.

I was glad to learn that you were all well and getting along so nice with the work. I was going to say (don't work too hard), but that will not make any difference. I know that you do. I wish you could have as many leisure hours as I do. We have more time here than we had at Taunton but do not know how to improve it so well because our exercises are not so regular. We do not drill but twice a day. But have more police and guard duty to do.

Many of our men have been sick since we have been here. So it makes it a little harder for the well ones. Diarrhea is the most common complaint. I have not seen a sick day since I have been here. In fact, I have felt better than I did while at Taunton. I have been rather costive but am in better condition now. Seven tomatoes and a piece of brown bread which I bought there on the ground set me all right. They are ripe and very good. Cost seven cents apiece.

We have fine weather here. Cooler than I expected. I am glad you have got your clothes. I have not received any money yet, but expect a little soon. A half a month's pay.

I want you to write me as often as you can if it is but little. It is now morning of the twenty-fifth and I shall not mail this until tomorrow. On my next sheet, I shall commence my memorandum with Sunday last.
Rufus

July 28, 1861
Camp Old Colony
Washington, D.C.

Dear Mother,
I have taken a very comfortable seat at the Captain's[18] table which he has loaned me under cover of an awning which projects from the back of his tent. I have as many different places to write as you receive letters. I wrote a letter of 4 pages to Ruth this morning and finished it in season to go to meeting which commenced at ½ past 10.

The weather is very fine today as it is about every day. It is now about 2 P.M. and pretty warm out in the sun. This morning it was quite cool and good air. I enjoyed the meeting very much this morning. Not because the sentiments were in unison with my own so much but because it was the place where I could go with a grateful heart and acknowledge the many blessings which continuously surround me. It seemed quite home-like to hear the bells over in Georgetown ringing for the morning services.

My health is very good today and I think that I enjoy myself about as well as I ever have in my life. Not that I do not miss my home. I can not think of anything that would give me half the pleasure that it would to spend a day with you. But I feel that I am engaged in a good cause. And being in the company of many kind friends and nothing to weigh heavily on my mind, I do not know why I should not enjoy my new life. And I think it has thus far proven beneficial to my health.

I like this place much better than I did Taunton. I think we had a few days there as warm as any I have seen here, though I think when I first arrived here that I noticed a difference in the air that I had never before.

One thing I enjoy very much is our good chance for washing our clothes and bathing. Luke and I start off about every other morning along the stream to a waterfall, where there is a first rate shower. I meant to have said that roll call is at five o'clock. We start immediately after that. Are not gone for more than fifteen or twenty minutes, for we have company drill for fifteen or twenty minutes and then breakfast.

We make a little improvement in our diet lately. We take a stick and run it through a slice of bread and hold it over the coals and toast it. And when we have butter with it as has been the case a few times of late, we think we were never so well fed before. We had a surplus of coffee which our orderly swapped for butter. The worst trouble we have now is the cooking but that I think will be remedied soon.

Mother,

It is now Monday morning. I was called to duty last eve before I could finish my letter and I have not time now. So good-bye. You will hear from me again soon.

Yours affectionately,

Rufus

August 1, 1861
South Abington

Dear Brother,

We received your letter Wednesday morning and glad enough were we to hear from you. Glad to hear that you were still in good health and spirits. I should like to have been with you when you went blackberrying but at all other times I would rather you would be with us.

I am making sewed army shoes for J. Lane & Company of East Abington. Now I suppose you would like to know how I came to get such a seat of work. Well, I will tell you. In the first place, I always thought I would like to know how to make sewed work so as pegged work was all played out. I went to see Mr. Samuel P. Reed, saw him make one shoe, thought I could do it, came home, cut me out a pair from some large pieces of bottom filling which I had, got them fitted, and made them. Well, they did not look very well, nor very bad, considering that my outer soles were but poor inner soles. Then, I thought I would get a pair out of someone's lot and try them. But I did not dare to show anybody my shoes, so I gave that up. Then, I thought of hiring a man to sew and stitch and I do the finishing.

But it is getting late now and I must bid you good night now, but will resume my experience tomorrow night with I hope of a better pen than I now have————

Sunday, August 4

I am sure I did not think it would be so long before I should resume my letter when I left off last Thursday eve, and the manner which I left off has since reminded me of a story which I read a short time ago entitled, "Regular Habits," in which the head of a family consisting of himself, wife, a son and daughter (the two latter being of the respective ages of nineteen and sixteen) had established for himself a code of regular habits, such as the rising every morning in winter at precisely 4½ o'clock and summer at precisely 4 o'clock to the great discomfiture of the rest of the household, for after taking his morning's walk of ½ an hour he would give them no rest until they presented themselves below. Well, this functionary becoming disgusted at length at the indolence of his family, especially his children, that he resolved to advertise for a tutor who, beside his other accomplishments, should assiduously adhere to a form of regular habits.

This advertisement happened to fall under the notice of a newly graduated member of college who having nothing in particular to do thought he would apply for the situation, which he obtained. Arriving at the station a few miles from the home of his employer, he was met by a young man who inquired if he was Mr.____. The tutor replying in the affirmative, he was invited to ride. The young man, being one of his pupils, who gave him an account of his father's management and wound up by declaring that his father did not understand himself and sister, and appealed to Mr.____ to defend them so touchingly that that individual thought that there must be something in it, and resolved to lay his plans accordingly.

So, after reaching their destination, settling the terms, etc. with his host, he was introduced to the family which he amused by telling stories. Being in the middle of the description of an arch which was only wide enough to admit of a very spare man, he said he saw a large man try to force his way through, getting however only his head and shoulder through.

At [this] juncture, the clock struck nine, whereupon Mr.____ jumped up, declaring that it [was] one of his regular habits to retire at just nine o'clock and walked out of the room.

"I should like to know what became of the fat man," said the son (whose name by the way was Rufus).

"He will tell you," said his father exultantly, "at precisely ¼ of 6 o'clock tomorrow."

Not being satisfied, however, he called to him to know what did become of him.

"He drew his head out and concluded not to go through," was Mr.____'s reply.

Next morning, after considerable shivering (for it was the latter part of November) and two or three times resolving to abandon his project, and as many to go ahead, he forced himself out of bed, dressed himself, and giving some half dozen raps upon the wall which divided his room [from] that of his hosts, succeeded in bringing him in his nightshirt to his door with the inquiries. "Why, sir, are you sick? Shall I send for the doctor, etc.?"

"Oh, no sir," said Mr.____, "but it is one of my regular habits to take some light refreshments at precisely three o'clock in the morning and, if you will be so good, as to show me the way to your larder, I will try not to disturb you in future."

Half asleep and more frightened at his sudden disturbance, the host started to obey. Upon reaching it, Mr.____ found plenty of good things and bidding his host good morning set himself in an easy chair in the parlor and commenced a very comfortable smoke from which he was aroused by a stern voice from the head of the stairs calling, "Rufus! Rufus! How many times have I told you not to smoke in the parlor?"

Whereupon Mr.____ presented himself and said he was very sorry if he had disturbed him but it was one of his regular habits to smoke after his morning's repast.

Discomforted and angry, he (the host) had to return to his bed.

But, alas, how soon to be disturbed, for Mr.____ no sooner than he found himself again victorious than he went to the piano and, being joined by Rufus and his sister, commenced playing and singing in a terrific manner.

This was the last "pound." Down came the host, half dressed, followed by his wife. Stalking into the room, he commenced to denounce the devoted tutor in all the evil comparisons of which he was capable. To which Mr.____ replied that he was only fulfilling that solemn compact which they has entered into—the care of the moral and physical growth of his children and ending with the assertion that it was one of his regular habits to sing an hour every morning.

This argument, the other could not refute. So he seated himself in a chair and prepared himself to endure it as best he might. But the time for singing was up. So they started for a walk and the old man fell asleep.

Now the amount of it was that others have ways and feelings as well as ourselves and the tutor took this way to let his host know it.

Now I have a great many things here to take up my mind and am not so mindful of you as I should be, though I am thinking of you every day. Yet when I left off the other night, I thought I could finish my letter tomorrow. Tomorrow came, I had to work late, was tired. I thought, so I will not write tonight but tomorrow and now I find myself with my letter unfinished but I will try to do better next time.

But this is not telling you how I came to get my sewed shoes. I said I thought of hiring someone to sew and stitch. With this design, started out. Met with no success. Brought up at Uncle Ames. About 9 A.M. went to work. Joshua worked until 2 P.M. Was told by Josh that I could make them as well as anybody. Stopped at J. Lane's. Told him what Josh said. Asked him for a case. Told him I would make a sample, if he wished it. But he said he would risk it. So I took them and come home. Have made 4 pair. Like them very much.

Everything is growing nicely here. Corn never looked better to me. Plenty of rain now, but it was _very_ dry until about a fortnight ago when it began to rain with a vengeance.

I have written so much that I am afraid Sophie and Mother will not have room. So I will close.

From your affectionate brother,
Edwin

[The letter continues.]

Dear Brother,

We were very glad to receive a letter from you and glad to hear you were well. I would like very much to visit you and see the camp and the country. I often imagine how it looks, but I suppose I have no correct idea of it. I read a letter from Mr. Bosworth,[19] which was published in the _Standard_. It was very interesting.

We had quite a time when Company E[20] came home. I think I never saw so many people together in South Abington. I did not know but three or four of the Company. They had altered so much. I was standing on Mrs. Woodsum's Store steps, when the Company marched from the depot and if I had not known they were coming, I should have called them all colored persons.

Edwin has written about his making sewed shoes. I think he gets along nicely. Henry and John are going to learn to make them next week or the week after.

Mother, Edwin, and I went to pick whortleberries Saturday. We started at ½ past four and got home at ½ past seven. We did not find very good picking, for someone had been before us and beat a path around every clump of bushes. We got about three quarts.

How I wish I could send you some pie, and I wish you were here with us every day when we sit down to eat, and I want you at home all the time. I have not been to see the farm this summer, but intend to the first opportunity. We have fine showers here almost every day or night. I wonder if it is much warmer where you are than it is here. Today is the most uncomfortable we have had for some time. Real dog days weather. Our garden looks quite well. The early potatoes are very small owing to the dry weather we have had for some time past. I am glad you can have blackberries. I would like to change with you. I should be willing to give you all my share of whortleberries for a few blackberries.

Business is as dull as can be. Men standing around with nothing to do. I heard this forenoon, that there were four men drunk Saturday night, three of them were singing and dancing on Mr. Ransom's steps, after the shop was closed till eleven o'clock. They were down back of Widow Bonney's house, the first part of the time.

Is it true that Captain Harlow has been promoted? We heard so. Captain N. Nash is dead. He was buried Saturday. Perhaps Father has written of it. Uncle and Aunt Partridge have gone to New Hampshire. He has gone to some doctor to see if that cancer can be cured, I believe.

Henry was here last night. He said, tell Rufus I shall send him a letter by next Sunday.

I do not know as you can read this letter. I have got a <u>hard times pen</u>. I shall lay all the blame on that, and say nothing about the blunders. Please do not forget to direct your letters to South Abington.

We shall expect you to write to us every other letter.

Your Affectionate Sister,

Sophie

August 1, 1861
Camp Old Colony
Washington, D.C.

Dear Father,

I received your letter today at twelve o'clock. I want to forward you a few lines today but I have but little time to write as it is now nearly four o'clock.

In answer to the last question which you ask, I have not met with any change which brings doubts to my mind of the truth of the doctrine of Universalism. On the contrary, I improve every opportunity to express it in word and deed.

Our fare is very good now. I will not attempt to answer your letter now, for tomorrow I shall have time enough. But have you received all the letters I have written home? This is the fourth, as you will see I have numbered it at the top and have written Edwin one.

My health is good. I was very glad to hear from you. Write again as soon as you get this. I do not know about our going to Washington but there is some talk about it. Inspection of arms now. So good afternoon. Rufus

August 2, 1861
Camp Old Colony
Washington, D.C.

[Dear Father,]

I penciled you a few hasty lines yesterday and today as I have more time I will try to give your questions a more definite answer. First, as to our going to the city of Washington. Yesterday I could not say anything very definite, but this morning I heard talk that makes me believe that we shall go there as a city guard. Captain, or rather Major, Harlow (as he was promoted to that office last Wednesday) says we are having a new uniform making at the city and another report, which I consider quite as good, says we shall go there within seven days. I hope it will be so, as it is considered a post of honor and no doubt our duties will be much easier.

The paymaster was here last Wednesday and we received five dollars and 86 cents each. He says our regiment is composed of the most intelligent men he has yet paid off and the Colonel told us a few days since that we have been here, we have the name of being the best behaved of any regiment that has come to Washington.

Now as to the effect of the battle[21] on our men. I do not know much of the feeling outside, but with us the feeling is: you will catch it so much the harder when we have an opportunity to engage you. I don't suppose the defeat has had a tendency to discourage our troops much because, as we understand it, we engaged them at a great disadvantage. I think you have had more correct news concerning the battle than I have, as I have not often seen the papers.

I see Charlie Shaw almost every day. He is not much disabled aside from the hurt which he had before he left home. I suppose he will be discharged. Hinckley was kept in the guard house about a week and then discharged without trial. I do not know that there are any that are not well disposed towards our company. I think he was a little guilty.

Our fare is very good now. There has been a great improvement within the last five days, although it has not been very bad except the first two or three days we were here. We have good fresh beef and salt beef, pork, and bacon. This we can have cooked in every variety of form we choose. Sometimes fried steak with new potatoes and onions, fresh beef soup, and salt, rice and sugar or molasses. Pea soup today for dinner, two slices of cucumber, and a little molasses on my bread. The two last named articles not in Uncle Sam's bill of fare today, but a treat from a friend.

We have got a first rate cook now. We agree to give him ten cents a month each. He is very saving too. He has not been cook but four days and has now a surplus of provisions worth twelve dollars. This will go to buy knickknacks. There is almost everything to sell on the ground in the shape of edibles.

Now in answer to the last question. Whilst I was at Taunton, I attended prayer meetings almost every evening. I was one of three or four who started them. The chaplain came in with us the second evening. I used generally to take some part in the meetings. I was often requested to read a chapter in the Bible at the commencement. I did not expect when I helped to start the meetings that the sentiments which I should hear would be in accordance with my own, but I thought they would do me good and others.

The next Sabbath afternoon, after you had visited me at Taunton, I spent an hour with the chaplain and with a few others, most of whom I was acquainted with. The subject of conversation was the difference of opinion betwixt them and myself. I gave them many good reasons why I was a Universalist. All seemed to listen with respect and none censored me for my belief. I cannot think how such a report could go from there. When I left home it was with the resolve that I would take good care of my moral and religious life and do all that I could to persuade others in the way which I believe is good. There is need enough of it here. You do not know how depressed many of the men are, even of our own company.

There is much more that I should like to write but I must close now. My health is good.

I am going to enclose six dollars to you. Five in bank notes and one gold dollar. Half of it belongs to William Howland.[22] Please give it to his wife. He has not written yet, but is well. I want you to use the three dollars I send, as you have need. I have enough left to stand me until I get more.

I enclosed a flower in my letter yesterday to Mother. I hope she has got it.

Rufus

August 4, 1861
Camp Old Colony
Washington, D.C.

Henry,

This is the stillest Sunday I have seen since I have been in camp. It is now twenty minutes past two P.M. and pretty warm though we are having a good breeze just now. The weather here for the last week had been warmer than we often see at home but I think it does not disagree with me for my health continues very good. I am feeling rather lazy today although I think I have not spent much of the time unprofitably.

I find the *Trumpets* which you sent me very interesting. I arose this morning at four o'clock, half or three-quarters of an hour earlier than I usually rise. Got my face washed and hair combed before any of the rest got up.

The order of exercises vary little on Sundays. They have been today as follows: roll call at five, breakfast at six, inspection at eight, police duty at ten, meeting at half past ten. Police duty is to clean up around the tents and tables. This we do every day. I think dress parade is the only remaining duty for today.

I have not much news to write today, so I will write just what happens to come to mind. We have not got to Washington City yet, though I still think we shall soon.

I have not told you anything yet about the soils and products of this place and the country which I have passed through. When I got as far as New Jersey, I expected to see the crops very much in advance of the crops at home but such was not the case. The soil through New Jersey and Pennsylvania and also here is composed of red clay at least along the railroad. The banks along the road are of a pale brick color. I saw a great many very large corn fields as I came through New Jersey and Pennsylvania but the corn does not look so even as it does at home. Some of it in the same fields looked three weeks in advance of the corn at home and some as much behind. I saw but few potatoes, but large crops of wheat and oats, which was mostly harvested. We have corn, potatoes, cucumbers and tomatoes here in the market now, though the corn is not very plenty yet. New potatoes are worth eighty cents per bushel. They do not take so good care of the gardens here as at home.

How are your tomatoes getting along? And the pears and apples, how are they getting along? You must write me another farming letter soon. Tell Edwin I am expecting to hear from him soon. I sent you six dollars last Friday, three dollars for Wm. Howland. Please write as soon as you get it. Don't work too hard.
Rufus

August 4, 1861
West Sumner, Maine

Dear Brother,

We received your letter this morning and were very glad to hear from you. And I now improve the first moments that I could get in writing to you. We have been to the village today. I went to meeting half a day. I think I am very smart. I am trying to do my work alone now. The baby is only four weeks old. Alice is a great deal of help to me. She is getting to be a great girl. The children are all well.

We received a letter from Henry last week which relieved our anxiety for I did not then know what regiment you belonged to and was fearful that you might have been in the great battle.[23] But it seemed still better to receive a letter from you telling us that you were well and contented. Still, I know that your heart must yearn for the old home and for the dear faces there. If we are ever so well contented, it will seem as though we must see father and mother and brothers. But we will all meet at the old home again, perhaps some Thanksgiving day. I do not believe this will be a long war. The right must conquer, and with Scott at their head, without much bloodshed. Perhaps, you will think I am very confident for one that knows so little about it but I always look on the bright side if there is any and hope for the best.

Albert is expected home this week. His wife has gone to Paris to meet him. He belongs to the First Maine Regiment. They enlisted for three months only Sunday the 11th.

I thought when I commenced this letter, you would receive it before this time but could not get time to write last Monday. Hiram[24] went on to the mountain blueberrying. He got about fourteen quarts of very nice ones. Albert got home last Tuesday. He has been to see us and we have been up there. He looks as fat and tough as can be. He says he had rather have given five dollars than not to have seen you. He was very near you several times. He will write to you soon. He says he knows how good it is to receive letters when away from home. I shall try to write often.

We had a letter from Mother last night. They were all well then. I have just got up from the table. We had beans and peas for supper. I wish you had been here to eat with us. I cannot write any more this time. Hiram wants that I should go to ride tonight so I shall have a chance to mail this letter.

Write soon and let us know how you get along. Be careful of your health. Hiram sent a letter to you last Saturday. I hope you will get it. "May the God of Battles preserve you," is the prayer of your sister.
Yours affectionately,
Ruth

August 7, 1861
Washington, D.C.

Henry,

We left Camp Old Colony yesterday morning at 8 A.M. We are located now about as near Washington as before although we had a march of about 5 miles. I do not like this place so well as the other. I miss the shade trees and the good water. We are encamped on a hill with low land all around but have only a small stream of water and a few springs which we have dug, but the water in the springs is very riley and always will be. I filter all that I use.

This is the 7th letter I have written you since I left Taunton and have received but two. I was very much disappointed today.

Last Monday, the day before we left Camp Old Colony, I was detailed as a Provo Guard. There are 10 of us and corporal and sergeant, one private from each company. I happened to be the lucky one, for I call it lucky. I have a fine opportunity to see the county. We can go and come when we please, that is with the corporal or sergeant. I saw more of Georgetown last Monday than I had ever seen before. Our business is to pick up those who run guard, report liquor sellers, arrest gamblers and capture rebels if we can find them.

Last Monday whilst we were at Georgetown, we had sat down to rest on the corner of a street in front of a large house. The man of the house came to the gate and asked if we would like a cold potato. I told him no for I was not very hungry and thought a cold potato was not a very great treat, but the corporal thought we had better go in. It was true. The potato was not very warm, but we had a dish of string beans, corn, tomato and a slice of pork. This was all mixed together. What is called succotash. It was very good.

I don't know how long this duty will last but I hope a long time for it clears me from all other duty and I think I heard the Colonel say it would last during good behavior. I like the men. They are all good fellows.

This morning we went out about a mile, picked a good lot of black and whortleberries. Picked up a few runaways.

I begged a few flower plants of a lady whose house I stopped at, which I am going to send you. One of them which looks like pusey is common at home. I send the seeds of that kind with a few slips and a few larger seeds which I do not know. The other is a pink, new to me, and very pretty. I hope Mother will make this live. I am writing very fast as I have got to go out again soon.

Direct your letters, Washington, D.C. 7 Regt. Mass M V care of Capt. George W. Reed.

Rufus

August 8, 1861
South Abington

Dear Cousin Rufus,

As Ann has written rather fancy, I will write very polite. I now take my pen to write you a few lines.

We are all well. I have just returned from Marshfield. Ann started for Weston this morning.

I must tell you about my visit at Marshfield. I went in the express wagon Mr. Fairbanks used to go in with two horses selling beer. We had a fine ride. Ruth Porter, Mrs. Norton's sister, you know who she is, an old maid. She frets and worries all the time. The first night we were there, she did not sleep a bit, so the next day she worried more than ever. Wednesday, the wind blew quite hard, so the waves made more noise. She said she could not sleep for that old roaring. That evening, when Mr. Norton came in, she was just as sober as could be. She asked him if the sea had not been roaring and carrying on terribly that day, so she talked all the time. She never was to a beach before.

We stopped at Mr. Earle's. It is a tip top one. There was thirteen of us. I did not catch but one fish and that washed away among the stones. He was alive when I found him, so I left him until after he died, then I carried him up to the house.

When we was coming home yesterday a shower came up. We all got out. I ran into somebody's house. I don't know who[se] it was. The [rain] felt very nice, so I did wish an old shaker on one that Mary knocked a great hole in. For when we were coming down a hill, I had my shaker in my hand. Mary almost fell out of the wagon. She struck my bonnet with such force as to knock her hand right through the side.

Almost everyone there at the shanties said they was glad I had come for I looked so thin, with my cheeks all fell in. So they thought I really needed to come.

Samuel Keene and all the Torry's were there next to us. Is it not nice to be down there? I love to stay there dearly.

I had a letter from Andrew Hinckley, Monday. He says it is a pleasant campground.

How do you like to be so near Washington? You have a fine chance to see so many different places.

I am going to take music lessons. I begin next Wednesday, so I will play a dancing tune when you get home for I am going to take light music.

I am glad to hear you have not had to fight any. I hope you will not have to.

As it is about dinner time, I must close. Please answer soon and direct to South Abington. You may write to Ann too, but Judson and I shall want some.

Next time I will try and write more news if there is any.

Good-bye,

Hannah

August 12, 1861

Dear Brother,

Although I have not received an answer to my letter which I wrote you a week ago, yet it has become one of my "regular habits" to write you every week, nothing preventing.

I have but little news to tell except that I have hired a gang. Four of us in all. The Rev. Mr. Hutchinson and son take the lasts and get the shoe ready for the outer sole. Also finishes them after they are in black. William Rich does the rest, except stitching which I do. We think we can make six pairs a day. We have not got to work yet.

We came together yesterday for the first time. Puttered a little. Finished my case. Equal to the making of two and a half pairs, which was very well, considering our company. There were three in at one time, making seven of us in all. Saying nothing about the ones and the twos which were in almost constantly.

We are going to work in Frank H's shop, there being more room. I am going in with my shoes tomorrow.

I have invented a jack for holding my shoe while stitching it. Perhaps, I can give you somewhat of an idea of it by the following.

Now suppose the figure 1111 to represent a board 6–4 inches, the mark 2 a staple, 3 a small block upon the board through which there is a pin to secure the heel of the last, 4 a block to secure the toe fastened by a sort of hinge to the staple 2, so as to allow it to play back and forth. a in 4, is an oblong hole through which passes the end. b of 5 which has a thread on it with a nut which is turned with the thumb and fingers and by the way which is an iron rod. The end c is turned up and flattened with a hole through it and is riveted to the block 3 at the point d. e is a hole through which passes a bolt which fastens the jack not to the bench, but to the side of a plank or board set upright. Thus bringing the jack sideways instead of flat on the bench as others are.

Now if you can understand it or not, you may think that I have taken a great deal of pains to do something which some other jack would as well do. But that is not so, for reasons. First, all jacks which require a strap would tax my inventive genius a great deal more to rig a pulley over which the strap must run. Second, the bottom or foundation of all jack fastening with a bolt and screw are so large that the thread would catch on them every stitch. But you will see that by rounding the corners, I have a bottom every way smaller than the sole of my shoe.

This may not have been very interesting to you but there is nothing interesting here to write about, so I have to pick anything I can. If there is anything that you would like to know about, which does not occur to us, just write it in your next and we will try to inform you.

Your letters are very interesting to us, though the last one was not half so long as I want them to be. Give us a description of the place, what you have to eat, what is going on, and everything. It makes it seem as though we were nearer each other if we know what each are doing.
All full
Edwin

August 14, 1861
Washington, D.C.

Henry,

I have an opportunity to send this to you by Samuel L. Snell,[25] a member of our company, who is to start for home this morning. My health is good. I am expecting to hear from you today. It is two weeks today since I have. I have sent you money. Have you received it? I will enclose a letter which I received from Hiram.
Yours in haste,
Rufus

August 14, 1861
Abington

Rufus,

I suppose that you have received a letter from Henry today. You ought to have heard from us before giving you to know that we had received the money you sent home. I believe all the letters you have written have been duly received.

Henry in his letter gave you an account of the farming. The corn fields do not look now as they did then. We have had the two days past as hard a northeast storm as anyone needs to remember. There has as much rain fallen, I should think, as there has been the three months before. The corn all lays flat to the ground but the sun will bring it up again, I hope.

There is such a sameness here, as you know, that we can get but little material to write about and may sometimes have to send our thoughts south and ask questions.

You gave a description of the soil and the crops there but said nothing about the fruit. Do they raise many apples and pears? And what is the prospect for a crop? Peaches, I saw mentioned in a paper, were in Baltimore for sale, I think. Is there many this year? It is thought here there has not been so little fruit for a number of years. The few apples, there is here, are so wormy that they do not grow fair. I do not know as we shall have a bushel of winter apples. Do they raise many sweet potatoes where you are? We cannot expect to have any this year. The rebels will want them all to feed themselves.

We had a letter from Horatio a few days since. He is at Winthrop. He thinks he shall make a stop there. He is liked there and thinks he shall have practice.

Business is as dead here as it was when you went away. Nothing but army shoes making and they are mostly sewed.

Mr. Hutchinson told me of a statement made to you from a writer here saying that Frank wrote that when you were expecting to go and reinforce the force attacking Manassas that you and Luke were <u>scared</u>. It was a different version from what I got from Mr. Hutchinson. He told me that Frank wrote he never saw two such <u>solemn men</u> in his life and his father told me (he received the letter I believe) that he wrote he never saw two such <u>solemn</u> and <u>determined men</u>, altering the case entirely. John has written to Frank so that you will get the truth before you receive this.

We are all well here. I do not know but you will get a letter from Edwin as soon as you do this one. He received one from you tonight.

Have they made a Colonel of Captain Harlow? We hear he is acting in that capacity. I shall give you a short letter this time. Mother thinks of writing in a few days. Take care of yourself as far as you can. Henry says that business is very good for army service shoes. They cannot get them made as fast as they want to.

Yours Affectionately,

R. Robbins

August 15, 1861
Abington, Massachusetts

Dear Brother,

We received your letter yesterday. Anything and everything from you
is interesting. I went with my shoes today. Mr. L[ane] liked all but the
sewing in of the welt or, as we should call it, the lasting. He said I took
too long stitches. He gave me $5.25 for 17 pair. I got another lot of 15
pair. I had 5 persons besides myself in the shop at one time yesterday.
Henry and Judson were two of them. They were at work. The other 3
spectators. Everybody thinks it is wonderful strange that I am making
sewed shoes, though a great many are going into it.

We read the account of the great battle near Springfield last night. We
regret very greatly the death of General Lyon,[26] though we cannot expect
to gain a bloodless victory. And we are thankful that those who are dear
to us were not exposed to danger, or greater than attends a soldier in
fulfilling his daily duties.

A very cold eastern storm commenced on Monday night last, which
lasted until last night (Wednesday). The wind was very strong, prostrating
corn and trees at a great rate. It blew out my best graft which had grown
about two feet. I was very sorry, for I prized it very highly. The corn will
come up again.

I think I read your message to Henry yesterday and I think he is making
amends by writing you tonight. Both my pen and ink are so poor that I
am out of patience with them. So I shall bid you good night.

[The letter continues.]

August 18th
Dear Brother,

I again take the first opportunity to write you a few more lines. It is a
beautiful Sabbath morning. The sun shines brightly, the air is cool and
refreshing, and everything looks cheerful and happy. It is just such a time
as calls forth the better feelings and perceptions of man's nature. Pleasant
thoughts seem to present themselves, as it were, unbidden. Thought of
good and the goodness of the world and of its supreme governor.
Thought of happy days past, happy scenes witnessed, and a happy looking forward to the realization of joy in the future and remembering
naught of the present but its joys. We shut ourselves up within our own
happy reflections, which reflections, however, are not selfish ones. No!
We close our doors only to the unpleasant but we welcome with open
hearts all generous and unselfish thoughts. We think of the absent and
though we drop a tear at the prospect of that absence being so pro-
longed, yet we quickly banish it and dwell upon the great joy to be experienced when our Father—whether in this vineyard or the immortal—

shall see fit to unite heart to heart and life to life, the members of his ever blessed family. And we hope and trust that we may be permitted to enjoy those pleasures which we have heretofore so long and tranquilly enjoyed while yet serving here on earth.

You will perceive by the train of thought in which I have indulged that my impatience has all subsided. It has with the clouds. And the storm passes every unpleasant thing from our lives. And happy are we, if we acknowledge it. Thrice happy, if we fully realize it.

We are all well. Sophie in particular. Henry did received your letter with the money. We have garden sand in plenty.

I will close and make room for Sophie.

From your brother,

Edwin

[Edwin has drawn this picture. It is unclear whether it is of himself, another, or simply a cartoon. A close inspection will show that he has written "Jeb" or "Jef" in the elongated chin. Perhaps it is a caricature of Jefferson Davis, President of the Confederate States of America.]

August 15, 1861
Washington, D.C.

Henry,

If I had not got that letter today, I had made up my mind to ask for a leave of absence long enough to come home and find out the reason but it is all right now.

I feel the best this afternoon that I have for more than a week. We have just had another moving, but only a short one about a quarter of a mile. The object, I suppose, is to secure a better location. We are now on higher ground and in every respect pleasanter. We have just pitched our tent and got things together again.

I was on guard, day before yesterday. It was a cold, not disagreeable day, but I got along with it very well. The wind was northeast, very heavy showers in the afternoon and towards night. Just such a northeaster as we have at home about the last of April or first of May. It cleared off about 12 o'clock that night. I do not like guard duty very well in such weather as that and felt a little down about it. But I had a streak of good luck before it was over. I was stationed near the cookstand that was cooking the Colonel's supper. He gave me three good, warm, griddle cakes with butter and sugar and a cup of tea.

My last watch was from 4 to 6 A.M. and there were then patches of frost in the low ground within 20 feet of my beat. I wore my overcoat and had to walk fast to keep myself warm. I am not on that Provo guard now. The sergeant got sick of it and gave it up August 16 [sic]. We are digging entrenchments now about ¼ of a mile from camp, fixing for a battery. Work 6 hours a day and get twenty-five cents per day extra pay.

I received a letter from Ruth yesterday at the same time I received yours. They are all well. She says Albert is going to write to me. I have not time now to write much and can't think of what I do want to write. I am glad Mother is going to write to me but I don't want to task her too hard.

Send me the *Trumpets* and see that I have one letter every week from you or Father or Mother. No matter how short, but the longer the better. I mean to write to James as soon as I can get the time. Tell him I think of him as often as once every day.

I want to know about my chickens when you write again. Write every particular.

Since writing the above I have been digging again for Uncle Sam. I told you we worked six hours a day. So we do, only we don't. The company is divided into two parts: first and second relief. The first work fifteen minutes and then the second relieves them whilst they rest for that length of time. So it is not very hard work.

Well, it is almost supper time now and Luke and I are going to make a little apple sauce for supper. I happened to pass through an orchard and picked up a few and as they are too hard to eat, I thought I would save them to cook.

I want you to tell me how the garden is getting along. I want to know if you have had any green corn yet. I have had two ears and some beets and cucumbers.

Well, now, Henry I will close my letter. I feel very thankful for the good long one you wrote me. It was just such a one as I wanted. Oh, how glad I should be to see you! I would walk ten miles tonight for the sake of being with you ten minutes. I am not homesick. I am having a good time here. But home—Oh, I tell you, now I know there is no place like it. Now, Mother, will surely think I am homesick but I can tell her of many a man in this regiment that would sooner grab for a chance to go home than he would for a handful of gold and yet none the less loyal to duty.

It is not with sorrowful and disheartened feelings that I contemplate home but with feelings of hope and pleasure.

I have been interrupted many times since I commenced this letter and as I know I must be again soon, I will stop now.

Yours Truly,
Rufus

August 18, 1861

Dear Brother,

We have not received a letter from you for a long time. We cannot but think it is because you have so much to do at this time. We hope you are well and we feel anxious to hear from you.

Edwin carried in his shoes last Monday. He got 15 pair more from Mr. Lane's and 12 pairs from N. Beal. Mother is stitching Mr. Lane's shoes. Uncle Partridge and Judson are making sewed shoes for a man in Joppa.[27]

Ann was here the other night, and she said she was going to give you a good scolding, because you have not written to them. She is going back to Weston next Saturday.

Business is about as dull as ever here. There is more done in East Abington. We saw some congress boots Monday, and Judson has had a chance to get some pegged work. I believe he likes sewed work pretty well. Edwin likes it much better than making Brogans.

I have been thinking to visit Mother Robbins[28] this week, but I fear I shall be disappointed. Mother Abbott[29] is so busy stitching shoes to keep Edwin at work, that she cannot leave them very well to go with me, and Edwin cannot stop his work to go, for he has so many working with him. So I must wait a while.

We do not see much of Henry. It is a long time since he was here. He came over one day to sew some shoes and I think that was the last time he was here.

We have got six hens from Father. Three are the Leghorns. They are doing nicely.

We saw Mr. Charles Curtis Monday, and he wished us to ask you to write to him. He said he would be pleased to hear from you, and would have your letter published in the *Abington Standard*.

I am afraid my letter is dull, but I hope you will excuse it. When I sit down to write, I cannot think of much to write, but if you were here, I could talk fast enough to tire your ears. Please write soon and as often as you can. I will try to write better next time. I have been working pretty busy this morning and my hand trembles.

From your affectionate sister,
Sophie

August 20, 1861
Washington, D.C.

Dear Father,

I have now a little leisure which I will improve in writing to you. It will be short for it is now ½ past 8 and at 9 our company will be marched off to the trenches again. We shall have to dig until 12, then 3 hours rest, commencing again at 3 this afternoon.

Since breakfast I have been fixing a place to dry my clothes. We have had a great deal of wet weather during the last 2 weeks. It is cloudy this morning but looks as though it would break away. I have been into the woods and cut 2 sticks with notches at the ends. These I have stuck up back of my tent about 8 feet apart and placed a straight stick acrost the top. This makes a first rate place to dry my blanket. I want you to understand that this is my invention and almost every man in our mess has followed my example.

We had for breakfast this morning rice and sugar, bread and tea, about as much sugar as you could take up on a spoon such as you eat bread and milk with and about 4 times full of rice. I can make ½ of the sugar do with the rice and the rest of it I use with the bread. I eat[30] my breakfast with a good relish and altogether there was enough of it.

Now I must work.

Well, here I am again. It is now about 1 o'clock. I have finished my work and eaten my dinner and have now 2 hours leisure.

For dinner we had bread and beef and 3 potatoes. I have not worked very hard this forenoon. When we work, our company is divided into 2 reliefs. The first relief works 15 minutes and then rests, whilst the 2nd work that length of time, and so on to the end of the 3 hours.

I have forgotten to tell you that we have had fair weather this forenoon, though it has been some cloudy. The sun has shone out a good part of the time and a good feeling air.

I was very happy to receive a letter from you last Sunday. I was at a place called Rock Creek. The way I happened to be there, our company were detailed as picket guard. Rock Creek is about 2 miles from our camp on the road to Harpers Ferry and the headquarters of our picket. We left camp Sunday morning at 7 o'clock and left at posts along the road 3 together about ⅛ of a mile apart. My post happened to be near the creek. Hobart,[31] Samuel's brother in law, and M. L. Sproull, the tailor's son at South Street, were left with me. We had a first rate time. Soon after we got there, I went to a house not far from our post and asked the woman if she would sell me a small piece of pork and lend me a pot to boil it in. I bought 3 ears of corn off her but when I got back I found that Hobart and Sproull had got corn, potatoes, cucumbers, and beets in great abundance. They said they went into the field and asked the man if we could have them. He didn't say anything so they supposed he was willing.

We fried most of the pork in one of the tin plates which we brought with us. The rest of it we put into the pot with the corn and potatoes. I never ate fried pork that tasted so good. We had plenty of bread and beef which we brought with us. And I think it was the best dinner I have eaten since I left home.

For supper we had more corn and some corn cakes which we bought at the house where we borrowed the pot.

After dinner, I sat down on my knapsack in the shanty built of brush and rails by the side of the road and wrote a letter to Hiram.

Next morning we were relieved at 7 o'clock and returned to our camp.

You ask about the fruit crops. From what I can learn the peach crop is rather small this year. I have not seen one large peach orchard yet in any of my travels, but I suppose there are many in our vicinity. Peaches are sold here on the ground from one to two cent apiece. I have seen 3 or 4 good looking apple orchards but not very full of fruit. I did not see so many fruit trees along the railroad as I expected to. They told me the soil was very poor along the road through the whole line. I have seen a few pear trees well loaded with fruit. But I could not learn any name for them. They are all sweet pears or early pears. Sweet potatoes, I think, are not grown very extensively in this part of the country, only a few for home use.

August 21st

This is another fine morning. The sun is shining out clear and we are having a good cool breeze. It begins to seem like September.

We commenced work this morning at 6 and were relieved at 9. They brought us 3 large guns last night. I should think they would carry a 36 pound ball. I think we shall mount 12 guns there. The works which we are building are about 5 miles from the city of Washington, on the road to Maryland, about 2 miles from the line. The ground is somewhat elevated and comprises about an acre, in the center of which is a small brick church.

Around this hill, we are digging trenches at the width of about 6 feet and about the same in depth. The earth is thrown up on the inside and sods lain so as to make a perpendicular wall. I cannot give you a very good description of it yet for I do not know how or where the guns are to be mounted. It will be quite a work when it is finished, but it is not ½ done yet. I like to work there. It is something new and gives me a good appetite.

Now the mail has arrived and I will go and see if there is a letter for me.

Yes! I have received Mother's letter as I expected and I feel very happy. But I am not going to answer it on this sheet but will very soon.

Well, now about that statement of Frank's. I think it was nearly 2 weeks ago, Luke received a letter from Hosias stating that Frank wrote to John stating that Luke and I were 2 of the soberest men he ever saw. It was very annoying to us to think that Frank should write any such thing about us when there was no provocation, as the inference was that we were scared. We went to Frank immediately and asked him if it was correct. He denied writing any such thing and told us he would inform John of the statement and we should be satisfied.

I am well satisfied now that there was no malice intended on the part of Frank or any one else. Even if there had been, it would not amount to anything. I feel very <u>confident</u> that when the time comes I shall have strength to <u>do my duty</u>. And I have no more doubts of Luke's courage and abilities to do his duty than I have of my own.

I thought I should write no more about it, but I will give you Frank's statement which he made when we asked him about it. He says, "Others as well as myself could not help noticing the difference between you and Luke and others about you and in your mess. They were cheering and swinging their hats. But you and Luke were about your business and seemed as unconcerned as though nothing had happened."

This was all true. Luke was very busy dealing out rations to the men in his mess as he took them from the cooks. And it seemed to burden his mind more than anything else.

I wrote you some time ago that Captain Harlow[32] had been promoted to Major. I will now say in place of Major Holman[33] [who] resigned. I have not heard of his being promoted again.

Well, what shall I write now? I guess I shall have to print this half of the sheet rather coarse.[34]

How would you like Father to have a farm out here? I wish you could see some of the corn fields here and then I think you would have a ready answer. I have not seen a farm here yet that I would swap mine for, though it were 40 times as large, if I have got to spend my life upon it. In a corn field of 10 or 15 acres, perhaps ½ of it will be pretty good. The land is very uneven out here and the corn which grows upon hills will never be worth harvesting except for fodder. But between the hills it looks quite well.

I suppose this is a very good market here, it being near the city. But I don't think that farming is more profitable here than at home. I have seen one corn field where the corn grew to the height of 16 feet. But I don't think the amount of corn will be much greater from it than we have harvested at home.

In one word, I don't like the style of the country out here. The houses are too far apart and I don't like the color of the ground. It looks as though they had been carting brick dust upon it all the days of their lives.

It is a hard red clay and after a rain it will stick to your feet like wax and the more steps you take, the more you have to lug.

We are expecting to receive our pay from the state soon.

Yours Affectionately,

Rufus

August 21, 1861
South Abington

Dear Brother,

I fear I shall not be able to write anything interesting, but I suppose you will excuse me if I am dull, for everything is dull here, I mean on the Mount and in the village.

You do not know how pleased we are when we receive a letter from you. I wish you could see Edwin when he brings one home from the office. He trembles like a leaf, he is so excited.

We looked for Father, Mother, and Henry last night, but were disappointed. I think Edwin has improved very much in stitching his shoes. He has quite a number of callers every day to see him work. I think he feels quite encouraged now. A few weeks ago, he felt downhearted and so did I.

But then it is natural for us to when we cannot see our way clear.

Our garden helps us very much. I hardly know what we should do without it.

We hear today that more volunteers are wanted as soon as possible. I think some of the members of Company E[35] will go.

Oh, how, I wish this war was over! It is hard for us to have our friends leave us, but not so hard for us, as for those who go from us and leave everything dear behind.

But we have one thing to comfort us at all times. We know there is One whose watchful care is over us in all place[s] alike. He will never leave or forsake us.

We read in the *Journal* that the Democrats in Maine held a convention on August 14th which broke up in a row.

From a long string of Resolutions, I will copy one. "Resolved, that in our judgement the discontented feeling, which has arisen among our brethren of the Southern States, caused by agitation of the slavery question, might have been quieted by conciliation and compromise equally honorable to both sections, and that a day of retribution will soon overtake the Republican leaders for their unwise and unpatriotic course in preferring to carry out a party dogma, to the preservation of a great and prosperous people from the horrors of civil war and national ruin."

They appeal to all true friends of the Union to join with them in an effort to save the Union. There were a few sensible ones, who thought the war was the only way to save the Union. I hope the Democrats will not make any more trouble, but I think they will if they have much encouragement. Don't you think they are about the same as secessionists? Perhaps you have read all this before.

It is getting late and I must close. Hoping to hear from you soon.
From Your Affectionate Sister,
Sophie E. Robbins

August 25, 1861
Sunday
Washington, D.C.

Dear Mother,

It is a beautiful Sunday morning. We have just got through with inspection of arms which comes between the hours of 8 and 9 and Luke and I have gone out into the woods a little way from the camp and spread our rubber blankets under the shade of a large tree where we can sit and read and write with comfort.

My health is very good and I can say with truth that most of the time I am in a very happy frame of mind. I know that you are very anxious about me and I often think how blest I am, that I have a home and friends to sympathize with me, but you say that you hope most. That is as it should be. I am glad that you can, for there is no need of any painful anxiety. Let us continue to trust in the One that will always take good care of us. I sometimes almost think that I am blest above every other man in the regiment and, with the exception of Luke and a few others so far as our company is concerned, I think it is true.

I suppose, there have been many letters sent home describing our situation as very bad. But with a very few exceptions, I do not find it so. So far as the food is concerned, I get along very well, when I have a good appetite. When I do not, as it is not often the case, I buy a little milk or some butter and toast my bread. I can buy cakes and pies or any kinds of fruit.

So far as sleeping is concerned I get along quite as well. I sleep at the end of the row, on one side of the tent and at the back part of it, next to Luke. I always raise the bottom of the tent a little so that I can have a good breathing hole and have a way of making my bed which is very comfortable and am more regular about my sleep than I ever was before. My rubber blanket, I prize above everything else. I spread it wherever I may. I can always keep dry with that.

I wish it were possible that the dream might be realized that you might see us just as we are but you would not find my trousers so ragged as you dreamed. With the exception of a little hole just below my right knee, which I tore (It is only large enough to crouch my pencil through) and a little rip at the pocket on the right side, they are as whole as they were the day I left home. They are not so clean as I wish but I have no trouble in keeping my drawers and shirt clean. I have been expecting a new suit so long. I think it must come soon. There is but little of the time when I am off duty that I am not washing or reading or writing. Two pairs of my stockings (my best ones) are nearly as good as when I left home.

I will now explain to you how we do guard duty. We are detailed now by company. It used to be so many men from each company. Tomorrow, I think, will be the day for our company to do guard duty and we shall relieve the company that is on today. Tomorrow morning at 9, we shall have what is called guard mounting. We shall form a line out in the field. The band will play while the officers are inspecting our arms. After the ceremony is over, we shall be marched off to the guard tents. There, whilst we are standing in line, the company will be divided into 3 equal parts called 1st, 2nd, and 3rd relief. It will then be 10 o'clock and the 1st relief will take the posts as they are numbered. When they have stood for two hours, the 2nd will go to their relief and then the 3rd and so on through the twenty-four hours. If I am on the first relief, I shall be at the post from ten to twelve A.M., four to six P.M., ten to twelve P.M., and four to six A.M. That is what is called two on and four off. Two hours duty and four hours rest, through the day and night.

When we have pleasant weather, it is quite pleasant duty but the last time I was on, it was rather a hard time but I did not take any cold.

I think we shall remain where we now are for a long time as we are posted at a place where we can do much for the defense of the city.

I received the *Trumpets* yesterday and was glad to see them. Tell Henry not to work too hard (I mean it!) and that I shall expect another letter next Thursday.

Now good-bye for a little while.
Affectionately yours,
Rufus

August 28, 1861
Washington, D.C.

Henry,
I feel very grateful for the letter which I have just received from you. It cheers me more than you can imagine. I am glad that you are having enough to eat. I should like to take a seat at the old table with you some of these lazy days which we are spending in camp. I frequently have spells of thinking of you at home and as often as it will I suffer my imagination

to take a turn homeward and take a view of you as you are seated at the breakfast, dinner, or supper table.

It was just before dinner that I received your letter and how natural it looked to see you seated at the table, spread with the luxuries from the garden as it usually is at this time of the year. Well, eat away. It won't hurt you if you have a good appetite. It is a joy to me to know that you can.

I too have eaten a good dinner today. You know I am very fond of stewed beans. I had plenty of them for dinner and they were well cooked.

I love, when I am making my home visits, to take my pipe after breakfast and walk out to the barn with you and take a look at my chicks and Old Nell and the pig but I can't seem to see him so distinctly as the rest of them. So please tell me in your next if he grows well this summer. Then I love to take a walk over to the farm but I know pretty well how it looks there now for you have given me a good description of it. You are taking more pains with the strawberry patch than I thought but I think it will pay. How are the water and musk melons getting along? I can buy a musk melon here nearly as large as my head for six cents and they are very good ones.

Well, now whilst I have room I must write you a few words of things which have occurred here. Twice, since I last wrote you, we had our ears pricked up with the prospect of a fight. One night last week, the pickets gave us a false alarm. It was about eleven o'clock and most of us were asleep but we were not long in getting into line. We stood about fifteen minutes prepared to march, were then dismissed to our tents, and the excitement was soon over.

It was a little different last night. I did not notice anything of it until dress parade and I think it was about that time the Colonel received the news that our services might be wanted for he hurried through with it, as fast as possible. We were then given as much ammunition as our cartridge boxes would hold, which is about forty rounds and I think the box will weigh, when thus filled, from twelve to fifteen pounds. We were obliged to keep them on all night, so that we might be in readiness to march at a moments warning but with us it only ended with a good night's rest. I managed to slip my box around behind me so that it didn't plague me one mite. All I had to do was to lie still on my right side and I was somewhat surprised to find myself so refreshed in the morning. I cannot learn anything satisfactory concerning this alarm but no doubt there has been a slight affair at Chain Bridge.

Well, it is now near the close of another day and I want to mail this tomorrow morning. So I will not try to fill another sheet. My health is good. I have gained about 2½ pounds since we left Kalorama. I weigh now 127½ pounds, without my jacket. So good night. Let me hear from you again soon. How is James' health? We are expecting to get paid again soon.
Rufus

September 1, 1861
Washington, D.C.

Dear Mother,

I can hardly realize that this is the first day of September for the summer has seemed to me very short. It is a fine day and I enjoy it very much. It seems just like the September weather we have at home. The sky is very clear and the sun scalds a little, but it is cool in the shade.

It is now about five o'clock P.M. I have just returned from meeting which was held in the grove near by. I did not like the sermon very well today so I will not say much about it but I could not help thinking what a contrast there must be between the one I was hearing and the one you had heard today. Oh, how I should like to have spent the day with you and heard Brother Crehore preach. I am afraid he will not be with you when I get back. You must do all you can to make him stay. I think of him very often and I wish to send him my best respects. I like to have you tell me what the text was.

Our company were detailed for guard duty yesterday. I wrote you last Sunday that I thought we should be detailed the next day and so we were, for picket, not for the camp guard, of which I am now speaking and as I expected. I like the picket the best for it is a good opportunity to see the country about us. But I had quite an easy time of it yesterday and this morning. I was detailed out of the regular guards as an orderly for the Colonel. This is quite an easy duty. All I had to do was to remain by the Colonel's tent and carry orders for him. The orders were so few that I will enumerate most of them. This was the first one. "Orderly go and tell the sergeant major, I want to see him." "Go and tell the captains of the companies that their men will come out for inspection this afternoon without their knapsacks." I spent most of the day in reading. I was dismissed last night at 9 had a good night's rest and was with him again this morning from 5 until 9. All I had to do this morning was to call the sergeant and buy the Colonel a newspaper.

I had almost forgotten to mention that I got a choice bit from the Colonel's table last night. And this morning after the Colonel had eaten his breakfast, the cook invited me to take a seat at the table with him. It was a good breakfast and I had a good appetite. After I was dismissed, I went down to the stream and had a good wash, put on my clean shirt and drawers.

I hear news tonight of a great victory achieved by General Butler[36] but I will not give you any of the particulars for you will get them in the papers before this will reach you.

Now it is Monday morning and I must mail this very soon. It is a very fine morning and I feel first rate.

Now good morning.

Yours Affectionately,

Rufus

September 1, 1861
Abington

Rufus,

We received your letter to Mother last week. Was glad to hear that you was well. We read the daily as it comes to us and keep ourselves acquainted with the movements of things in and about Washington, but do not often see your regiment mentioned.

You wrote you were digging trenches and fortifying yourselves. I suppose against an attack. It seems there are to be heavy guns planted there. Now a query: Are you going to learn to use them as artilerist or are there men to take charge of them. I think from what we read that you expect the rebels are about to make a move upon you, that they mean to attack Washington. I hope you are ready for them and that our troops will give a good account of themselves.

I sometimes wish I was there to do my part. In fact, was there any position I could fill being competent in all respects to do it, I would accept it. I would place myself for the defence of my country against slavery and oppression. If it may not be so, then I will hope that those who are there will stand up bravely in defence of all that defined in one word that is worth defending (**liberty**) that lost, life is worthless and I have no question but they will. And the south will soon be made to feel and understand that their case is hopeless.

I should think from your letter to me that you was not well pleased with the section of the country you are in as a farming country. It may not be the fault of the land but of the mode of cultivating it. Is it done by free or slave labor? That, as you know, makes a vast difference. Southern land, or plantations as they call their farms, do not yield all that free labor could make them. And I have read cases where the land has been put under the management of free labor it has richly paid.

It may be that too many slaves had to work on the corn field you described. And may it not be that as slave labor is so cheap, in the southerner's opinion he can get rich even if he gets no crops? I should think that so near Washington farming would pay well. At any rate, I believe New England farming would. You may have a wrong opinion of the land as I had in New York. I thought that it was worthless, yet was told it was very rich land for crops of all kinds.

I do not know of anything especial here in Abington to write about and yet there may be many things that would interest you. Army shoes are brisk (sewed). Pegged workmen are learning to sew. There are no pegged shoes to be had. I expect Henry and I shall have to learn a new trade. They pay as high for the best as 50 cents per pair. Edwin expects that for those he is now making. He has got four or five workmen: Frank's father and brother, Hector Foster, and two others. Make 7 pair per day. I suppose that when Henry gets the strawberry plants all set and the corn is topped that we shall try it, if other work does not come on to prevent.

I have heard that Jenkins Lane has 500 at work. A number of others have or are going into it. I do not think there will be much other work done except California work. Something doing now in that. It is said that the sewed work will be demanded at the west. I think the shoe trade is going to change about but few pegged shoes will be made.

It has been so dull here that we have raised no money to pay Mr. Crehore anything on subscription. We do not know as we can keep him this winter. He stands engaged until the first of November giving him, in the meantime, the right to engage elsewhere if there is an opening for him. I hope as there is some change in business that it will be so that we can keep him. They have no meetings at North Bridgewater.[37] We tried to get him in to preach half the time but they were as poor there as we are and had to stop.

Do you have meetings in the camp now? I presume you do. I was glad that you was one to start extra meetings and that you took part in them (although you was supposed by someone to have changed your belief on account of it). Your company has the name of being the best company as regards moral principles and I hope it will be kept so and no better means can be used to that effect than to have meetings and attend them. And as you are situated, you can throw a strong influence on the right side. And I would not say you alone nor would I be so sectarian that I would not unite with all of every sect to use an influence for the moral welfare of the company. Yet I would say that you can do much individually for some are too ignorant of Universalism as to suppose that one who believes in that doctrine can have nothing to do with meetings particularly if they be prayer and conference. And when they see a universalist engaged in those meetings then, of course, it must be that he has changed his faith. But convince them to the contrary and give them to know that you are in earnest and are looking for the elevation and advancement of mankind. They can scarce believe it then, as I said before. Your engaging in those meetings gives you an opportunity to know an influence to draw in some that perhaps are not in the habit of attending meetings of any kind. Looking for your own religious and moral advancement will command the esteem and respect of those who do not accept your faith and give some perhaps to enquire into your principles and in so doing to accept and believe. I shall send you this week some more *Trumpets* and I would ask here, "Do any of those of opposite faith read them?" I would say to you, read them and then send them out on a mission of good.

When I commenced this, I did not know as I should fill half of it but I could perhaps fill another sheet.

Edwin is here. He brought up your last letter from you. When the rebels call you out again, I hope it will not be in a rain as I understood it was. We want you to give full particulars of events with you and let us know about your health and all that regards the position of things that you may write. We are all well and send our best love. Mother will write soon.

Yours affectionately,

R. Robbins

September 1, 1861
Abington

Dear Brother,

As I can send this in father's letter, I thought I would write you a few lines just to let you know that we are all well.

I am going in tomorrow. I have four besides myself at work. I will second father's request that you should write all the particulars about your affairs, if you have time.

I received your letter Friday eve. I am going to write you a long letter soon.

It is so dark that I cannot see the lines.

Edwin

September 1, 1861
West Sumner

Dear Brother,

Perhaps you think I have forgotten my promise to write often to you. But I have not. My time has been so much occupied within two or three weeks that I could not get a chance to write till now. Estus and his wife are down here, so when we don't have company we go avisiting. There was fourteen here yesterday counting the children besides our family and Fred's which will count ten. We have enjoyed their visit very much. They will go back this week. It will seem rather lonesome when they are gone.

Hiram has gone over to Canton today to carry Columbus to join his company. They will start for Augusta tomorrow. And some time this week will go on to Washington. He belongs to the Eighth Regiment. Horatio Bisby is the captain of his company. The other officers are not chosen. I am afraid Columbus will be homesick. He never was away from home before. But his courage was good. He has been wanting to go all summer. We only had four days notice of his going. He signed the papers last

Wednesday. Captain B. was in the battle at Bulls Run. He belonged to a Mass. regiment. He says he only wants a chance at them again. He has been trying to get Hiram to go, but it was too short notice. Hiram thinks it is his duty to go. Perhaps it is, but I try to make him think it is not. What do you think about it?

I am really afraid he will go when Albert goes. I am very selfish, I know. But I can't bear to think of his going but I had rather he and all my friends should go than to have the South gain the victory. Albert expects to go again soon. The papers that he signed specified that he should serve three months out of the state and two years in the state. So the governor can compel them to stay at the barracks near Portland, which Albert says he shant do. He had rather be in active service than stay there. He thinks the whole regiment will go soon. Columbus says he hopes he shall be near to you and can have a chance to see you if you find out where his regiment is encamped and can have leave to go and see him. I wish you would. It would be very gratifying to him and to his friends.

Also, perhaps my letter will not be interesting but I do not know what to write about. There is no more news but war news.

Hiram has just got home and what few thoughts that I had are all gone. For he is determined to go when Albert does. He is writing to father and mother to see if they will stay with me this winter. I will close now. It is getting late and I want to write a few words to mother. We have not had a letter from them since I wrote to you. We received your letter a short time ago. Hiram will write a few lines.
From your affectionate sister,
Ruth

[The letter continues.]

Brother Rufus,

I think I shall see you within a few weeks, if nothing happens more than I know of now. And hope you will write so I may get a letter from you before I start. And I will close by wishing you good success in all things.
Your brother truly,
T. H. Barrows

September 2, 1861
South Abington

Dear Rufus,

The girls say your letter must go tonight. It is nearly nine o'clock but I must write a few lines. We are well. I am trying to make a few army shoes as they are all the fashion. I do not like them. I also think I should rather wear them than make them. Business is awful dull except the army work. I pity you if you have to wear some. I have seen they have to make them better than they did.

Corn looks first rate about here, potatoes will be rather small. I shall have any quantity of pumpkins and squashes. I should like to send you a pie. I have bought two more pigs. The one I got last spring has got promoted to be a hog. I like housekeeping first rate. My wife sends her respects to you. I expect to take more comfort after there has been a few more victories like the one Butler has had. It will close these troubles I think and then business will be good.

I must close. I hope you are well. Excuse this scribble won't you. I am summoned to send it. Please answer soon.
Judson

September 4, 1861
Washington, D.C.

[This letter is written on Edwin's letter of September 1.]

Father,

I have just received your letter and feel anxious to write you a few lines before I have to go to work at the trenches again.

I am a little short of paper just now. So I improve the blank which I find in Ed's letter and it will be as much as I shall have time to fill this time.

There has been considerable fighting around us during the last few days and we are expecting to march at any time. Should not think strange if we should have orders to march tonight, but I cannot tell you where. I don't know who will occupy the forts which we have built. I don't think we shall. We have finished one and the guns are mounted—10 in number. We shall have another ⅔ done tonight. We are putting it along as fast as we can. Our officers are not very communicative. We don't know anything more than 10 minutes before it happens.

My health is good and I feel ready to march at a moment's warning and think I can do a good execution. I think the rebels are anxious to attack Washington. But I can't make up my mind that they will. I think it will be a dangerous operation for them.

I must close now. Write often. It does me good to have a letter. Two in prospect now: Mother's and Edwin's.

I will write again tomorrow if I have time.
Yours Affectionately,
Rufus

September 5, 1861
Washington, D.C.

Henry,

I will try to write you a few lines today although it will be under rather unfavorable circumstances as we are on picket today and it is raining quite hard. I am out about a mile and a half from camp, seated on my knapsack, in a shanty by the side of the road, built of rails and brush wood. We have managed to keep pretty dry so far by means of a large rubber blanket which we have spread over the top of our shanty, but it drops pretty fast all around where the blanket does not cover.

I feel quite anxious to write you a few lines today as the one I wrote yesterday will lead you to suppose that we marched last night. Indeed there was a strong probability that we should. The cooks were at work half of the night cooking rations for us to carry.

Well, it rains so now that I can't keep my paper dry and my left knee is getting a good soaking. But I am not faint nor discouraged. I think I am engaged in a good cause and keeping as dry as possible. I do not know now what to tell you about our marching. It may be very soon and may not be for a long time. Father says he doesn't hear much about the Seventh Regiment. I suppose it is because we have not yet had anything to do. But I think I can say with truth that are willing men and there will be loud cheers when we have orders to march. We know that we have a work to do and are anxious to be about it. It is my impression that General Couch[38] will not return home with his men without doing his share of the work.

Now I am going to tell you what has happened since I commenced to write this letter. First, I have eaten a good dinner of stewed beans. You know it is my favorite dish and it is well that I am fond of them as we have them quite often of late. They were cooked on the road just below me. When we are on picket, we bring our own provisions and cooking utensils with us. I was seated on my knapsack with my plate on my knees and had nearly finished my dinner, when Brown[39] of South Abington came through with the Captain's dinner and the mail. He gave me a letter, but I could not guess who it was from. But when I opened it, I was pleased to find that it contained three. One from Judson, one from Ann, and one from Hannah. Ann wrote me a rather saucy letter, but nevertheless, she wrote many fine things. I think I will pay her back with the same coin. Judson and Hannah were very polite and I mean to answer their letters very soon.

This morning before I commenced to write this letter and before it commenced to rain so hard, I took a walk to a neighboring house and asked a young lady (the old folks were not at home and she was pretty besides) if she would let me walk around under the trees and pick up a few apples. She was very willing. I asked her if the big black dog which was barking at me would interfere and she said, "Indeed Sir, I reckon not. He will only bark at you." So I bid her good morning and went and filled my haversack with good apples for cooking. They were all ripe, but most of them were too sour to eat in the hand. I got about half a peck and they will make a good lot of sauce. I will have some tonight for supper.

I don't think it will rain so hard tonight. The end.

Rufus

Judson's letter was written with a pencil and was difficult to read. Are mine so?

September 7, 1861
Abington

Dear Son,

I received your last letter Wednesday evening and felt very thankful to you for it. The same evening we received one from Hiram and Ruth, informing us of his intention of enlisting for the war. He expected to go in four weeks. Should go with Albert. Fred and Columbus have gone to Augusta to join a company there, which will leave (he says) this week for Washington.

Yesterday, James told us he had just received a letter from Hiram in which he wrote that he and Albert should leave immediately to go with the company from Augusta.

Hiram gave your Father and I an invitation to go down there this fall and do his harvesting and stay the winter. "If you will come," he says, "I will give you a living through the winter." Ruth writes, "If you will come, you shall have the warmest chamber and be waited on like a lady." She says, "Kill the old horse, sell the cow and hens, and Henry can board out until his fall's work is done, then go visiting." Ruth says nothing would give her greater pleasure (except Hiram's staying at home) than to have us come down there, for she expects to be very lonesome. (I do not know how many servants there would be to wait on us, but I should think we should need one to take care of those two babies.) But the poor child did not stop to consider, when she made the request, how hard it would be for us to leave our home, to say nothing of the duty that keeps us here. Horace is going to do Hiram's work if Father declines the invitation. I intend to write to Ruth soon for particulars.

[The letter continues.]

Sunday, the 8th

Josiah brought us a letter from you last night. He said he had got one from Luke too. He brings most all of your letters to us. He goes to the office about every night on horseback and when we hear the horse coming up the yard, we know there is a letter from you.

Last night I could not make up my mind whether it was best to look for a letter or not, but could not help watching for Josiah's return, and sure enough we got one. I sometimes feel as if we didn't write to you as often as we ought to, if you feel as glad as we do to receive letters from you. And no doubt you do, but there is this difference. We can't write anything about home that you already don't, as it were, know for you must think of us as doing the same things and about at the same time that we have in the seasons that have past; but we can have no idea of what you are doing nor where you are, only when you write to us.

I think of you these cool nights and your one blanket, on the ground, when we need two on a soft bed to keep us comfortable. I wish that you would let us know if there is anything we can send you. I heard that some of the company sent for things and several families made a box of things and sent it to them and we will do the same, if you will let us know what would be most acceptable.

The next time you write, I want you should tell us who is in your mess and how many in a tent and whether the officers have to do any digging or hard work of any kind. Who is colonel of the regiment now? We have heard that Couch was promoted.

Henry asks that I must ask you if one blanket keeps you warm. He has just gone to bed and father sits on the lounge reading and I am sitting in the bedroom, writing on the stand. It is warmer in here and I could be by myself.

Edwin has been up this evening and Augusta called in a while. So you will see that I have been interrupted some since I commenced to write.

Have you received a letter from Anne P.? She said that she had written to you. She has gone back to her school again.

Father is hurrying me, so I must close this letter soon, or he will come in again and ask me how much longer I am going to write. It don't seem as if I had written a very good letter but I will try and do better next time. I can't always put on paper thoughts and feelings as I would like to but know that you will gladly receive it such as it is.

We are all as well as usual and I hope that this will find you so and that you will remain so until you return to us in safety which time I hope and pray is not far distant.

From your affectionate mother,

ASR

September 9, 1861
Washington, D.C.

Henry,

I have time this morning to write you a few lines, just to let you know that we remain at the old camp yet and no particular prospect of leaving immediately, although we hold ourselves in readiness all the time for we know not the day nor the hour when the order may come to march.

My health is good and we are living as well as usual and not over-worked. We are to commence work on the trenches this morning at nine unless it should rain too hard. We have had very pleasant weather since last Wednesday until this morning. It bids fair for a rainy day.

I had the satisfaction of seeing my old friend, Joseph Collins, yesterday afternoon. I was very much surprised to see him. He came on with the new recruits from South Abington. He is annexed to Company I. He says he was at High Street week ago last Saturday. Saw you and Father at work in the field but couldn't tell what you were doing. He says the corn looks first rate and that you have got it all topped. You had better believe I had a great many questions to ask about you and a few more than he could answer. Willard Lincoln is one of the number. He has joined Company A.

We are not paid off yet but I think we shall get it this week. Two months pay, I think.

Tell Edwin when he writes again to enclose a thread to me such as he sews his shoes with, an awl too, if he can spare one. I want to sew a tap on to the toe of my shoe. And I want you to send me as many envelopes as you can every time you write. And not make your letters too heavy, about the size I have been using. They cost one cent apiece here.

Now good morning. It looks more like fair weather now.
Rufus

September 18, 1861
Washington, D.C.

Henry,

I hardly know what to write you this morning as I have no news to tell you and it seems as though I have written all there is to write of things about camp.

Perhaps a few words about our new Colonel will be as interesting as anything I can write. He is a very smart man and I think will make better soldiers of us than we could ever have been under Couch or Lieutenant Colonel Green,[40] who was at the head of us from the time of Couch's promotion until Colonel Davis[41] took command of us about two weeks ago. We are now under the strictest military discipline. Every order has to be obeyed to the letter and the slightest offense subjects us to some kind of punishment. It is quite a common thing to see men standing upon the top of barrels from six to twelve hours for not being present at roll call or talking in the ranks. We have to be very prompt when we are on drill, handling the musket, and marching to the best of our ability. We have a company drill in the forenoon and battalion drill in the afternoon, commencing at three o'clock. Yesterday afternoon, we had the smartest battalion drill of all. When we left camp for the large field about half a mile from camp where we have our battalion drills, there was every appearance of a shower near at hand and the Colonel cut his garment according to the cloth exactly. I believe he got as much work out of us in one hour and fifteen minutes as we usually do in two hours. He marched us back to our camp and dismissed us just as the shower struck and it was a right smart one, as the folks say out here.

Well, it is nearly nine o'clock now and I shall have to go digging soon but I go with a light heart for I am expecting a letter from you when I get back.

Well, I have returned from digging. Read your letter and eaten my dinner. Wednesday is the day I get all your letters and papers. Your letter was the right kind. I always want to know what you are doing. Anything, no matter how trifling, in or about the house, is a sweet crumb to me now.

But I don't want you to work too hard on those shoes just for the sake of bragging about it. How I should like to be at home this fall and help you husk the corn. Perhaps some day when you are husking it, I shall be at work popping the rebels. I feel well and strong as though I would like to do some of that work for my country before I come home.

Now I must stop again for the Colonel orders us to move our tents. We have only got to arrange them differently on the same field to avoid the low places which some of the companies now occupy.

[The letter continues.]

September 19th

We are not detailed for fatigue duty today (that means digging) so we will take part in the drills. I didn't receive Ed's letter yesterday, so I shall look for it today. That letter which I received from Ruth and sent to you, I answered immediately and advised Hiram not to enlist if he had not. I am expecting to hear from him soon.

I shall not mail this until tomorrow morning, so I will tell you if I have any mail today. I hear a little something almost every day that inclines me to think that we shall not remain here a great while longer, though nothing

very definite. I sent Father a paper last Sunday. I mailed a letter with my
check last Friday evening. I think you have received it about this time.

Three hours later
Since writing the above, we have had our company drill and eaten our
dinner. No mail for me today. Luke and I booked our names this morning
to go to the city of Washington. Two from each company are permitted
to go daily. There are sixteen ahead of us now. I think it will be the only
chance I shall have to see Hiram and I doubt if I do then.

I must close now, so good-bye.
Yours Affectionately,
Rufus

September 22, 1861
Headquarters 7 Reg't.
Camp Brightwood

Dear Father,

I received your letter yesterday, also one from Edwin about noon. I
should have written an answer to you so as to have mailed it this morning
but we were permitted to go bathing yesterday afternoon and I don't like
to let such opportunities to wash my body and clothes pass unimproved.
Rock Creek is the name of the stream where we go. It is the same stream
which ran near us at Kalorama. It is about half a mile from us now and,
as we approach, it is a wild looking place. It is down a very steep hill
through thick woods. It is a wild, gloomy looking place but I love to stop
there a while and see the water tumbling and foaming among the rocks.
Just before we arrive at the creek, we pass a large spring of water called
Crystal Spring. It is beautiful water and I never can drink of it without
looking, or at least thinking, up with gravity to the kind Father who
placed it there.

I am cook's mate today. My duty consists in drawing water and cutting
wood. There are two of us besides the head cooks so I am not obliged
to work near all of the time. I was detailed this morning but did not
commence the duty until about noon, as Sunday morning inspection
usually lasts until about that time.

We were on guard Friday and it was a very pleasant day and night. I
like these pleasant moonlight nights when I am doing duty. I was on the
third relief so my watch came from 7 to 9 P.M. and from 1 to 3 A.M., giving
me the 4 hours from 9 to 1 to sleep and from 3 to 5. I like the third
relief best, because we are not called up but once in the night.

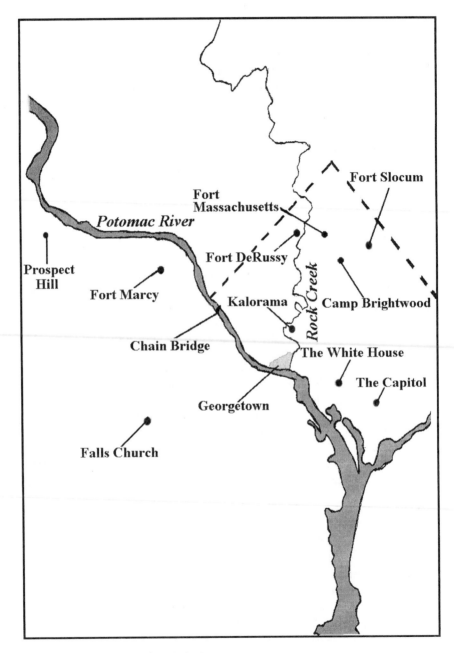

Washington, D.C., and vicinity.

Yesterday morning, after we came off duty, we commenced pitching our new tents. They are very small, but I like the setup as the old ones leaked when it rained very hard. There is not much spare room in the new ones but, as there are only four of us to a tent, I like the company much better. Luke, Henry Beebe[42] and Jacob Harden[43] and myself occupy one. We have bought straw enough at the cost of five cents apiece to cover the floor with a good thickness and we four are so well agreed that we can have things in good shape.

Now about the clothing. I am not particularly in need of anything now but I don't know how soon I may be. If the weather should continue a month longer about as it is now, I shall have clothing enough to keep me warm. The two shirts which were given me at Taunton are all that I have received. I don't see but they are about as good now as ever, except they are getting rather short. They are not much longer than the under-shirts I wore at home.

Now if I can have two good long flannel shirts to put on by and by and take the ones I wear now for undershirts, I think that will be the best arrangement. If you can have the color about the same as I wear now I shall like it. I should like to have my army brogans sent on or a pair of boots. If the brogans are in good condition, I wouldn't go to the trouble of getting my boots. My kipers would slip at the heel too much.

I don't think of anything else that I am in need of. If I get short of money, I can tell you of it and you can send me a dollar. I don't like to have too much about me at a time.

My health is good. I will write you again soon but must close now for supper is ready and I must help the cooks.
Yours Truly,
Rufus

September 28, 1861
Washington, D.C.

Henry,

This is a very fine day. I had almost said, "October day," for it seems so much like it. Yesterday was a stormy day. It commenced with a north-easter which lasted about 3 hours and then about 9 o'clock A.M. turned into a southeaster. A real squally day. It did not rain very [much] at any time but the clouds were black and heavy and the wind blew a gale. Some of the tents were blown over, but ours stood it like a major.

Our drills were dispensed with through the day. So we had quite an easy time. I felt very lazy all day and about all I did was to write a letter to Ed.

We have been at work on the fort today. Commenced at 10 and returned at 1 with a good appetite. We had beef soup for dinner. It was very good. But I didn't feel quite satisfied, so I finished up with 2 molasses cookies and a piece of cheese, which cost me 3 cents, and a good slice of frosted plum cake, which Jacob Harding received from his folks today.

The fort which we are at work on now is the second one which we have commenced. I thought when we commenced it, it would have been finished before this time. But we have not worked on it so steadily as at first. We are at work on the magazine now and have almost completed it. When that is finished, it will take but a few days to complete the rest.

The magazine is in the centre of the fort, is about 75 feet long, about 20 wide. The way it is constructed, a trench is dug the length and width the magazine is intended to be to the depth of about four feet. Then, hewed logs about 12 feet in length are stood up close together around the edge of the trench. The top is covered with heavy hewed logs. The top is then covered with sand to the depth of about 4 feet. It is banked up at the sides and ends with the same depth of earth with the exception of the doorways which are 3 in number and all on one side. Sods are then lain from the bottom to the top all around it as you would lay flat stones in building a wall.

The trenches around the fort are about 12 feet wide and 6 deep. The earth is thrown up on the inside so that we are surrounded by a thick, high wall.

[The letter continues.]

Sunday
September 29th
The drill overtook me yesterday afternoon before I had time to finish my letter.

The weather is very fine today. About as it was yesterday. Last night was very clear and still and the coldest one we have had yet. We spread our rubber blankets on a good lot of straw and slept with our jackets, blouses, and overcoats on. The blouse is a very long, loose garment, resembling both jacket and shirt. I drew my cotton stockings on over my woolen ones, rolled up in my blanket, and slept as warm as a pig.

A little before 12 o'clock the cooks were called up to make coffee for us. It was said that we were agoing to march right off. I got up a few minutes after and went down to the cookstand to hear about it. I asked but few questions. Consequently learned but little. But as much probably as I should, if I had asked more, as I was satisfied no one there knew much more about it than I did. So I came back and went to bed again.

I arose this morning a little before 5, folded my blanket and put my things to rights in the tent, washed my face, and had a few minutes to spare before roll call. So I went down to the cookstand again to see what progress they were making there. Found them boiling the same coffee, but they didn't know why any better than when they commenced.

At roll call, we learned that our troops had made an attack on Munson's Hill and retaken it. This was the cause of the alarm.

Inspection commenced this morning at ½ past 8 and lasted until 20 minutes of 12. Most of my time before that was employed in cleaning my gun and equipments.

Since that time, I have had nothing to do but to attend to my own wants. I have eaten my dinner, stewed beans, been down to the stream, washed myself, and exchanged my clothes. It is now 5 o'clock and supper will soon be ready. Dress parade soon after. So my time to write will soon be at an end.

We are hearing guns and are ordered to remain near our tents and be in readiness to march, but I don't think we shall this time.

I have not heard from Hiram or Ruth since the letter I sent home. I think I shall write to Ruth tomorrow.

I am writing now by candle light. Supper and dress parade are over. We had hominy and molasses. We have that with sugar or molasses for breakfast or supper almost every day. We are having as good bread now as I want to eat. I buy a small piece of cheese almost every day to eat with it. It tastes the best of anything I eat and just offsets the hominy which is very loosening.

I am well clothed now. So I don't want Mother to feel too much in a hurry about getting my shirts ready. Those and the army brogues are all that I want.

Your last letter gave good satisfaction. I think buying the pigs is a good idea. Don't be in too much of a hurry about getting into the shop. It will take some time to do all your harvesting.

Tell Augusta I should be very glad to walk in. Perhaps I may some time very unexpectedly. I think it was three months last Wednesday since I left home.

Now good night.

Rufus

October 2, 1861
West Sumner, Maine

Dearly beloved husband,

I received both of your letters yesterday. The first one Adna brought down just after noon. The other Horace got in the evening. You see,

Jackson village is getting to be quite a city. They have the mail twice a day.

And now I have set down to write you a good long letter. You don't know how anxious I have been to hear from you. But you did not say a word about yourself, whether you were sick or well. I have felt worried about you for fear you would be sick again. Be very careful of yourself for my sake. We are all well here except slight colds.

I suppose you want to know how we got home nicely and without any accident. We came a part of the way behind Deacon Joe Barrows. He made a great many inquiries about you. He wanted very much to know how much money your four brothers sent home. But he did not know exactly how much. He was a little too inquisitive. We left him at Winthrop. He went down through Leeds. We stopped at Wayne at noon to rest. Got home here about sunset. Fanny knew the way home. She never missed a road.

We did not happen to fall in with any of the folks from this way till we got to Buckfield. They overtook us there. We started before they did. I was not near so tired when got home as I was when I got to Augusta.

I was up that morning in season to see the regiment pass down the street. So was Nelly. When she heard the men hurrah, she would hurrah too. She could not think what made her mother so sad. She talks more about you now than she did before we went down to Augusta. The children want me to give their love to you and tell you that they have been good. If they don't behave just right, I ask, "What shall I write to father next time?" and they calm down pretty quick. But they are very good most of the time. Henry worked all the day yesterday picking potatoes. Horace said he worked first rate. He has dug potatoes two days and got 40 bushels. He says they turn out well. Today, he has been to Paris to cattle show and has just got home. He cut the corn up and shucked it last week.

I expect your folks will move down here soon. They have drove their cows down and I take care of the milk. I don't expect it will make my work any easier when they come down. Your mother's hand plagues her very much. It pains her all the time. I have not seen her since I got home.

R. Dean is getting well. He is able to set up now. Albert's Ida is sick but is some better today. She has not had a seated fever but came very near it. Perhaps you had best not say anything to Albert about it, for he would be likely to worry about her.

They say now that they don't think they will try to do anything with the first regiment. It will cost them more than it will come to. They are so stubborn.

Moses Pulsifer has been to Lewiston with a load of butter and got 14 and 15 cents a pound for it. I think I shall keep mine a while before selling at that price.

Most everyone at the village went to cattle show today.

I had a letter from Mother last week. They were all well. Then she wrote that Henry was at work on his first case of shoes. Edwin has been to work some time on the army shoes for J. Lane, East Abington. He has learned to make

[The remainder of the letter has been lost.]

October 3, 1861
Thursday
Washington, D.C.

Dear Mother,

I received your letter yesterday afternoon about 3 o'clock. The mail was about two hours later than usual so two anxious hours were past betwixt fear and hope. It is now about 9 A.M. and a very fine morning, warm and pleasant. My health is very good. This cool weather makes me feel strong and hearty.

Last Monday was a day of unusual excitement with us. We were expecting to march at a moment's notice. Through the whole day, orders were given and countermanded in quick succession. About 1 o'clock P.M. we were ordered to be in readiness at a moment's warning to sling our knapsacks, as the assembly roll would beat in a few minutes. Just at that time, letters were placed in my hand from Hannah and Almira. I opened them, but didn't expect to have time to finish reading them. But the roll didn't beat. But our company were on guard that day. We were ordered to our posts again and remained on duty until six, when we were again drawn in company, formed with knapsacks slung, expecting to march at seven. I don't know what the occasion of all this was but I think there must have been skirmishing somewhere and General Couch meant to have us ready. We shall march when the time comes, but when that will be, we do not know.

I have not heard from Hiram yet. I wrote to Ruth Tuesday. The 9th Maine Regiment is encamped within two miles of us. As soon as I had finished reading your letter yesterday, I went to the Captain and asked leave to visit it. He said he was willing but knew the Colonel would not give me a pass as he had just refused Lieutenant Mayhew.[44] I am going to write to him. Perhaps his Colonel will let him come to me. It seems rather hard when he is so near and I can't go and see him.

The box which the DEA[45] sent Luke's things in came yesterday about two hours after I received your letter. It was directed to Jacob Harding. He had some cakes in it which he has given me some of.

I have concluded not to have the boots or shoes sent at present as I drew a good pair of service boots last Monday when we were expecting to march. I didn't dare to risk the old ones on a long march but perhaps can wear them two or three weeks longer in camp and save the new ones until we do march.

The weather will not be such as to need boots before the first of December and I shall want another box by that time. Tell Henry I will give him some instructions about them soon enough so that he can have them ready as soon as I shall want them. I want the shirts and a toothbrush. Two quarts of doughnuts. That is all I can think of.

I have just received a letter from Ann. Tell Hannah and Almira I will answer as soon as possible. I have written in such a hurry, I don't know if you can read it. I want to write another today.

We are having quite an easy time. Now sleep warm every night and enough to eat. I will try to write to James soon. Where is Sam? Tell me something of him when you write again.
From Your Affectionate Son,
Rufus

[The following note was enclosed.]

Wm. Howland has sent some money home to his wife and has not yet heard from it. Tell his wife he wants to hear from [her] soon. He directed his letter to Julia Howland. He is well.

October 13, 1861
Sunday
Washington, D.C.

Henry,

I received yours and Mother's letters last Wednesday and they gave me a very comfortable feeling which has not left me yet. My desire to see my home again and share the labors with you has not abated in the least but I can wait with patience and feel very contented so long as I can hear that all is well at home.

I have no news in particular to write this time. We remain yet at the old encampment but have frequent orders to get ready to march. Yesterday afternoon, two days rations were given to us with the expectation that we should have orders to march but there was but little excitement about it. And by this time it has about blown over.

It was a sure thing that I did not want to go this time or at least I was not quite ready. I wanted my clothes to dry which I had just washed and I wanted to see the box before we started. I expected it yesterday but shall not be much disappointed if I don't see it until Tuesday as it has taken eight days for some of them to come through. When I get my new shirts and boots, I shall have clothing enough for any weather that may come and by the way, you have not made a very fatal mistake in sending the boots. Those boots which I had of Jacob's[46] were very good ones but as soon as I commenced to wear them, I found that one of them was too large over the instep and slipped badly at the heel. So I had disposed of them at cost but I wish you would, if it will not be too much trouble, get that pair up for Jake as I wish to adhere to the bargain which I made with him. Follow the directions as near as you can which I gave you last week and let me know as soon as you get this how soon they will be ready. I would like John Maloy to make them and leave them with the DEA[47] until called for.

I am not going to write much more. So I will commence to tell you what little news I have. Reverend Mr. Edwards made his appearance amongst us last Tuesday night. We were very glad to see him.

My health continues good. My weight is now 137 lbs. I think I have gained it very fast since cool weather commenced.

Before I forget it, I will tell you that I received your letter last night. I have been thinking of having my daguerreotype taken but have been waiting until I went to the City. I can get one taken here for fifty cents but they are poor things. I like the photographs which they take at the city. They get six for 150 cents but I shall have to wait until I get paid off again, which will be in about three weeks.

We are having quite pleasant weather now but quite cool.

Now I want to say a few words to Mother. I don't think your pink will ever blossom. I had but little hopes of it when I sent it but I am glad the others live. I have no fears but the shirts will be all right. I shall write to you as soon as I get the box.
Yours Truly,
Rufus

October 14, 1861
Monday
Washington, D.C.

Henry,

I have but a few minutes to write, but I want you to know as soon as possible that the box had come. I am the happiest fellow you ever see.

My shirts, Mother, are just right every way. I have taken the strings off of one of them and put it on over a clean one which I put on yesterday. I hope it will be as cold tonight as it was last night, so I shall be better able to realize the comforts of a good, long, warm shirt. You don't know how thankful I feel for what you have sent me. The boots fit me exactly. They are as easy as my old shoes and don't slip at the heel. I am not sorry that they are Kip.[48] I think after I have worn them a short time, I can put the inner soles in. The grapes were almost spoilt. I found one bunch that was pretty good. The pears had commenced to rot, but most of them were first rate and so were the apples. I gave one of the potatoes to Captain Reed. They are a wonder to all. The cake is in good condition. I believe I have received all you sent.

Now I must leave for camp drill. It is four o'clock.

Well, my boots have behaved first rate. I think they will soon learn to drill as well as my old brogues. I shall have to put a stamp on this or it will be a day later before you receive it as I am too late for Bufington to frank it tonight.

Yours Truly,
Rufus

October 20, 1861
Sunday
Washington, D.C.

Dear Edwin,

I received your letter last Thursday late in the evening after doing a hard afternoon's work. We left camp that afternoon at ½ past 1 and marched out 2 miles towards the city to a large level field in company with 3 other regiments (The New York 27th, Rhode Island 2nd, and Massachusetts 10th) for a brigade drill. We were commanded by General Buell and he kept us at it nearly as long as we could see. It was easily 8 o'clock when we got back to camp and got our supper.

I took my plate of rice and sugar to my tent so that I could have a light to eat by. I was so busy with my supper that I had forgotten that it was possible that I might have a letter, but someone gave it to me before I had finished it.

Well, I have but a short time to write, so I must commence with a few of the indispensables and leave the rest for another time. I suppose you will be glad to hear about the boots. They fit me first rate. I am very much pleased with them. They have already done me good service, as we have had heavy rains and it has been very muddy.

I feel very thankful to Sophie for the very nice cake which she sent me. I wish I could send her a good lot of chestnuts which I picked up this morning.

I am on guard again. <u>Provo</u> as it is called. I hardly know the meaning of the word, but I know what my duty is and I like it, as it is quite easy to perform, especially today. I commenced it Friday, was stationed at a house about ¼ of a mile from camp, alone to see that he[49] did not sell liquor to the soldiers and that [they] didn't molest his chestnuts.

Yesterday, I was stationed on the road with 3 others to stop the market men as they returned from the city and see if they brought liquor with them. Our orders were to take it from them unless they showed us a permit from General Couch to bring it. Today, I am stationed acrost the road opposite our guard tents to guard a gentleman's house and the grounds around it from intrusions of the soldiers. I am alone but my duties are not very arduous. There are plenty of chestnuts about the place and I have permission to pick up as many as I please. There is a singular fruit here, which I have tasted today for the first time in its ripe state, which I must give you a description of. They are called persimmons. They are about the size of our common plums and about the same shape. When ripe perfectly, they are very good, sweet but not sickish, but if not perfectly ripe, woe unto the man that sets his teeth into them, for he will get his mouth puckered as it never was before.

I have forgotten to answer Sophie's question about the stockings and blankets. I do not need them now and, if I should have them when we move, I should have to leave them behind.

Now good night. Let me hear from you again soon.
Rufus

October 23, 1861
Wednesday
Washington, D.C.

Henry,

This is the fifth day that I have been Provo Guard. In my last letter to Edwin, which you have probably seen, I gave a slight account of the last few days previous to writing him. I yet remain at the same place and I am having quite an easy time.

I am but a few steps acrost the road from the campground, so I have an opportunity to see all that is going on there. The house is quite a good looking one and very pleasantly located about hundred paces back from the road and entirely surrounded by a chestnut grove but far enough apart to admit driving amongst them with ease. There are two gentlemen with their families occupying the house at the present time. One of them, the proprietor, is a master workman at the Capitol, a stone worker, I believe, though his business is not very thriving just now. This is his summer residence. The other is an overseer of the place, a small farm being attached to it which he carries on with the help of his two black servants. One of them is a slave and owned by someone at the city. The other is not and says he never will be. There are two servants kept in the house, though the mistresses of both families seem to be workers. One of them is a New England woman, lived in New Hampshire until within a few years. They all seem to be very good people. At least, they are very kind to me.

Yesterday was quite a stormy day, but it did not trouble me much as I was provided with a small store room at the back of the house which I used as a sentry box. Towards night as my labors were about to close, I begged leave of one of the servant girls to take a seat at the stove in the cookroom. I found I was very welcome, so I pulled off my boots and gave my feet a very comfortable warming.

The New England lady commenced frying doughnuts as I was about taking leave of them. She requested me to stop a few minutes longer and eat some of them. Of course, I accepted the invitation and I can testify that 5 of them were very good.

Perhaps you would like to know by what rules and regulations I am governed in my present circumstances. My orders are to keep the soldiers from filling their canteens at the well and to keep them from committing depredations about the place. At such times as I think all is quiet about the place and no need of action on my part (and that is most of the time), I devote to reading, writing, eating chestnuts and persimmons. I am not subject to any roll calls. I leave camp soon after breakfast, go to dinner when it is ready. My duties for the day are done at supper time and it is now about that time so I must draw my letter to a close.

I received your letter on Monday and one from Father the Wednesday before. I am sorry to hear that the pigs are sick but I hope to hear that they are well when you write again. I will feel very thankful even though they are not, if I can hear that you are all well.

My health continues good. We shall look for the box tomorrow or next day. I must close now or you will not get this [this] week.
Rufus

October 31, 1861
Thursday
Washington, D.C.

Henry,

I thought I should certainly receive the letter today which I was looking for from you yesterday but I am doomed to a second disappointment. I don't know the why, so I will not complain.

This is the first opportunity I have had to write you since I last wrote. We are having so many brigade drills which occupy the whole of the afternoon besides the two drills in the forenoon that I have but little time for anything else.

We are having very fine weather now, though rather cool but not cooler than I expected at this time of the year. I am well prepared for it as far as clothing is concerned and I like it much better than the warm dog days weather which we had a month ago.

My health is good. It never was better. I have a great appetite and everything I eat tastes good. We did not get the box until last Saturday. It was miscarried. The pears and apples had rotted some but not very badly. They were first rate. We found everything in good condition and very acceptable. Jacob is very well pleased with his boots. They are full up to his expectations.

I was released from the Provo duty last Friday. I was on seven days and had quite a resting spell.

I think we shall be paid off again next Monday or a week from next Saturday. Our dues this time are twenty-six dollars and there are four dollars due me now on a pair of boots which will make me thirty dollars in hand on payday. I shall send you twenty and perhaps a little more.

I had subscribed two dollars for the purpose of conveying the dead bodies of two our soldiers home. They were embalmed at Washington. The expense was about $100 to each body. Their names are James Harvey[50] of Taunton and August F. Elms[51] of Hanson. Both of our company.

It seems now to be the general impression that we are to remain here or at the city this winter in barracks.

I have not heard from Hiram since the letter I sent you from him. I am expecting to soon. It is nearly drill time again, so I must close. There was two brigades at our drill yesterday afternoon. About eight thousand. Quite a sight to unaccustomed eyes. Give my respects to all the neighbors.

Yours Affectionately,
Rufus

November 1, 1861
Friday
Washington, D.C.

Henry,

It is now about two P.M. I have just finished reading yours and Edwin's letters which I received about half an hour since. I have just finished my dinner and was having a good smoke when the mail wagon drove in.

Now let me tell you what I had for dinner for I don't like these stories about stinking meat and wormy bread. I have never seen anything of the kind with the exception of a few times last summer and then I believe it was unintentional. We had stewed beans for dinner and plenty of good sweet pork cooked with them and it was as good a dinner as I want to eat. We take a loaf of good sweet white bread every morning which lasts us through the day. A few words will tell the whole story. We have enough to eat and that which is good. And Luke will tell you the same story.

My eyes have been sore but not very. They are not quite well now, but much better. I am using a kind of medicine which I think will cure them in a short time, which is the pith of sassafras wood, soaked in cold water. A portion of it dissolves and makes a kind of gummy substance, which I think will cure them in a short time. Nearly a week ago my weight was about 140 and I think I am gaining.

I do not think of any news to write now. So I will close as I shall have to go on drill again soon. I have not heard anything about crossing the river lately and I don't think we shall at present. Do not be over-anxious about me. I am taking good care of myself.
Rufus

November 6, 1861
Wednesday
Washington, D.C.

Dear Father,

I have not been disappointed today but have had the pleasure of reading a good letter from you and it makes me feel a wonderful sight better. What new things have come to pass since I left home! You don't know, Father, how much I should like to be at home with you a little while—a long while if the work was done. But when I receive a letter, it increases the desire to see Father and Mother so that I verily believe that time can never wean me from you. I suppose Grandpa will be with you before this reaches you. Oh how I should like to see him. Well, I have a big hope that I shall see you all again.

We have not changed our quarters yet. There are a great many stories in circulation concerning our future prospects. Some say we are going to the city, others to Virginia. I cannot give any kind of a guess now where our next quarters will be. I hope something will be done before a great while. I think there is no doubt but General Scott has resigned. I do not learn that McClellan[52] intends to pursue any different course. I do not see why they have kept us here this length of time. We did not expect to remain here after the first of October. Our quarters are comfortable enough here. We do not expect to fare so well anywhere else. But we are impatient to begin, so that in process of time we may see the end.

In my last letter to Henry, I told him we should probably be paid off again last Monday or next Saturday, but I begin to think now that it will be as much as ten days after next Saturday.

I am glad to hear that business is good with you. I hope it will continue a long time, but it seems curious to hear that you are making sewed shoes. Who would have guessed that things would have taken such a turn a few years ago?

My eyes are much better, almost well. The fruit which came in the box I shared with the rest, and they in turn shared their butter, cheese and molasses with me. We have lived high since the box came.

I shall write again soon.

Rufus

November 12, 1861
Tuesday
Washington, D.C.

Henry,

I don't think I shall have time to write you a very long letter this time, but I feel anxious to write you a few lines as I learn from a letter which Luke received yesterday that we are soon to have another box.

I don't write now because there is anything that I am particularly in want of, but more especially, if perchance you should receive this before you send the box, that you may have the satisfaction of knowing that I am not in need of anything more than I have reason to think you intend to send, with the exception of a pencil. If you get this before you send the box and can as well as not, I should like to have you send me one of Faber's No. 2. You will find them at Mr. Dyer's.

And now as my time is growing short, I must bring my letter to a close with you, for I want to tell Mother that I shall be very grateful for anything that she may send me and although I shall not be permitted to take a seat at the Thanksgiving table with you this year, yet my heart's thanks can go up with yours with more fervor than ever before, for the kind Providence has blest us with life and health. You will miss me I know, but I hope not with feeling of sadness. I would have you share with me the feeling of gratification of being engaged in so good a cause and one which I verily believe must prosper in the end.

I suppose Grandpa is with you now. Tell him I think of him every day and some day I am going to put them (my thoughts) on paper and send them to him. Tell Samuel he owes me a letter, and I want it pretty soon.

You will hear the news of the success of our fleet at South Carolina before this reaches you. So I will not say anything about it.

I must draw my letter to a close as it is almost drill time again. My health continues to be good, although my eyes are not quite well yet. But they do not trouble me but very little. They seem to be entirely well until towards night they commence itching and burning, though not near so bad as at first. I am going to try plantain leaves with milk, bind them on at night. Do you think that will be good? They don't run but very little.

We are expecting the paymaster every day. I shall write as soon as I get it.

Yours Affectionately,
Rufus

November 14, 1861
Thursday
Washington, D.C.

Henry,

I read your letter last night after returning from brigade drill. It was 3 o'clock yesterday before the mail got in and we left about 2. But I felt very confident when I left that I should have the pleasure of reading a letter from you when I returned. And I was not disappointed with its contents. It was an interesting letter to me and I hope you will never borrow any trouble on that account.

The one finger mittens are just what I want. They are quite fashionable here now. The Fall River company had quite a lot of them come the other day. I suffered more the last time I was on guard from cold hands than anything else. And they will be lovely too at morning drills.

Our drill yesterday consisted chiefly in firing blank cartridges. We fired 7 rounds and had quite a noisy time for a little while. Company K and F fired the best.

I have just signed the pay roll a receipt for our pay. So I think we shall see the pay master soon. Perhaps, he will commence this afternoon. But we don't much expect him before tomorrow.

The weather has been quite pleasant for the last few days. But it has commenced raining since I commenced writing.

The drum has just beat for the afternoon drill. But I think it will be dispensed with.

It is not cold today but we have some very uncomfortable ones and some that are much warmer than we get at home at this time at this time of the year.

My eyes have not troubled but very little since last Tuesday. If they behave as well tomorrow, I shall pronounce them well.

I shall write again soon.

Rufus

November 20, 1861
Washington, D.C.

Dear Mother,

We have just lit our candle and by the light of it I must write you a few lines to let you know that our barrel arrived here this noon and we found everything in good condition. You have sent me more than I expected but not too much. It will last a good while and Mother will seem nearer to me while I am eating it. If you had had nicer cakes than the brown loaf, which I found on top, it would not have been more acceptable. It tastes so natural it almost seems as if I was home. The pies are as whole as when you took them out of the oven. The chicks I have only seen enough to know that they are such. I believe they are in good condition and tomorrow we will have a feast of fat things. I wish you could receive this tomorrow that you might be certain that I was having Thanksgiving with you.

Tell Edwin I am very much obliged to him for the cake, although I don't think that all the praise is due to him. When I write to Sophie I will find out more about it.

We are going to have the day to ourselves tomorrow and passes are to be granted to visit the regiments about us. I think the day will be passed very pleasantly.

I received your letter tonight just before I commenced writing. I should like to write a great deal more, but it is not very convenient tonight. I am glad you sent the comforter, although, I could have got along very well without. But it will not come amiss. I have slept cold but a very few nights. You must think of me now as sleeping as comfortably as if I was at home.

My eyes have troubled me but very little for the last week. They are always worse after being on guard but I don't think that will affect them much now. I will not keep anything from you. You shall know when I am not well. I have written more than I expected to when I began but not all that I wished to. The light does not my hurt eyes at all tonight.

Give my respects to all my neighbors and friends.

Yours Affectionately,

Rufus

November 21, 1861
Washington, D.C.

Dear Brother,

I think you will be glad to know as early as possible how we have spent our Thanksgiving. So whilst the day is passing, I will improve a part of the time to give you an account of it.

We are having a good time. The weather is so fine and other things being equal, we can't very well help it. There is but one improvement which we can imagine that would add to our pleasure. That is that we might spend the day at home with our friends. But we know that you are with us and we with you, even though we are absent in body. The old yellow tub at my elbow is evidence enough of this.

It is about twelve o'clock, so I will now commence to give you an account of the manner in which we have spent it. We were up at half past five, roll call at that time. At half past six, we were seated in our tent around the cover of that old yellow tub, eating that nice chick which Mother sent to me. It was good, so they all said, and I should have known it, if they hadn't. With Luke's pies (cranberry and mince) and the bread and butter, it was little more than enough for our breakfast (four of us). After breakfast, our ideas were up for going to the city. Our company officers were willing. Lieutenant Gurney[53] was the only one not on duty. He signed a pass for Luke, Jacob and myself and told us to carry it to Major Harlow. He signed it and then it had to go to the General for his signature. He was not at his office, but had given his aide instructions how many to sign. He had not commenced to sign them when we got there but there was a great crowd about his house and we were not among the fortunate ones. It was something of a disappointment to me as I was very anxious to go and get my Ambro taken. But I am not agoing to give it up. So I shall stick now for a pass until I get one. I saw him give passes to some this morning that had been stood on a barrel for running away.

Now, I will rest a while as I have given you the substance of our fore-noon work.

Well, it is nearly four o'clock and I have been having Thanksgiving about after the old fashion. Jacob's box came today about noon. We dined at two. A piece of roast pig came in it which with some of his pies and cakes, we had a good dinner. He had some plum pudding, but we forgot all about it until after we had finished our dinner. I have been kicking foot ball a while this afternoon. No lack of numbers and a merry time. After getting tired of that, Luke and I took a walk for a short distance out of camp. We went up as far as Fort Mass, the one which we made first. When we came back, we stopped at a Brightwood store and weighed ourselves. My weight is 145 and ¼. Luke's, I believe, was 132.

We are to have an oyster supper tonight for the whole company. The expense to come out of our company fund. I have eaten quite a hearty dinner, but I think I did my part with the oysters.

I believe I should have been as happy today as it is oft the lot of man to be if I could have had my Brother Henry with me. How I should like to have shown you about the camp. My cup would have been full. But I have had a good time and I am thankful.

I will now write a few lines which I omitted in my letter last night to Mother. I shall not part with the stockings which she sent me, although I have now on hand with them three pair of new ones and the two pair that I brought from Taunton with me that are worth something now. One pair of my new ones I received from the U.S. two weeks ago. They are very large and pretty good. The charge for them is 24 cents.

A box came to us last Tuesday from the Ladies of Center Abington, of which Mrs. Dennis Powers is at the head, containing stocking and hand-kerchiefs. They were distributed after the fashion of the grab box at our dances. I paid four cents for a ticket, which went towards paying the transportation and drew a pair of first rate stockings. Great care was taken in knitting them and the heels are run. They are not quite so soft as Mother's, but they are good ones. I have got a good pair of cotton draw-ers, furnished by Uncle Sam and am going to have another pair soon. They are warmer than the woolen ones.

I have my washing done since the weather has become cooler. I gave a Negro woman a pair of my old woolen drawers that had grown too small for me for washing two shirts and a pair of drawers and stockings. They charge 5 cents apiece.

It is a long while since I have heard from Ruth or Hiram. I think I sent you the last letter I received from them. I have not written to Ruth as often as I ought to. Is Ann at home now? I owe her a letter and have for a long while, and also to Hannah, Almira, and Judson. I have not had time to answer them. Give them my best respects and tell them how it is. I shall try to soon.

My eyes have not troubled me any today. My health was never better. I have tried some of the pears. The yellow ones are very good. I am afraid I have got more than my share.

I must close now although I leave a great deal unwritten. Let me hear from you soon and send the *Trumpets*.

Yours Affectionately,
Rufus

November 30, 1861
Washington, D.C.

Dear Brother,

I have finally succeeded in getting a pass signed to go to the city. I seen a great many wonders there, but I can't tell you much about my visit this time as I am writing by candle light and our evenings are rather short as we have roll call at 8 and taps at ½ past.

I went to the city last Tuesday. Started about 9 with Sergeant Brown.[54] Our pass was written to be in camp again at ½ past 4. I did not expect to go that morning. Consequently, I had but little time for preparation. So I hope you will excuse any imperfections which you may discover in my appearance. That morning I had 6 photographs taken at the cost of $2.00. I couldn't have a smaller number of that kind taken and I thought they would be the most convenient kind to send. I am going to send one to Ruth and one to Uncle Ichabod's folks to Almira or Hannah. I forget which it was that requested it. I can tell when I refer to their letters. And one to Ann. If she is not at home, you will tell me if she is when you write. One to Edwin, and one to Uncle Sam, and one to Mother.

I received a letter from Ruth a few days ago. She and the children were well. It contained about the same news from Hiram that your last did which I received Tuesday eve after returning from the city. I should have delayed writing until tomorrow, but I shall be on guard and shall not have an opportunity.

Henry Beebe's box has come. I have got my mittens. They are good ones and the pencil and eye water. My eyes are well now and I hope I shall not have any use for it. I shall write you again soon and tell you something of my visit.

Yours affectionately,
Rufus

P.S. I should have written before but didn't receive them until today. Mother must take her choice of the 3. They are the best ones. I want you to take particular notice of my boots.

December 2, 1861
Washington, D.C.

Dear Brother,

I have just discovered my mistake. Instead of sending you three of my photographs as I intended, I have sent you something else but I don't know what. I don't feel like writing much this morning, as I am just off guard, but I want to rectify my mistake as soon as possible. I feel very sorry that I have made such a mistake for I am afraid you will be unable to understand my letter and, moreover, as I had not informed you that I had been to the city, I was in hopes they would be something of a surprise to you. But you will understand it now.

In my haste to finish my letter last Saturday, all before roll call, I suppose I enclosed an envelope containing a letter instead of one containing the pictures.

Here's a bit of news and will close. (Perhaps it will not prove correct but I think it will.) We are informed that our regiment is to be set at building barracks a short distance from where we now are for our accommodations this winter.

My health is good. Eyes a little bad today because I didn't sleep last night. But the medicine helps them. I shall give you an account of my adventures at Washington soon. We had a very little snow last week.
Yours Truly,
Rufus

December 8, 1861
Sunday
Washington, D.C.

Dear Father,

I received your letter last Tuesday and am very much obliged to you for writing me such a long one. The papers I didn't receive until yesterday and today (just now). I have finished reading a few lines from you and Henry.

I narrowly escaped being on guard duty today. It is all the leisure day we have and only half an one at that as inspection usually occupies most of the forenoon. Some that were on guard with me last Sunday complained to the Captain that it was too bad to stand guard two Sundays in succession. So he detailed the guard for tomorrow to take our places. I am very glad of the change (though it was none of my getting up), for it is a very pleasant day, the warmest I think I ever knew in December.

After inspection, I took my towel and clean clothes and went to the brook and had a good wash and feel very much better. I don't know how late in the winter I can continue to bathe in the brook. But I have been favoured with a pleasant day once in two weeks during the last two months.

The blue birds were singing this morning the same old tune they sing at home. And if I had been there, I should have thought it the last of May. But we had all kinds of weather here. We have not had snow but once and then but very little. But it was so cold a few nights since that the water froze in our canteens hanging in our tents. But we slept warm. We have got comforters enough to keep us warm even if the weather should be a great deal colder than we have yet had. I will tell you some time how we make our beds. We have got four comforters. Nat Noyes sent two to Luke and Jacob.

I want to write a few words about my visit to the city. I saw wonders. Oh, I told you that before. Well, after getting my pictures taken, my first visit was to the Capitol. Well, what can I tell you of a building which covers over 3 and ½ acres with only the space of one short hour to see it? I visited but a small portion of the building although I tarried but a short time in any room except the one which contained pictures representing scenes of the Revolution. They were splendid. That is all I can tell you.

I saw from the gallery the hall of the representatives. That is a pretty room. The seats are arranged in half circles in front of the Speaker's desk and covered with green velvet. I didn't see the Senate chamber. The door to the main entrance was locked. I could have seen it, if I had had time to have looked for another way. It is said to be very much prettier than the representatives'. I find that I had a very limited conception of things before I saw.

My next and last visit was to the Patent Office. That is a very large building and contains a little of almost everything. Among the things which interested me most was the clothes worn by Washington when he resigned his commission at Annapolis. The coat was blue cloth fronted with yellow buckskin vest, breeches were buckskin the same as the front of the coat. I saw the sword which he used in his country's service and his cane. I saw two guns which was presented to Jefferson by the Emperor of Morocco (Beauties). That is all the description I can give you now of them.

I saw a great many things which I should like to tell you about but I haven't time now but when I get home I shall have a long story to tell you. My health is good and I am accumulating much grease very fast. When I was at the city in the Patent Office, I weighed 147½. Last Thursday, I weighed at two places. First time at quartermaster's 151. Being a little frightened at my weight there, I went over to Brightwood store and

I found the exertion of the disagreement in the scales cost me ¼ of a pound.

I am going to send you the two remaining photographs (I have sent one to Ruth.) Keep the best one and dispose of the other as you think best.

Yours truly,

Rufus

[The following was enclosed with the above.]

Dear Mother,

I want to tell you not to attempt to write to me when you don't feel able to. As much as I love to receive letters from you, I had much rather think that you are resting. Only write when you can with ease. I shall write you again soon.

Yours affectionately,

Rufus

December 17, 1861
Washington, D.C.

Dear Brother,

I am going to try to write you a few lines this evening, although I have nothing in mind just now that seems to me will be new to you as I suppose you will have the pleasure of reading the letter which I sent to Edwin last Sunday.

My 24 hours of guard duty expired this morning at 9 o'clock. The weather was very fine especially last night. It was very calm and mild and not a cloud during the whole night to hide the moon from my view. Did you notice the eclipse? I think you did not. You should rise early if you want to see the wonders of nature. I think it commenced a little after 2. As I was on the first relief, my last watch was from 3 to 5 so I had an opportunity to watch its progress but I will not make a long story of that as I suppose you can get a more correct account of it from the *Old Farmer's Almanac* than I can give you. I don't suppose if I had been comfortably in bed I should have taken the trouble to rise for the sake of seeing it. But when the sergeant calls out, "Fall in first relief!" and it is a General House offense to be missing about that time, it is well enough to have something of that kind to while away the time.

We have 7 tents for the guard, each of which will comfortable accommodate but 4 men and 3 of these are usually filled with prisoners. So you can imagine what kind of accommodations we guards have at night when we are not on the watch when I tell you that the whole guard numbers 57 men and but ⅓ of them are on duty at a time and the other 2 parts are not allowed to go farther than speaking distance from these tents day nor night without special permission from the sergeant of the guard and there can be but 2 absent at a time and but a short time at that excepting as each relief are sent to their meals as near the proper time as circumstances will admit.

The 3 last times that I have been on guard before last night I have not attempted to sleep. Even if there was room in the tents, I don't like to pile in with all sorts in such close quarters. We always have a good fire near the tents when on a cold night not less than ½ a cord of wood is consumed. But this does not always add much to our comfort for when the wind blows hard, we have plenty of smoke on one side and cold on the other. When I was at home reading of soldiers and camp fires, none of these discomfortures ever occurred to my mind.

But this is not very sensible in me to be enumerating these petty hardships when the only effect will be to add more to your anxiety for me. I am in hopes that we shall soon be provided with better quarters when we are on guard.

Last night, Charlie Reed[55] and I found better. Our sutler has put up a new building very near the guard tents which is not quite completed. So Charlie and I got consent of the sergeant to make our bed there and the old comforter and my woolen blanket and an equal amount with which he was provided made us a comfortable bed which we occupied from 11 until 3.

I am never troubled about going to sleep. 5 minutes is usually enough to send me off to the land of dreams after I have put myself in a sleeping position. I usually spend the remainder of the forenoon after being relieved as I have today in sleeping. I can then make my bed in my own tent and am not subject to any duty again until after dinner.

We have been at work this afternoon on our barracks. We are not making very great progress on them but I am not in much of a hurry as I am very comfortable in the old tent.

I must stop now for tonight, for I hear the drum beating for the last roll call. But I shall try to fill the remainder of this sheet tomorrow as our company is detailed for Grand Guard to Fort—Well, I will call it (Deruser[56]) or something that sounds very much like it.

December 18

I will now try to give you an account of myself and things at Fort D. But I must state in the first place the object for which our company was detailed. Perhaps it will not require a long explanation as you will readily perceive that a fort without a guard is worse than useless. A new company is detailed every day for that purpose. Sometimes from the N.Y. Regiment and sometimes from ours.

Well, arriving at the fort, our company is divided into 3 squads. One to guard it, myself being among that number. The other 2 are stationed at cross roads to guard against the approach of enemies. 20 of us are retained at the fort and all we have to do unless an enemy should approach us (which is not very likely) is to take turns standing at the gate and cry out, "Grand Rounds," when the officer commissioned for that purpose comes around to inspect the guard. He comes once in the day time and once at night. No matter if we are all asleep, the sentinel calls out, "Grand Rounds. Turn out the guard." And in less than no time every man must be out from under his blanket and in line with his equipments on ready to present arms. Immediately after which we are dismissed. And if he has then any orders to our captain, he delivers them and goes his way. And there is one more required out of our squad to guard a house about ½ a mile from the fort. This guard is relieved every 2 hours. The object of having a guard there is to keep soldiers that may be strolling about from stealing poultry or visiting the premises too frequently for any purpose.

I am expecting to relieve the guard there at 5 P.M. It is now near 3 o'clock and I must hasten to give you a short description of it. But I hardly know how to do it. Perhaps the description which I gave you of Fort Slocum will answer for this. Only it is finished in more workman-like style. It mounts 7 guns. The largest one, a 32 pounder, weighs 8,000 pounds. In the center of this fort is a log hut in which I am seated. It is quite a cozy place. But one room about 15 by 25 with a row of benches around it and a fire place in one corner.————

Thursday, December 19

I did not have time to finish writing all I intended yesterday. I am now in camp again and have but a few minutes to write. I told you yesterday I was expecting to relieve the guard at the farm house. I did so last night from 5 to 7 and again this morning at the same hour.

I am going to give you an idea some time of the farming operations here. But I have only time now to say that the sun never shone on a brighter morning than this. The big bellied old fellow gave me a good breakfast. I could not leave my post to take a seat at his table. But he brought me out on a plate a large piece of corn cake, a white bread biscuit, and a sausage and a cup of tea.

I have just received Father's letter. I am sorry to hear that Grampa is sick. I am afraid I shall not meet him again in this world.
Rufus

December 22, 1861
Sunday Eve
West Sumner, Maine

Dear Brother,

I received your last letter week ago last Thursday containing your picture. This is the first opportunity that I have had to answer it. I have but little time to write tonight for it is already past nine but I want to thank you for that picture. I think it looks just like you, although I have never seen you when you had so much beard round your mouth. Fred's wife says she should know that picture if she should see it in heaven. She is queer, Sarah. I should be so lonesome enough if she should move away.

Alice called it the President at first. Then she said it was Uncle Rufus. I think your moustache and soldier clothes make you look first rate. I have shown the picture to quite a number and they say it is a very good looking picture. But there I shall spoil you. You will be getting too proud.

The last letter that I received from Hiram was dated the second of December which was twenty days ago. He wrote that he had written to you and Henry, Father, James, and Augusta. But he said that when the last mail came in he did not get a letter from anyone. He thought that it was rather too bad. You said in your last letter that you would write as soon as you knew how to direct them so I will write it down here:

Company F

9th Maine Regiment

3rd Brigade

Sherman's Division

New York

care of Colonel D. D. Tompkins, Supervisor Master

I had about as lives write a whole letter as to write the directions.

You must excuse this short letter for my head aches so, I can hardly write. We have all got bad colds and Nelly is the most sick, but I am doctoring her up. I am in hope she will be better in the morning.

From your sis,

Ruth

December 29, 1861
Sunday
Washington, D.C.

Dear Brother,

I will again attempt to write you a few lines although as usual my beginning is at a late hour, not exactly evening, but about three P.M. I received your letter last Thursday. It contained much that was interesting to me.

I am afraid you are striving too hard against the hard times. Fifty cents a day with three leisure hours each day will be worth more to you at the end of the year than a dollar a day will without. I hope you will take my advice and let the evenings at least be free from care.

I did not expect to hear that Grandpa was better. It seems as though his end was near, and yet I cannot give up the hope of seeing him again. Please tell me when you write again if he is able to converse.

We occupied our new quarters last night for the first time. They are not quite finished but with a little extra exertion yesterday we were enabled to make them quite comfortable last night. Our work yesterday was sewing the tents together for covering the barracks and finishing our fireplace. Each mess worked by themselves, as each have a house of their own. The company is divided into four messes with a sergeant at the head of each. We succeeded in finishing our fireplace as we have a good mason in our mess (Sylvester,[57] one of the Scituate Boys). The covering was all ready at sunset to throw over the ridge pole but we didn't have time to fasten it. Fortunately, it was a very still night, so it answered every purpose.

I am more pleased with our new quarters than I expected. Our bunks are roomy and it is very pleasant to lie in them and watch the fire. I am seated on my old yellow tub by the side of my bunk. The old tub has been a source of much happiness to me. It is a part of my home and I prize it more than anything I have got. I find it very convenient to keep my stockings, needle book, papers and various other things in.

Well, I have not time to write much more, so I must tell you that the baked beans which we had this morning for breakfast were very good. Mr. Taggard[58] is a very good cook. This morning was the third time that he has treated us to baked beans. For dinner, we had corned beef and bread for dinner and rice and molasses for supper. The Thanksgiving stores lasted us four about a month. It was common prepared as long as it lasted.

I am blest with a good appetite and good health. That is all now. So good evening.
Yours Truly,
Rufus

NOTES

1. This line is not in Rufus' handwriting, and was probably added by Alice Robbins.

2. Faneuil Hall in Boston was a meeting place for patriots prior to the outbreak of the Revolutionary War.

3. Benjamin F. Hutchinson, 37, Corporal, Company K.

4. Frank Erskin, 18, Private, Company K.

5. Thomas Sherman, 29, Corporal, Company K.

6. Rufus has drawn a dash. Apparently, at the time of writing he did not know, or remember, who the other man was.

7. Franklin P. Harlow, 33, Captain, Company K, Major, August 1, 1861, Lieutenant Colonel, October 25, 1862.

8. Rufus has drawn a line across the page here. He then resumes the letter on July 8.

9. Edward M. Bain, 27, Sergeant, Company K.

10. Joseph W. Brown, 22, Private, Company K.

11. Joshua F. Winslow, 35, Corporal, Company K.

12. Rock Creek.

13. Andrew Hinckley, 18, Private, Company K.

14. Probably Abijah L. Mayhew, 39, 2nd Lieutenant, Company K, 1st Lieutenant August 1, 1861, discharged September 23, 1862 with a disability.

15. Franklin P. Harlow, 33, Captain Company K, Major August 1, 1861, Lieutenant Colonel October 25, 1862.

16. Luke B. Noyes, 24, Corporal Company K, Sergeant Major November 1, 1862, 2nd Lieutenant June 18, 1863.

17. Nahum A. Reed, 18, Private, Company K.

18. Franklin P. Harlow, 33, Captain, Company K, Major August 1, 1861, Lieutenant Colonel October 25, 1862.

19. Probably, John C. Bosworth, 35, Sergeant, Company K, 2nd Lieutenant March 26, 1863.

20. Company E of the Fourth Massachusetts Volunteer Militia lays claim to being the first Massachusetts Company to report for duty in answer to President Lincoln's April 15, 1861, call for volunteers to defend the Union. The period of enlistment of the men of Company E was ninety days. The majority of Company E came from South Abington.

21. Battle of First Bull Run fought July 21, 1861. The Seventh Regiment was not engaged.

22. William F. Howland, 26, Private, Company K, discharged September 23, 1862, with a disability.

23. First Battle of Bull Run fought July 21, 1861.

24. Ruth's husband.

25. Samuel L. Snell, 19, Private, Company K, discharged August 1861 with a disability.

26. On August 10, 1861, Union general, Nathaniel Lyon, was killed at the battle of Wilson's Creek in Missouri.

27. A section in East Bridgewater, Massachusetts.

28. Rufus' mother.

29. Sophie's mother.

30. Rufus regularly uses "eat" instead of "ate" as the past tense of "eat."

31. Most probably Elbert F. Hobart, 29, who, according to records, was mustered in to Company K on June 15, 1861, as a musician.

32. Franklin P. Harlow, 33, Captain, Company K, Major August 1, 1861, Lieutenant Colonel October 25, 1862.

33. David E. Holman, 55, Major, Seventh Massachusetts Regiment, re-signed August 1, 1861.

34. By this, Rufus means that he will have to write using rather "large" letters so that he can fill up the remainder of the sheet of paper.

35. This is the same Company E of the Fourth Massachusetts Volunteer Militia to which Sophie refers in her letter of August 4, 1861.

36. In late August 1861, General Benjamin F. Butler of Massachusetts, who had commanded the garrison at Fortress Monroe, led the infantry contingent of a naval assault on the Confederate forts guarding Hatteras, North Carolina. The Confederate forces were defeated, with Butler's troops occupying the forts.

37. North Bridgewater is now the city of Brockton, Massachusetts.

38. Darius N. Couch, 38, Colonel, Seventh Massachusetts Regiment, Brigadier General U.S.V., September 4, 1861.

39. Probably Joseph W. Brown, 22, Private, Company K.

40. Chester W. Green, 49, Lieutenant Colonel, Seventh Massachusetts Regiment, resigned November 22, 1861.

41. Nelson H. Davis, Colonel, Seventh Massachusetts Regiment September 4, 1861, Assistant Ins. General U.S.A. November 18, 1861.

42. Henry W. Beebe, 27, Private, Company K. Died of wounds, May 3, 1863, at Fredricksburg.

43. Probably a misspelling of "Harding"—Jacob Harding, 19, Private, Company K.

44. Abijah L. Mayhew, 39, 2nd Lieutenant June 15, 1861, 1st Lieutenant August 1, 1861, discharged September 23, 1862, with a disability.

45. Daughters of East Abington.

46. Probably Jacob Harding.

47. Daughters of East Abington.

48. Untanned calf hide.

49. That is, the occupant of the house.

50. James G. Harvey, 18, Private, Company K.

51. Augustus F. Elms, 21, Private, Company K.

52. General George McCellan.

53. William H. Gurney, 32, 1st Sergeant, Company K, 2nd Lieutenant July 15, 1861, 1st Lieutenant July 12, 1862, Captain November 1, 1862.

54. William H. Brown, 39, Sergeant, Company K.

55. Charles W. Reed, 19, Private, Company K. Killed May 3, 1863, at Marie's Heights, Va.

56. Fort De Russey.

57. Charles F. Sylvester, 18, Private, Company K.

58. David P. Taggard, 38, Private, Company K.

Henry Howard Robbins, 1830–1903. Courtesy of Richard Robbins.

Edwin Ruthran Robbins, 1839–1918. Courtesy of Richard Robbins.

Sophia E. Abbott Robbins (wife of Edwin). Courtesy of Richard Robbins.

Ruth Partridge Robbins Barrows, 1833–1929; and Thomas Hiram Barrows, 1828–1864. Courtesy of Richard Robbins.

Franklin P. Harlow, First Captain, Company K. From Nelson V. Hutchinson, *History of the Seventh Massachusetts Volunteer Infantry in the War of the Rebellion of the Southern States Against Constitutional Authority* (published by authority of the Regimental Association, 1890).

This camp was at the junction of 7th and 14th Sts. Washington. From August 1861 until March 1862

9737444
7th MASS
INFANTRY

14th St—

Tent

CAMP BRIGHTWOOD

Col. N. H. Davis, 7th Mass Volunteers.

Entered according to act of congress in the year 1862 by L. H. Bradford in the Clerk's office of the District Court of Mass.

7th St,

Camp Brightwood, Washington, D.C. The handwriting is that of James E. Seaver, who on June 15, 1861, was mustered into the Seventh Massachusetts Volunteers at the age of twenty-one as a 1st Sergeant of Company D. Seaver has identified the camp streets by company and the location of his own tent. Courtesy of the Old Colony Historical Society, Taunton, Mass.

Fort Massachusetts, sally port, and soldiers, 1861. National Archives and Records Administration.

Interior of the Upper Battery at Chain Bridge, Washington, D.C. Originally published in *Harper's Pictorial History of the Great Rebellion* (1866).

Darius N. Couch, First Colonel, Seventh Regiment Massachusetts Volunteer Infantry. From Nelson V. Hutchinson, *History of the Seventh Massachusetts Volunteer Infantry in the War of the Rebellion of the Southern States Against Constitutional Authority* (published by authority of the Regimental Association, 1890).

Carver Hospital, Washington, D.C. National Archives and Records Administration.

LETTERS FROM 1862

January 1, 1862
Washington D.C.

Dear Mother,

I think I should not attempt to write this evening but for the desire to wish you a Happy New Year, and I think you will be some happier if you receive this next Saturday eve.

I was on guard again last night. My turn comes once a week. I was on picket guard with Corporal Samuel Foster.[1] We were detailed for regular guard but there is always a picket guard taken out and it was Foster's turn to take charge of it. And he had liberty to select his men to go with him. Robinson,[2] one of the Scituate boys, M. Penniman[3] of South Abington, and myself were the ones selected. We were posted not far from the camp on the road leading to the city for the purpose of examining the passes of such soldiers as came our way. If they are without passes, we have to take them back to camp. At night, no one is allowed to pass without the countersign.

We had a tent by the side of the road and a good fire to sit by. It was quite pleasant sitting by our fire last night. The weather was very fine, hardly cold enough to freeze. We talked the old year out and the new one in. We talked of the fine picture we should make seated around our cheerful fire. How the inexperienced would envy us if they could see it. But we all agreed that we would willingly exchange our situation for a comfortable bed. But I like it much better than I do regular guard. It is not so tiresome as it is to walk a beat two hours at a time.

My eyes trouble me but very little now and only when I have been on guard and then the medicine which you sent cures them very soon. Others have tried it with the same effect.

My clothes are all good. I have got a very pretty blue frock coat, large enough to wear over my two jackets. I didn't have it when I had my pictures taken.

I received a letter from Ruth yesterday. I will send it to you as I have no time to tell you what she wrote. I have got paper and envelopes in plenty. I sold a part of that which you sent me to accommodate. We cannot have any more franking done. I am out of money, but I have got a dollar order on the Brick Store to buy butter. I will tell you more about it next time. I think we shall be paid off again next Saturday.

My health is very good. I must close now with a Happy New Year to all.

Yours Affectionately,

Rufus

P.S. I am by accident obliged to send you a small portion of my candle.[4]

January 29, 1862
Washington D.C.

Dear Brother,

I have been waiting as patiently as possible for the mail to arrive, hoping that it will be my good fortune to receive a letter. I now hear that the mail has arrived and 5 minutes more will decide the matter which is of so much interest to me. It is later today than I ever knew it to be before.

It is now nearly seven o'clock. Dress parade at half past four and then supper (rice and sugar) but I eat toasted bread and butter. I have got rice enough for the present.

Hold! here comes the orderly with the mail. A whole handful of letters and papers so I guess there is one for me. (Now listen.) H. P. Beebe, A. Lufkin,[5] Frank Hill,[6] Rufus Robbins. Here, this way! In the bunk writing. Now hold on a bit and let's read it. Well, not quite so long as I get sometimes, but a very good letter.

I am glad to hear that Grandpa is some better. I pray earnestly that his life may be spared until I return home. As soon as I read that John Bouldra[7] was coming, the very thought occurred to my mind which you suggested, before I read what you had written. I will do all I can to shield him from the bad influences which will certainly surround him. His brother is well. I was on guard with him the day that I received your letter making inquiry about him and mentioned the same to him. But I forgot to mention it when I wrote.

I think I am as well satisfied with the new horse as you are and that is, I think, saying a great deal. But, as you say nothing of his looks, I have made up my mind that he is rather different in that respect. I would rather have Mother's opinion on that matter.

I must close now as the drum is beating for the last roll call. My health is good.

Yours Affectionately,
Rufus

January 31, 1862

A little later the same day.[8]

It is now about dinner time and it is raining quite hard. We hear that Old Taggard, the cook, has burnt the beans. So Luke and I conclude not to go down to dinner but stay here and make a toast.

So I will say good-bye until after dinner.

Well, the toast was pretty good. Luke toasted the bread and I made the butter. A spoonful of flour and a lump of butter, about the size of an egg, boiled up with 3 gills[9] of water made us a good dinner. Is that the way Mother does it?

Have you heard the news of our success at the south? I suppose you have, or will at any rate, before this reaches you. So I will not attempt to tell it.

I sent Father a paper last week. I think Hiram must have seen some of the fighting. I have not heard from him or Ruth for a long while.

I have just received Henry's letter and I feel very grateful for it and Mother's too. The words of advice and encouragement which it contains will be a great help to me. I will say to Henry that I am glad he has subscribed the six dollars for me, for I feel as willing now as ever to help the cause along and I am glad you could give me so good an account of our church and society affairs.

Our new colonel takes command today—D. A. Russell[10] of Boston. We all think he will be the man for us. We are all out with Raymond.[11] He doesn't know enough to command us as he should, at least some think. It is possible that we may leave this place when the mud dries up, but nothing is certain. We are anxious to share the honors with our brethren in arms and all are tired of staying here.

As soon as you hear from Ruth or Hiram, let me know.
Yours Affectionately,
Rufus

February 2, 1862
Washington, D.C.

Dear Brother,

Since I last wrote you, I have been a little unwell, but today I am much better. I could say quite well, but I feel a little weak yet from the effects of a diarrhea and physic which I have taken. I will give you an account of my sickness from the commencement and how I think it was brought on.

Last Thursday morning I had to go on guard and, at the same time, we were having a cold northeast rain storm. And mud as it has been since the first of January most of the time from two to six inches deep. I don't think I took much cold, though my feet were wet and cold most of the time during the twenty-four hours. But the fatigue of walking eight hours in the mud and water when I was on duty (as I was obliged to if for no other reason to keep warm) is enough to endanger the health of anyone. Then the hard bread, which was all we could have for supper (as the ovens had given out so that they couldn't bake bread for us), I think was another cause as I have never eaten of it without feeling bad effects.

I was taken with diarrhea, Friday morning, which lasted me through the day. The doctor came in about eleven o'clock to see how things were looking in our mess, whilst I was lying down. I told him I was sick. He wanted to know what the trouble was, so I told him, "Headache, sick at the stomach, pain in the back, and diarrhea." "Well," says he, "trouble enough for a stormy day. Come down and I will give you a dose of salts." But I didn't go for them, but took a good dose of my rhubarb root, which I think is the best physic I ever took. I had a good operation from it and with that my diarrhea left me and I felt much better. I didn't eat anything until yesterday morning when I went to the store and bought a little flour and made some gruel. I couldn't get milk then, so I had to take it without. But it answered very well as I eat it with a good relish and I could think of nothing else that I could. About noon, I bought some milk, a pint for 5 cents, and made some milk porridge. I didn't put much water in, as I was very sure it was one quarter water when I bought it.

Perhaps you may think that I am a bungler at making porridge, but it is not so. My first attempt was a success. And I have had some experience at the business as I have been nursing several sick ones since I have been in the army.

Well, I am making a long story, but I am bound to tell the whole of it. So I must tell you what I had last night for supper, and all the particulars of how the pudding was made and baked, may occupy another sheet of paper.

Receipt for the pudding made by Charles Knott[12] of Scituate.

> Crumb baker's bread into a 2 quart pan until it is filled. Add ½ pint of milk, three eggs, rest water because there wasn't any more milk. A good lot of raisins. Do sugar, spice, and salt to suit the taste. Now take the old fashion bake kettle such as we used at the barn to water the hens. (Ours was borrowed off an old Negro woman who lives near our camp.) Set your pan in containing the pudding and bake in the fireplace until it is done.

¼ of it was my share, which cost six cents, though from the whole cost, there must be a deduction of 3 eggs as there was not so many needed as was at first supposed. But we are to have a rice pudding for supper and they will be used for that. I didn't eat any of the raisins, as I was afraid they would hurt me, and not all of my share of the pudding, so gave some to Luke.

I slept well last night and when I was arose this morning, went to the doctor's to get excused from inspection, reminding him of my condition yesterday. He excused me and ordered 2 pills for me, one to be taken this morning and one tonight. But I have not taken either of them and think I shall not.

Whilst the company were out on inspection, I gave my neck and head a good washing, then went to work getting my breakfast. I made a toast. Took a little flour and butter and boiled in water the same as I make porridge, with the exception of the butter, and I made a good breakfast.

It is now nearly four o'clock and I have eaten my share of the rice pudding. I had a good appetite as I had eaten nothing since morning. And it was very good. And I think I feel as well as ever.

I dreamed of being at home last night and Mother told me that I looked as lean as a crow. I could not help looking in the glass this morning to see that it was so. I think she would not say so if she could see me. And it was also a reality to me for a while that our new horse was guilty of running and breaking the carriage.

We are having a fine day, the first one for more than 3 weeks. A few of them will make a great improvement in our camp.

I hear that Edwin has got a daughter and I am very much pleased, as I suppose he is.

Write soon and let me know if I have been dreaming.

Rufus

February 5, 1862
Washington, D.C.

Dear Brother,

Your letter has not reached me today, but I will write you a few lines this evening as I think you will expect to hear from me next Saturday eve.

My health is now as good as ever. I was quite well last Monday and, notwithstanding the thick snow storm we were having, engaged in a speculation which net me clear profit. 12 ½ cents.

Since we have lived in barracks, it has been quite fashionable for one and another to cook messes of various kinds to suit the tastes of their companions. For the sake of the profits, for instance, Andrew Hinckley fries buckwheat cakes which he sells for 5 cents apiece. Others peddle knickknacks, such as combs, pencils, paper, pamphlets, and newspapers. I felt that day like doing something for my country, so I proposed to Charlie Knott of Hull some corn. So we went acrost the road to a Mr. King's and bought 14 ears of corn for which we paid him 14 cents, then bought 3 cents worth of saleratus.[13] Borrowed a kettle at the cookstand and went at it. We had very good luck considering it was our first attempt and it sold very quick at from 5 to 10 cents according to the amount we put upon a plate. And the demand was greater than the supply. We sold 42 cents worth and had one plate left to divide between us.

We have now about 4 inches of snow and yesterday and today very fine weather. I did my washing yesterday, the 2nd time I have attempted it since I have been in the barracks. I have a barrel sawed in two for a tub. I had quite a large wash: 2 shirts, one pair drawers, towel, handkerchief, and one pair stockings and mittens.

We had a target shoot this morning, distance 180 yards, bigness of a man. Fired 2 rounds. A few hit, but I was not among that number.

This afternoon, we had a battalion drill of an hour and ½ and fired 10 rounds of blank cartridges.

I got my boots tapped yesterday. Frank Hill, Sergeant, of our mess is our cobbler. He is from East Bridgewater. I had the ones which you sent me put on and a lighter pair with them. That and fixing the heels cost 62 cents. I use a kind of blacking which is very good for keeping out water.

I go on guard again next Friday and I think I shall come off with dry feet.

Now, good eve.
Yours Affectionately,
Rufus

February 12, 1862
Washington, D.C.

Dear Father,

I feel that I owe you a much longer letter than I shall be able to write this evening but if I delay it until tomorrow, you will not receive it Saturday evening. It was nearly 5 when the mail arrived tonight and dress parade and supper consumed the larger part of two hours so I am rather late.

I should have informed you some time ago that I had received Brother Crehore's letter, but it escaped my mind. I have made several attempts to answer it, but have not succeeded to my satisfaction. But I hope to be able to soon. His was a good letter, full of encouragement and good news. He spoke of our church affairs, of the progress they had made, and my desire was to be one of the number.

I have seen much of the workings of evil since I have been here, more than I ever dreamed of before. And more than ever do I realize the necessity of a firm belief and trust in God as I have learned of Him at home. I sometimes think of the little ones in our Sabbath School. What if they should be called in a few years to the school where I am now? Will it not be well for them if they have had faithful teachers and learned their lessons well? Surely it will, for the burden of a soldier's life is enough without the burden which sin imposes.

I have but little more than time enough now to tell that I am now as well as ever and answer Mother's question concerning our fare. In my next letter, I shall give you more particulars but I can say now that our fare is very good and we have enough of it. Our ovens are now in good repair and we have now every day a good large loaf of nice bread.

The weather has been very fine for the last few days. I do not like to stop now as I have much more in mind that I should like to write. But I shall write again soon.
Yours Affectionately,
Rufus
Tell Sam I do not want to see him here.

February 19, 1862
Washington, D.C.

Dear Mother,

It was my intention when I last wrote you to have written again before this time and I am afraid as I told you I should write again very soon my delay has caused you much anxiety. I must tell you that I have not been

quite well, as I have had since last Friday a pretty severe head cold. My teeth
and head have ached at such a rate that I could not think. But I am well
now. I feel today like a new man. And I am glad that I can tell you so for I
know it would cause you much anxiety to know that I am sick.

I don't know as I had really ought to say that I have been sick for I
have had a good appetite all the time and a plenty of good food to eat.

I was on guard last Friday and since then I have had but very little to
do as it has been stormy every day since. Since the 1st of January we
have had but very few pleasant days. Most of the time the weather has
been much like our spring weather at home and I have set it down as
impossible so long as we have such weather as this to avoid colds.

But the folks here tell us that we shall soon have better weather. The
March winds will soon dry the mud up and we shall see them planting
by the middle of the month. We are having good fare as we have had
most of the time since we have been here. Sometimes I think too good,
for there is a great deal wasted. There is more bread and meat thrown
into our fireplace every day than Henry's pigs could eat. In the course of
a week we have for dinners stewed beans and soup of fresh beef and
potatoes and fried steak and what the cooks call "smothered meat," which
is very good. And when the cooks don't bake beans often enough for us,
we go to the cookstand and get 3 quarts of beans and a piece of pork
and bake them ourselves. We had some baking last night for breakfast
this morning and they were very good.

I little thought when I was about to become a soldier that I should
have such good fare and be comfortable in so many respects. It is true
there are many disagreeable things about this life but the greatest trouble
that I have is that Mother is feeling too anxious about me. I shall always
tell you when I am sick so you will not need have unnecessary fears long
at a time.

My companions are all good hearted fellows, always ready to lend a
helping hand when one is in distress and at all times cheerful and accommodating some rousing good times. We have but all agreed that it
will be a joyful day when we start for home.
Rufus

                    February 23, 1862
                    Sunday
                    Washington, D.C.

Dear Brother,
    I don't know of any good reason why I shouldn't write you a few lines
this evening as my health is quite good and am also in pretty good spirits.

Somewhat better, I must say, than I felt at this time last night. I was detailed for guard duty yesterday morning and that, as I have hinted to you before, is not a very pleasant duty at this season of the year.

It was something of a disappointment to me to be on guard yesterday, as it was you know the anniversary of Washington's birthday, and was observed with us as a holiday. We were not favored with very pleasant weather, as it was cloudy all day and a part of the time raining and mud ankle deep. But all that did not prevent the sports of the day as they had planned them. Our camp duties were all dispensed with except guard duty, target shoot in the morning, and evening parade.

The sports of the day commenced with a foot race around the camp. There were but six entered for this. The prizes were 2, 3, and 5 dollars. They ran singly, and some of them barefooted with nothing but shirt and trousers on, and the mud flew right smart. I had a good view of them at the commencement and end of the race. I was on guard at the time and they ran past my beat.

The next was the sack race. The style of this is to place each one engaged in the contest in a sack long enough to tie up around his neck so that he has no use of his limbs outside of the sack. Then, the one that by springing (as you see it would be impossible to run) arrives at the point first wins. This was the occasion of a great deal of merriment, as some of them soon found themselves in a very helpless condition having fallen and not able to rise without assistance.

Jumping and wrestling were other sports enjoyed in. But the drop race— next to catching the greased pig—was considered the greatest feat of the day. The plan of this is to drop potatoes along in a straight line at regular intervals, say about six feet apart. A box is placed at one end of the line from which the racer starts. He picks up the potato first nearest the box, puts it in, and then starts for the next one, returning with it to the box the same as the first, and so on to the end of the line. The distance accomplished was $1\frac{3}{4}$ miles and in the space of 14 minutes.

Next came the race for the greased pig and with that ended the sports of the day. Much more pleasure was anticipated from this than was realized, for the pig was not disposed to act well his part. The pig wouldn't run. Consequently, there couldn't be any race but he was finally caught up by one of the party who had volunteered for the race and carried to his quarters.

I witnessed most of the sports of the day. Although when I was not on my beat, I had to remain near the headquarters of the guard.

I felt rather tired this morning when I came off guard but was well and had a good appetite. Mr. Taggard had a plate of good baked beans for me. After I had eaten them, I got Frank H.[14] to cut my hair and trim my whiskers. Then washed up and put on my clean shirts and drawers and a new pair of sky blue trousers and then went to bed feeling as comfortable as you can possibly imagine and had a first rate nap.

Awoke about 3 o'clock just as the mail arrived and received letters from Almira and Hannah. Almira tells me she is very pleased with my picture. I haven't time to write much more now.

Our new Colonel is very strict, but I think we shall like him. We are hearing good news every day from our army at the south which is very encouraging.

Nothing said about our leaving here at present.
Yours affectionately,
Rufus

February 26, 1862
Washington, D.C.

Dear Brother,

There were twenty letters received in our mess today and this evening nearly that number of our boys are writing home. Those not writing are keeping remarkable still. We have some calm times but they come so seldom that they don't pass unnoticed. I suppose you have already guessed that I received your letter but to make you quite sure I will say that I have.

We have had fair weather today or what we call fair weather nowadays for the sun has shone a part of the [day] and we had no rain until this evening. It is raining quite hard.

Last Monday the wind blew furiously. A large number of trees in the grove adjoining our camp, where our cook stands, are now blown over. Some of them falling upon the cookhouses but without doing serious damage. The coverings were blown off from some of the barracks which were most exposed. One of the patients in the hospital thought he was on the water and asked if they were going home. The flapping of the canvas covering his barrack he supposed to be sails. There was a soldier killed in the New York 36th close by us. A pole fell and struck him on the head which caused instant death. It is reported that there were three wounded at the 9th Rhode Island camp. Buildings were unroofed at the city. One of the general's orderlies received a wound there by the falling of timbers but not fatal. His horse was injured at the same time and died a few hours after I believe.

I receive all the papers though they are longer on the road than the letters. Our papers say that Savannah is ours but Nashville is not confirmed.

[The letter continues.]

February 27

The rain is over and we are having a very fine morning. The news of the victories are very cheering. We think this war must soon close. Some think we shall march soon but nothing sure.

I had my tooth out last Tuesday morning. It ached badly Monday night and I parted with it with a good will. Dr. Adams is a good dentist. It took a strong pull, but it is all over with now and no soreness. I must close now or you will not get this Saturday evening. My health is very good.
Yours Affectionately,
Rufus

March 5, 1862
Washington, D.C.

Dear Father,

Another Wednesday evening has come. It finds me seated with pencil in hand to tell you that I have read your letter and am glad to hear from home again. I should have written you last Sunday but I came off guard that morning feeling somewhat exhausted and could not deny myself the pleasant nap which I am in the habit of taking after such occasions.

We had orders to march last Thursday to the city but we knew not where we were to go from there. We all felt it a sure thing that Friday morning would not find us here. When we formed company for evening parade, Major Harlow told us we should have to fight soon. But General Keyes countermanded the order before nine o'clock. So we remain here yet but are under marching orders.

Some think we shall march before Saturday night. I don't think we shall leave quite so soon as that but don't think we shall remain here another month. I think we are seeing easier times more than we shall after we march. But we are anxious to leave. We have been here so long it is getting an old story.

Pleasant weather is not very plenty with us yet. We had about nine inches of snow last Sunday and a powerful rain Monday night.

My health is good and I have an excellent appetite. We have some doubts about being paid off this time at the usual time. It should come the 15th of this month. Perhaps it will. Uncle Sam keeps us very much in the dark concerning all his dealings with us.

I believe we have got as good a colonel as ever commanded a regiment. He is a captain in the regular service, was in the Mexican War. It makes a great difference whether we have a real or a sham colonel. He is a very pleasant man, but we have to toe the line.

I am very anxious to see home again, but am not homesick or discouraged but am looking forward to the good time coming. I am not unmindful of the goodness which has preserved me thus far and pray for help to lead and keep us all in the path of duty.

I think I shall write you again Sunday. I am prepared to march at a moment's notice with clean clothes and good boots.

Yours Truly,

Rufus

March 12, 1862
Prospect Hill, Virginia

Dear Brother,

We now find ourselves acrost the Potomac River about fifteen miles from the city of Washington. We moved in a direction a little south of west. The three brigades—Couch's, Grayham's, and Peck's—moved together. We broke camp last Monday morning about eight o'clock and arrived here about sunset of the same day.

I don't know how long we shall remain here. We expected to move again the next morning but for what place we are not sure, although it was rumoured that we are going to Winchester.

I will not attempt to tell you of the rumours which I hear concerning the evacuation of places in this vicinity, for before this reaches you, you will have probably more accurate accounts than I can now give you from the papers. And concerning the movement of this portion of the army, you cannot be more ignorant than I am at present. We may stop here three or six months, or may move tomorrow.

I can tell you that I think that there will be but little more fighting. It appears to me the rebels are giving up their strongholds and are afraid to meet us. I have no time to write particulars now as the mail will leave soon.

I am well and hearty and ready for anything that comes along. Our disappointment was very great when we found that we were not to march again the next day.

Say to Brother Crehore that I have received both of his letters. Give him my best respects and tell him he must think as kindly as possible of my delay.

Direct your letter the same as ever, only omit Camp Brightwood.

Yours Affectionately,

Rufus

March 16, 1862
Camp Brightwood
Washington, D.C.

Dear Brother,

I think you will be somewhat surprised to learn that we are again at our old camp. We have not had any fighting to do but have had a hard time since we left here last Monday morning. I will proceed at once to tell you our adventures.

I retired a little later than usual last Monday night without any knowledge of our marching the next morning. About half past twelve, the orderly came in and told us to be in readiness to march the next morning at seven. There was no more sleep after that.

Our brigade moved together. The morning was somewhat rainy. We had a hard march to Chain Bridge as that was the muddiest part of the way. We halted three times before crossing the bridge to rest and after marching about a mile on the other side of the bridge, we halted quite an hour.

I understand that our Colonel told General Couch that he was marching us at an unreasonable rate. I think we were ordered to Winchester but the news of the evacuation of that place and Bull Run caused General Keyes to order a halt at Prospect Hill. This place is about fourteen miles from our camp and seven miles from Chain Bridge. We had guard mounting as soon as we arrived at Prospect Hill and as the guard are detailed alphabetically and had got to the R's, it was my fortune with the three Reeds—one of them the Captain's brother—to be detailed to stand that night and until 4 o'clock the next day afternoon. There were four detailed from each company in the brigade. There were seven reliefs. So I had to stand only two hours that night and two hours the next forenoon. I felt a good deal like crying when I found I had got to do guard duty that night for I was very tired. I was on the second relief and I stood from nine to eleven.

I then spread a rubber blanket on the ground and laid down with one of the Reeds, covering ourselves with our woolen blankets. It was fair weather then, though quite cool. I went to sleep as soon as I laid down, feeling quite warm and comfortable. I think it would be a strange sight to you to see soldiers sleeping on the ground, using their knapsacks for pillows and covered with their white woolen blankets, and snoring as loudly as if they were at home in their beds. After sleeping two hours, I awoke feeling a little cool. So I sat around the camp fire until morning. I did not sleep again until two o'clock the next afternoon. It was quite warm then and I had a comfortable nap of two hours when the new guard was marched on and I was relieved.

All the shelter we had all the time we were out of camp was huts made of pine boughs but these afforded but little protection from the cold wind.

Wednesday was a very warm day—warmer than you will see probably before the middle of May. Thursday and Friday and in fact ever since Wednesday the wind has been northeast.

I wish I could give you a description of our encampment at Prospect Hill. It is a large plantation owned by the heirs of Commodore Jones. One of them is at Fort Pickins another commands the *Merrimack* and one is in jail at Washington—a secessionist. You can have but a small idea of the vast territory which could be seen from the top of this hill. At night 500 camp fires and perhaps twice that number were visible. Within a mile of us, not less than 20 acres of young pines were cut for building bough houses.

We left Prospect Hill Friday morning and returned to within a mile of Chain Bridge. We halted by the roadside until nearly dark then went back into the woods to spend the night. I made my bed with Lieutenant Mayhew and slept comfortable until 4 o'clock. It rained some in the night and wet our blankets. I stood by the fire until daylight then went to the cookstand and got some sugar and coffee, which I boiled in my dipper. A slice of fat pork and hard bread was my breakfast. I thought of home and the breakfast you were eating but yours could not have been eaten with a better relish than was mine.

I tried to write you a few lines after breakfast but it was so misty then that I could not. The place where we were encamped looked some like the hills in Maine where we went swimming. The trees were mostly oak and pretty large. It commenced raining hard early in the forenoon and continued to pour all day. We contrived to shelter ourselves with our rubber blankets but it was too cold to remain under the cover of our blanket-house all the time So we were obliged to get out.

Ed Hutchinson[15] is waiting to take my letter to you, so I must finish. My health is good. I think we shall leave here this week. I am glad you sent me the stamps. I have got paper enough. I have got no money, but I can get things at the sutler's without. I am afraid you can't read what I have written. I received a letter from Ruth this morning. She is well.
From your brother,
Rufus

March 18, 1862
Tuesday
Washington D.C.

Dear Brother,

In my letter to you, which I sent by Ed Hutchinson, I tried to give you a description of our last week's work to Prospect Hill and our return. I didn't write all I wish to as I was short for time and what I did write I am afraid will be difficult to understand. I meant to have told you of our Saturday night's march from Chain Bridge. We left Prospect Hill Friday morning and returned to within a mile of Chain Bridge where the division was halted to wait for further orders, but not receiving any, the General ordered us on a little farther towards Chain Bridge to a piece of woods to rest for the night. I cannot give you a better idea of the place where we stopped than to compare it to the woods in Maine about Hiram's place. It was very hilly country on one side of the road and the trees were mostly fallen and lying upon the ground. It was nearly dark when we arrived at this place so we could make but little preparation for sleep. But sleep I did, and in the morning awoke very much refreshed. This was Saturday morning.

It began to rain hard at ten o'clock and continued to until twelve o'clock Saturday night. The road was flooded with water and the mud was ankle deep. We pinned our rubber blankets to frames which we made from branches of trees to protect us from the rain. But it was too cold to remain under shelter all the time so we were exposed to the rain whilst warming ourselves by the fires which we built the night previous. Thus we spent the day, the most disagreeable one I ever experienced.

It was getting along in the evening and we were expecting to spend another night there when the order came for us to get into line and be ready to march immediately. It was dark and the men were scattered far and near through the woods. Drums beat and the officers shouted. The men cheered for we were glad to leave the place though we knew not where we were going. Our company officers were as ignorant as we were. We thought most that we were going to the city, then by transport down the river to Norfolk. At nine we were on the march. From Chain Bridge we came back to camp by a different route, through Georgetown and Washington. The distance was ten miles. We took this route to avoid some bad hill we should have the other way. The mud, a part of the way, was almost up to my knees, but the rain had thinned it so it was not so bad.

At one o'clock our mess was all in our barracks. I was in at half past twelve. You can't imagine what looking creatures we all were. The sick ones, which we left behind, had hot coffee for us when we came in. They heard that we were coming. We soon had on dry clothes and went to bed. The two last days have been very busy ones, cleaning and drying our clothes, guns, and equipment. I have got two clean suits again, one on my back and another in my knapsack.

We expected when we came into camp to have marched again before this time. I think now we shall start tomorrow morning for Alexandria and probably from there to Norfolk. You will know if we move when you receive this. But perhaps I shall not be able to tell you for a certainty where we are to go.

It is surprising to me that myself and all of us could pass through so much fatigue and exposure and yet remain in such perfect health. One year ago, I feel sure we could not [have] endured it, but we have been gradually prepared for it.

When I marched through Baltimore last summer, my knapsack was such a burden to me that I couldn't see the sights. But I took it along on my last march with surprising ease, notwithstanding the additional heft caused by our clothing being wet. All my rigging, including overcoat which I wore, could not have weighed less than 45 pounds.

The next time you write send me a few postage stamps, not more than 12. I will write as often as I want them. They are as good as money, will answer the same purpose, and the most convenient way of sending it.

I must close now, but will write a few lines in the morning to let you know if we do go.
Yours Affectionately,
Rufus

March 18, 1862[16]

I have again a few leisure moments to write tonight and I feel sure now that we shall not march tomorrow. The order was countermanded about two hours ago. I suppose the reason why we do not go tomorrow is because the means are lacking for conveying us down the river. That seems to be the talk within a few hours.

I would write you a few lines in the morning, but I shall go on guard. My guard comes about once a week, and guard at the fort about once a month.

The weather has been quite pleasant today. And if we have a good day tomorrow, guard duty will not be very hard.

Send me an envelope when you write. I have got paper enough.
Rufus

March 23, 1862
Washington, D.C.

Dear Brother,

I don't know whether it is best to tell you the feelings which possess me today, and I might say, even longer—for ever since we returned from our march (I am going to tell you) I have felt very discontented and by spells almost discouraged. You know me of old as one of the discontented kind, subject to ups and downs, but perhaps by this time had hoped better things of me.

We are pinned here now to this place, in my opinion so long as the war lasts or during our term of enlistment. Last winter we were looking forward anxiously for the spring to open, feeling quite sure that we should then be removed from this place to a new country and perhaps more active duties. I have no doubts you have thought us very fortunate in being permitted to stay here so long and so in some respects we have. We have had an easy time, enough to eat and drink, and better quarters than many of the soldiers have had, but you don't know, and never can, until you try it what a tiresome life it is to be pent up seven months on one plot of ground with nothing in particular to interest you. It is the same old story day in and day out and no prospect of anything different.

When I last wrote you we had just returned from a hard march and whist I was telling you about it, I was elated with the prospect of moving again soon, but that is played out. And there is now no fear that Couch's Babies will ever be tired with another march, unless he should hear that the enemy were retreating from some place and then he might say, "Come on my brave boys."

Now I have told my story—done a little grumbling and feel better. I went to meeting this forenoon. Ten of us got a pass signed by the Colonel. The church where we went is about a mile and a half from our camp. We have all attended a meeting there once before. I wrote to Edwin about it. It is near the soldier's home. I think I wrote Edwin something about that place. The church was built in 1719 and rebuilt in 1770. The text today was Paul to the Romans 12C–12V, continuing instant in prayer. It was a very good sermon. The congregation was mostly soldiers, from privates to Brigadier Generals. They have an organ about the size of ours and four good singers.

We are not having much pleasant weather yet. My guard duty last Wednesday commenced quite pleasant but it was a very rainy night. The storm continued until Friday morning. It is not very muddy here now. The ground is quite solid. I find that old March is quite as successful in coming his shifts over us here, as at home. But not quite so successful at blowing cold, but sometimes rather rough.

The grass is growing in spite of him. The birds and frogs sing us merry songs night and morning. I suppose they are feeling more contented than I am.

But really, I am feeling better than when I commenced writing. I must close now.

Yours truly,

Rufus

April 7, 1862
Warwick Court House

Dear Brother,

I suppose you are feeling very anxious to hear from me. I have just finished my breakfast and word has come that we can send our letters if we have them ready in a half an hour.

We left camp near Newport News last Friday. We are now near the enemy and expect to have something to do soon.

My health is good and I feel that I can do my duty. We have had some hard marching. We rested all day yesterday and perhaps we shall not march today.

I received your letter Thursday last. I wrote you that day but couldn't send it. So I send this in place of it. I must close now. Do not feel too much anxiety for me. I am getting along first rate.
Yours Affectionately,
Rufus

April 18, 1862
Camp Near Yorktown

Dear Father,

I received your letter yesterday containing a few lines from Mother and Henry. I was glad to see it. How glad I cannot tell you. The mail leaves this morning at ½ past 10. It is almost that now but I have time to tell you that I am well.

Our regiment have not seen any fighting yet although there has been some smart skirmishing near us. I don't know how soon the attack will be made upon Yorktown but I think soon. We are now within 4 or 5 miles of what I imagine to be the scene of action.

My courage is good. I feel confident that we shall be successful. We have got one of the best colonels in the world to command our regiment. We were called up twice last night but made no advance.

It is reported that the *Merrimack* is sunk. I am afraid it is not true.

We are having very pleasant weather here now. The apple trees are almost in blossom. I am glad to hear that Grandpa is out again.

Next September is the time that I have set to see my home again. Whenever it may be, if I can see you all will my cup of joy be full. But God knows what is best. I must close now. Send me a few postage stamps when you write again.
Rufus

Mother,
Be of good cheer and hope for the best.
Rufus

April 25, 1862
Warwick

Dear Brother,

I will take advantage of this opportunity to write you a few lines this morning. Company K is on picket duty today. I escaped with several others by being on fatigue duty yesterday. When we came in last night, they were gone and will not be back until four this afternoon.

When I last wrote you, we were some 4 or 5 miles nearer Yorktown than now. That you may better understand things, I will give you an account of our marches since we left Brightwood.

Fortress Monroe was our first stop, although we didn't camp there. Camp Smith was our first camp. A days march brought us there from the fort, the distance being only about twelve miles. We were then within four miles of Newport News. We stopped there about a week and then came to this place (Warwick Court House).

I suppose we are now, by the most direct route, only twenty-six miles from Fortress Monroe. If you can find Warwick Court House on any of the newspaper maps you will be better able to judge of our location than I can tell you.

Well, what I want to tell you now is of our march from this place to another, some 5 miles nearer Yorktown. This took place last week, Tuesday or Wednesday. We camped within two miles of rebel entrenchments.

Last Friday, week ago today, I went out of camp far enough to see them but I took care to keep Uncle Sam's guns between me and them all the time. I went as near as we were allowed to our earthworks (500 yards) and the rebels were about the same distance beyond. Sharpshooters were engaged on both sides, our men doing great execution with their telescopic rifles. As sure as a rebel showed himself above the entrenchment, he was a dead man. This was to prevent their mounting guns and what they had already mounted, they can only use at night as our sharpshooters pick their men off too fast. Our big guns are covered, so that they were giving them a few shells once in a while when they didn't behave pretty.

I suppose you have seen an account of the skirmish which took place near there, in which one of the Vermont Regiments was so badly cut up. The rebels were rather noisy at night, whilst we were there. As near as I can learn, some of our men were at work nights too, near their windows digging rifle pits. This called out 2 or 3 regiments of them and they kept up a running fire to drive us back. When our men retreated, then our works would give the rebels a few shells and drive them back.

Just after retiring Sunday night, our regiment was called out to occupy a place in the edge of the woods, near the scene of action. They were firing briskly on our right and continued to at intervals through the night. And we expected to have work to do before morning but we heard more than we saw. We came in the next morning about ten o'clock.

We came back here last Wednesday to a better camping ground than we left. It is a very pleasant place in the edge of a forest, a large farm in front, a large peach orchard immediately in front of us, and an old apple orchard in blossom with a few pear trees on our left and good springs of water. I don't know how soon Yorktown will be ours, but I think McClellan will make sure work of it when he does begin and I think with little loss of life on our side, and I hope with but little on the other.

I received a letter from Hiram the other day, which I will enclose. My health is good and I have enough to eat. But somehow lately in my wonderings home, I find myself seated at the breakfast table with you eating warm potatoes and johnnycake.

There is a good time coming, but God knows when and where, better than I.
Rufus

April 27, 1862
Sunday morning
Warwick Court House

Dear Brother,

I received your letter last evening, with the postage stamps. I am well this morning. Have eaten a hearty breakfast of salt horse, as the boys call it (but what might be more properly called rather hard salt beef) and hard bread and a pot of coffee, which I made myself and a small piece of cheese which I bought off the sutler to top off with. Perhaps you recollect the size and form of the tin dippers which were given to us whilst we were at Taunton. They hold more than a pint, deep and smallest at the top. They were dippers at Taunton, but we call them pots now. I have got the one which I marked at Taunton, and it has ever been a faithful servant to me.

We have made our own coffee since we have left Brightwood. Coffee and sugar are dealt out to use twice a day, a large spoonful each night and morning. I mix mine in the little oil silk bag which Mother made to keep my Bible in and have a supply on hand all the time as the rations are more than I want to use, except when on the march. If we halt for half an hour when on the march, coffee making is a lively business. Fires are made and the pots go on at short notice but sometimes we are caught right in the middle of it. The order comes, <u>fall in</u>. Sling knapsacks. Take arms. Right face. Forward march. And away we go with the coffee half cooked turned upon the ground. You know, I was always a lover of coffee, but I prize it now more than ever.

We have been a little short of provisions until today on account of the bad passings. You have no idea of the conditions of the roads out here. I pity the poor mules. They fare worse than the soldiers.

We are building what is called corduroy roads through the swamps to Fortress Monroe. (<u>Log Roads</u>.)

Do you think I am ever discouraged? I am sometimes and I will tell you what plagued me and how foolish and short sighted it was. It was just one week ago this morning that we returned from our night watch in the edge of the woods which I told you of in my last letter. It rained when we started out and continued to until after we returned the next morning late. It was very dark when we marched and we had to march through mud and water nearly up to our knees. I had nothing but shoes. I had to throw my boots away on the march from Camp Smith to this place. They were so run over so at the heels that I could not go through the march with them. They lamed my ankles so that they could be of no further use to me. I had a pair of shoes strapt to my knapsack which I put on.

Well, to return to the morning of my tribulation. Arriving at camp, found my blouse very much out of repair. Shoes full of mud, wet, sleepy and tired and no clean clothes except a dry pair of socks. What could I do? Put my clean socks into those wet and muddy shoes? Pulled off and washed my feet. Whilst doing this, happened to think that it was possible that I might borrow a pair of old dry ones. Went to Uncle Taggard, the cook, (he didn't go with us) and got a pair. That was a great relief to me. Washed the mud out of my shoes and hung them up to dry. Pretty soon, the sun came out warm, and I soon forgot that I was wet. But I was thinking what shall I do for a pair of boots? Within half an hour, I had bought a pair of quite good ones for fifty cents and sold my shoes for the same price.

Next trouble, when shall I do my washing? No pond or brook fit to wash in. No tub or soap but I will try. Went to Uncle Taggard again and I borrowed a water pail. Found a small piece of soap, heat some water and in a few hours my clothes, two shirts, trousers and stockings were clean as ice and drying fast, and troubles were all gone. Had never felt so helpless and discouraged as I was then. And I feel that it has learned me a lesson to trust more fully in the kind Providence which cared for me then in my straight.

We commenced this morning to draw full rations of everything that the law allows. Had some very nice stewed beans for dinner. Are to have rice and molasses for supper and a ration of tea.

We have got a very pleasant camp. Good springs of water with running streams to bathe in. I can't tell you any news but I doubt not things are progressing as fast as possible.

I love to read your letters. I am home. Neighbors and friends about town—those interest me. I want to see my home. Yet money could not tempt me to leave the army now. I shall see joy when and where God wills it, so I trust. I have never felt better to do my duty.

I send home for postage stamps because it is rather difficult getting them here at times. The six dollars which I reserve has so far been sufficient for my wants. If I want more, I will tell you. I must close now. May God's blessing be with you all.

Yours Affectionately,

Rufus

April 27, 1862
Sunday
West Sumner, Maine

Dear Brother,

I will now take this opportunity to write to you. It is a long time since I have heard from you. I do not owe you any letter but I feel so anxious to hear from you that I thought I would not let that make any difference. Perhaps you have not received my last letter. It was written so long ago that I don't remember the date, but think it was some time in February.

I have received five letters from Hiram this past week, but they were written sometime ago. The last one was dated April 8th. They were all well. Albert has been promoted to second lieutenant. Hiram likes very well where he now is. I suppose it is a very pleasant place but there are some disagreeable things out there such as alligators and snakes. Hiram says that he dreads the snakes more than the rebels. He thinks there is no prospect of their having any fighting to do which I am very glad of.

I feel anxious to hear from you once more. Father wrote that you had left Washington and I am fearful that you are before Yorktown, perhaps before now that you have been in battle.

I can realize nothing of the horrors of war, nor do I wish to. It makes me shudder to think of it. It is sad to think of the many lives that will probably be lost in that terrible battle. I hope that your courage is good for I fear that I can write nothing that will cheer you up as the day of battle draws near.

My heart grow faint and sick to think perhaps I shall never see my dear brother again but we must put our trust in God. He is all powerful to save and notices even the fall of a sparrow. Oh, may He keep you and save you.

I know there is but few lost in battle compared with the many engaged in it and you are as likely to live as any one. I know it is no worse for me to lose friends than for others, but I am very selfish. We do not know what is in store for us and it is well that we do not. But we know that all things are ordered for the best and we should try to be reconciled to whatever may befall us.

Perhaps you will think I am writing rather a desponding letter, but I can't help writing such as I feel.

We are all well as usual and hope this will find you in good health and spirits. I have not heard from home lately. There is no news to write.

Write to me as soon as you can. Perhaps you are not permitted to write. Let me know what division and brigade you are in so that I can tell where you are. When I see anything in the papers, I always wonder if Rufus was there.

The children send their love to you. They talk a great deal of you but they are not old enough to realize where you are or for what purpose. I must close now for it is getting late. So I will bid you good night.

May the God of Battles keep and preserve you—is the sincere prayer of your affectionate sister.
Ruth P. Barrows

May 3, 1862
Warwick

Dear Brother,

I must write you a few lines this morning. I am feeling very comfortable just now. I am out of camp about a mile and half on picket. We are to stop here two days. I am seated in a shed made of boards, sufficiently large to accommodate the six of us, the number detailed for this place. Other squads are posted near us, so that we have a force near us of not less than 150 men.

Our post is within 75 paces of the Warwick River. We are in thick woods, though we occupy a little opening. One of our number is stationed close to the edge of the river to watch the rebel pickets on the opposite shore and a gunboat which lies down to our left about three-quarters of a mile. I think Mr. Gunboat will not give us any trouble for he knows very well that we have batteries on our side of the river, not very distant from us, that would take care of him at short notice.

I told you at the commencement that I was feeling very comfortable this morning. Let me enumerate the causes and then see if you have reason to doubt.

In the first place, my health is good, so I feel at liberty to enjoy all the pleasant things which nature has thrown around me and they are not few.

It seems to me sometimes that we have mistaken the month, that it must be June instead of May. The trees are almost in full leaf and the birds are singing in their branches as if it was their last chance.

The river adds much to the beauty of our place. It is a pretty sheet of water not quite half a mile right in front of us, running nearly straight at our left a long distance but on our right rather winding. It looks very pleasant on the opposite shore. I think there must be some nice farms there. Three houses in view, one of them large and good looking. But we have got some pretty farms on our side. The one in front of the grove, where we camp, cannot be easily beaten, though I have nothing to say in praise of the buildings. Three hundred acres are stretched out before us, as pretty lay of land as you ever saw. This is very flat country but the farm which I am speaking of now is a little rolling.

I should judge the number of young, though bearing, peach trees on the place to be about one thousand, a few old apple trees and three or four large pear trees, though much past their prime. Capt. Young, the owner of this place, on our approach took his Negroes and horses acrost the River Warwick and is now in command of a rebel company.

I must now draw my letter to a close. But two things occur to my mind which I have not told you which add greatly to my comfort.

I will mention first the good wash which I had the day before yesterday and the clean clothes which I had to put on after my bath. That was worth one thousand dollars.

I will speak next of the content of my haversack. I crammed it full this morning to take on picket with me. My little bag full of coffee and sugar, one pound cheese, one dozen cookies, and one dozen hard bread. And they will bring us some soup for dinner.

I can give you no news as to our progress on Yorktown, although I am expecting every day a movement onward to that place. You had probably heard some strange stories concerning our regiment being badly cut up, and especially Company K. You must be rather slow to believe, especially such stories as that. It all springs from our night in the woods. Some of our men gave wrong answers when questioned by men of other regiments, which answers, I suppose, reached the ears of reporters of the press.

Yours Affectionately,

Rufus

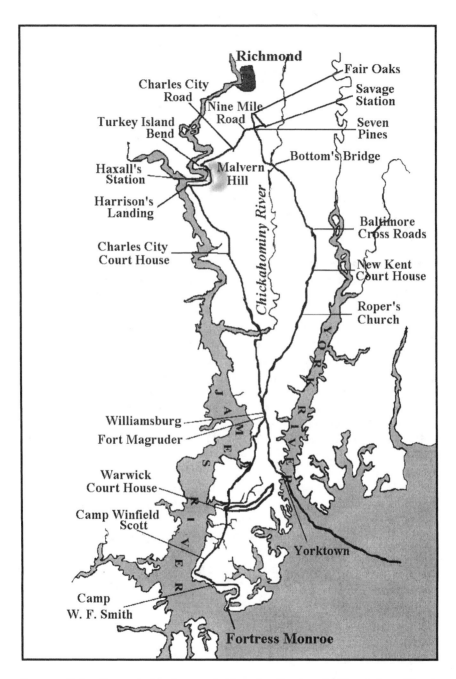

Route of the Seventh Regiment during the Peninsula Campaign, March 24, 1862–August 29, 1862.

May 8, 1862
Williamsburg, Va.

Dear Brother,

I improve the first opportunity to tell you something of the scenes which I have passed through since I wrote you last Saturday. I was then on picket as my letter will tell you, expecting to remain there two days. But the next day (Sunday) we learned that the rebels had left Yorktown. We received the news about noon and, soon after, an order to go back to camp and join our regiment. We did so as quickly as possible and arrived just in season to move with our regiment.

We made a march of about 8 miles which brought us to a large plantation, where we halted for the night. It was about 10 o'clock when we halted and we set about making such preparation as we could for a night's rest. I slept very comfortably, but when I awoke in the morning found it was raining very fast. You can imagine the consequences. Everything wet. Guns, equipment, knapsacks, and blankets—all as wet as water could make them.

I was not very wet when I turned out as I happened to lie on a slightly elevated spot. But some of the boys much to their grief found themselves when they awoke in a puddle of water. But it made but little difference, as we were all alike in that respect in a short time. The rain continued until 12 o'clock that night.

We commenced our march at 7 in the morning and another 8 miles over such a road as you can never have any conception of brought us to within one mile of Williamsburg and close to the battleground. I never had such a pull before. I believe we all had to use strength that had ever before lied dormant within us.

I think by this time you have become quite as anxious to know what part we took in the action. It was but slight and yet called very important. It was between 2 and 3 o'clock when we arrived near the scene of action. We were immediately formed in line of battle and as soon received an order to advance. We took our position in the woods to keep the rebels from charging upon our batteries.

I can't give you a description of the battle. There was great loss on both sides. I think you will see all the particulars in the papers before you get this.

We had a warm place in the woods. Shot and shell from rebel batteries was very plenty for a while. I must close now for we shall be on the move soon. We had 2 men wounded, one of which died.[17] Sometime during the night 2 shells struck near the center of Company K but all the damage they did was to throw dirt in our eyes. The 7th behaved well and have had due praise.

Yours Affectionately,
Rufus
P.S. I received Mother's letter and the paper. I am well and all the rest.

May 11, 1862
New Kent County, Va.

Dear Brother,

I closed my last letter to you rather abruptly and I haven't time now to write many particulars. But it will be a satisfaction to you to learn that I am well. I think I have seen some hard times and I should love to give you all the particulars, but the mail leaves in two hours and I must write a few lines to Ruth. I have neglected her sadly, and she is feeling very anxious about me. I received a letter from her last Thursday night which I shall enclose with this.

To assure you of the continued good health which I have enjoyed, I will say that my weight this morning was 145 pounds, a loss of only six pounds since last winter.

It is Sunday and a very fine day. A day of rest with us. I thought when I closed my letter to you last Thursday that we should march that afternoon, but we did not until the next morning. We marched about twenty miles Friday and eight yesterday. We are going to Richmond.

Perhaps you will think it strange that I am not able to give you correct information concerning the battle at Williamsburg. It was nearly three o'clock when we arrived at the ground, and as our position was in the woods, we were unable to see any of the fighting. But we saw shot and shell enough to satisfy us that they are dangerous things. Our Brigade General gives us great credit for our coolness. All the particulars that I can give you is that our loss was great, but the rebel loss much greater. I don't know the number engaged on either side, but I think when the battle began in the morning that our side did not number more than 16 Regiments, 16,000.

Co. K was one of the companies detailed to go to Williamsburg with a part of the prisoners which we took. We went up with 225 of them. I conversed with some of them. I think full one-half of them were not interested in the cause which they represented but some were as unyielding as tigers. I think the number of prisoners which we took will not number less than 500. They took not less that 100 from us, 80, I hear. Their next stand will be near Richmond but I think it will be a feeble one.

I want you should write to Ruth and let her know where I am. Send me the newspaper and write often. There is no regular times to send our mail now, so you must not feel worried if you don't hear from me so often.

Be of good cheer all of you. I think of home often, but not with regret that I left it, for there is need of me here.

We shall continue our march again tomorrow morning. The roads are good now. I feel much interest in my travels through the country. I feel that the fighting is about over and have great hopes of being with you again next September.

I don't know what to tell Mother to send me. My clothes are all good. A little writing paper, a towel, and a cheap jackknife is all I can think of now. I shall write again as soon as possible.
Yours Affectionately,
Rufus

May 15, 1862
New Kent Courthouse, Virginia

Dear Brother,

I don't know how you would have enjoyed my bed last night or my breakfast this morning but I can tell you that they were both very agreeable to me. I awoke once in the night and found it was raining quite hard. And the first thought that came to my mind was, oh how wet my blanket is getting. I put my hand out and found it was dry. Then I came to my sense and recollected that before retiring we had built a tent of our rubber blankets. A feeling of satisfaction came over me and I soon fell asleep again.

My breakfast was fried pork and hard bread, hard bread fried in the fat. My health and appetite continue good. I do not now crave food that I cannot have so much as I used to. Pork and hard bread are the staples now but we have beans and rice, when we stop in a place long enough for the cooks to prepare such food. Coffee enough always.

We have made another move since I last wrote you. You must now look on your map and find New Kent Courthouse. You will find us four miles in advance of that. Twelve miles from where I last wrote you and now thirty miles from Richmond. Our last march was a hard one, although we only made twelve miles.

How can it be, you will ask, such hard work to march especially when you only go twelve miles? Well, I will tell you. Mud ankle deep when it rains. But our last march hot, dry, and dusty.

We broke camp to come here Tuesday morning. Seven o'clock the order read. But it was nine before we moved. Marched about forty rods. Bugle sounds to halt. Stand 5 minutes with knapsack on, then throw it off and sit on it one half an hour. When the bugle sounds to move again, move twenty paces. Toot goes the bugle. Halt. Throw off knapsack and sit down. But at the same instant bugle says up again.

Well, to sum it all up, I have learned that halts in marches, like notes in music, may be long or short. It is difficult for me even to understand the causes of all these delays. But there are sixteen or twenty thousand of us on the road. Several long mule trains and batteries. Perhaps they have stopped to water, perhaps a bridge needs a little repairing. We only know it is a halt, perhaps for one minute and perhaps for two hours.

That night at sunset we had come seven miles and between that time and twelve o'clock that night we accomplished the remaining five.

I made a cup of coffee before I went to bed and then I laid down feeling very tired, but as comfortable after I got to bed as I ever felt in my life. I love to sleep when it is pleasant weather under that big roof where the moon and stars are fixed.

We were awakened by a company of cavalry in the morning which passed near our heads. I heard one of them say, "Sleep on boys. We won't harm you."

I can tell you no news except the report that we have surrounded and taken a large lot of prisoners near here and most everybody thinks the rebs will do more running than fighting.

I think you have done well to dispose of so many trees and vines.
Yours Affectionately,
Rufus

May 18, 1862
New Kent County, Virginia

Dear Brother,

We continue to advance towards Richmond. When I wrote you last Thursday, the distance was about thirty miles. It is now about eighteen. We have come the last two days a little in advance of our main army. There are three regiments of us infantry, one battery, one cavalry. Our Colonel Russell had command of the whole. We are feeling the way along and driving in the rebel pickets. We have met with no resistance yet, but supposed last night that we had advanced about as far as we could with safety with what force we had. I think we shall get to Richmond without any fighting and it also seems to me that there can be but little after we get there. I think they are afraid of us, and not without good cause. For unless they can crawl out at a pretty small hole, we will soon have them in a tight box.

We are resting today and I am improving it to the best of my ability. It is a very fine day, only pretty warm. I suppose you would like to have me write you a long letter and give you all the particulars of my journey here. I would but I feel too lazy. I will tell you lots of war stories when I get home.

I would show you some of my farms out here. The one that I am on now is a fine one. I call it mine because the proprietor is gone. We find many such places. The rich ones run, but the poor are not so much afraid of us. He has left us a fine peach orchard, peaches as large as the end of your finger. Also some fine looking apple trees full of fruit, about the size of the peaches. Apple trees look much better out here than I expected to find and are full of fruit. We see peas in blossom and potatoes six inches high. Corn about the first hoeing, not much planted. But large fields of wheat.

I am expecting to receive a letter from you today, but I shall have to mail this before I get it, as was the case last Sunday.

I got up early this morning and had a good wash and put on my clean shirt.

The next thing I did was to wet up some meal, which Luke gave me, to cook at the halves. I wet it up about as thick as I should for chickens, put in a little salt, then take out a spoonful and put it into a thin cake and fried it in pork fat. It was Indian meal and was very fine. They were very good.

I think we shall move on a piece again tomorrow. I must close now as the mail will leave soon. I have been looking for some flowers to send to Mother, but I can't find any that I can put in a letter.
Yours Truly,
Rufus

May 28, 1862
Henries County, Virginia

Dear Father,

Frank Erskin[18] brought me last Friday the package of things which I wrote for and a letter from you and Mother. I accept them as presents from each of you. Father sent me the paper, and Mother hemmed the towel for me. It is just what I want. Henry I give credit for the knife. It has two blades. I only expected one. But I should be loath to part with either of them now. The little one is just what I want to sharpen my pencil and clean my nails. I have lost my knife which I brought from home or rather Henry Beebe lost it. I lent it to him about the first of January and he laid it down carelessly and someone picked it up. It was hard for me to become reconciled to my loss but there was no help for it.

I have not written since the 28th [*sic*]. I told you then that I wrote you every week and sometimes twice. I think you receive most of my letters. But I sometimes think not quite all. I think I receive all yours and the papers. I have received two since they were mailed. The last one Sunday evening, the first one just before the Battle of Williamsburg with a letter from Mother.

We are now eight miles from Richmond. Have now got our toes about on the fighting line. We have been here since last Sunday expecting every day the fight would commence. We privates know but little of what is going on. It is reported that the rebel force is about three miles in front of us. I think there is no mistake about that unless they have retreated since yesterday. There was heavy firing on our right yesterday, which continued most of the day. And the story has just come into camp that General Porter[19] whipped two divisions, captured 1300 prisoners and a big gun. I am inclined to think the story is true as it came pretty direct from our colonel's mouth. If we fight them, I have no fears as to the result. We have got a large [force] to bring against them. (Gen. Keyes has just brought the news which I have written above to Gen. Couch. So it is true.)

We are having very fine weather, and my health is very good. I must close now as the mail will leave soon.
Yours Truly,
Rufus

[The letter continues.]

You shall hear from me again as soon as possible, but you must not feel concerned if not <u>very</u> soon as our mail leaves very irregularly.

I received a letter from Edwin the twentieth, my birthday.

I have a minute more to write. What shall it be? (A trifle.) I had some huckleberry sauce yesterday. I picked a few green ones and stewed them in my dipper, sweetened with the sugar which was intended for my coffee.
Rufus

June 8, 1862
Fair Oaks, Virginia

Dear Father,
I received the letter, which you was writing me last Sunday, last evening with the paper. Your letters and papers come to me as regularly as if I was no farther from you than the city of Boston.

I should be glad if I could give you a history of the past week, but this little sheet would contain but a small part and perhaps I shall not have time to fill even this, although it is Sunday morning and we are anticipating a day of rest.

I am well and strong and feel equal to the task which is before us. We are going to Richmond, when McClellan says the word, rebs or no rebs. I don't know how determined resistance they will make next time. But I think their troops have lost some confidence in their ability since the last battle.

When the attack was made Saturday noon week yesterday, things were not quite as they should be. Casey,[20] as I understand it, occupied the ground where the attack was made. He was asleep when one of his aides came to him and told him that the rebels had assembled a large force in front of him and appeared to be making preparation to come down upon him. His answer was, "Then we shall have to do the best we can," and continued on in his repose. He had but few pickets out and I hear that they had stacked their arms and were playing cards. All were expecting an attack but Casey was not on the alert, else we should not have lost any ground.

But as I wrote you in my last, the rebs occupied our camp that night. But I don't know how much of the damage which I sustained is chargeable to them. It matters but little since my knapsack, which I left snugly packed, was opened and part of my things carried off. I found my portfolio which you made for me with nothing in it. My knapsack was empty when I found it, but I found my testament, towel, and woolen blanket. My loss was two pairs of socks, two rubber blankets, two shirts, one [from] Taunton and one that Mother made for me, a piece of tobacco, and my paper.

I think we shall have a new supply of clothing soon. At any rate, as soon as we get to Richmond I am anticipating better things there, though I am getting along very well now.

Perhaps it will be something of a disappointment to you that I have not told you any war stories. I leave that for the papers and when I get home, if my life is spared. I have heard the bullets whistle very near to my ears but none of our company have suffered by them yet.

Yours Truly,

Rufus

June 14, 1862
Seven Pines, Va.

Dear Brother,

Perhaps you will not be able to find Seven Pines on your map and may perhaps think it somewhat remote from any place which we have before occupied. We are now about seven miles from Richmond. I wrote you from this place, just previous to the Battle of Fair Oaks, telling you that we were then on the eve of a battle. I recollect the expression which I used (that we had our toes then about on the fighting line) which may be of some help by way of recalling it to your mind.

I think it was the next morning, after writing that letter, that we moved to the right some three miles to Fair Oaks, where we had the battle. We were then about 5 miles from Richmond. Since then, we have had several encampments and have finally come back to occupy this place again.

I suppose you have by this time learned most of the particulars of the battle and are aware that that was not the final, that there is yet another pending before we get to Richmond.

I feel tired of this warfare but I am not discouraged. I feel great confidence in our General McClellan. I feel that he is doing all that can be done and I think today we can show the enemy a stronger front than ever before.

A year has passed away since I have been in the service. The days and months have seemed short, but the year to look back seems long. It is not quite a year since I took my last leave of you. I shall never forget the few hours which I spent with you then. The remembrance is worth more to me than gold.

My health is good. I think it was never better. When I think of the exposure which I have been subjected to and I know not how to account for the large share of good health which I have enjoyed during the past year, save that it be by the working of a kind Providence.

We are having pretty warm weather now, but it does not disagree with me. I love the summer as well as ever. The trees, birds, and flowers more than repay the little inconvenience which I suffer from the heat.

By the way, I must tell you of the roses which we have out here. This is a great country for roses. I have seen several varieties here which are new to me. One is the Yellow Rose. I did not know that there was such a flower in existence. I don't think I shall be able to find any of my rare kinds before mailing my letter, but I am going to try to find one of some kind to send to Mother.

I dreamed of being at home last night. It seemed to me that we were all dismissed until the first of February. I saw Mother, but I don't recollect seeing Father or Henry. I shook hands with Grandpa and told him he was looking much better than I expected. I should like to hear from him when you write again.

I told you a short time ago that I had lost a part of my clothing. But the only loss, which I much regret now, is one of the shirts which Mother made me, but I have replaced that with a government shirt which is pretty good. Our quartermaster has ordered a new supply so there will be no lack of clothing here in a few days.

We were paid off again last Monday. Please tell me as soon as you receive the amount which I allotted. You have not mentioned receiving my first allotment (This is the second.) though I presume you have.

Our sutler has come up with us again, so I have got a new pencil and a little paper. If you send me a few envelopes occasionally, as you have been in the habit of doing with stamps on, they will be very convenient. I can get paper enough. I don't think of much more to write so I will go and look for the rose and when I get back perhaps I can tell you that I have received a letter from home. I received another paper last Thursday.

Well, whilst searching for roses, I met with a soldier of the New York 55th Regiment, who gave me a nice magnolia that will be new to you. I shall only send you a few rose buds this time.

The mail has not arrived yet I am waiting very impatiently, again with pencil in hand to write you a few lines before it is quite too dark.

I had not long to wait before receiving your letter. It was all good, but the last part. I am sorry to hear that you are not well. I hope it will prove but a slight illness. Father wants to know our position in the battle and Mother is feeling anxious about me. I wish she could know tonight how comfortable and happy I feel. I shall write more in the morning.

[The letter continues.]

June 15, 1862
Virginia
Dear Mother,

Father tells me that you are feeling very anxious about me. I do not wonder at it, since you have heard of our loss. But things are not so bad with us, as one who can know only in part would naturally suppose. I do not mean ever to represent things in a more favorable light than they will bear and in this case I can tell you truly that my loss thus far has been of but very little inconvenience to me.

I wrote you last Sunday the extent of my loss and perhaps it will be well enough to repeat it again today, as you possibly may not receive that. I will tell you in the first place that we did not return to our camp again as a company. But a detail was sent from each company to find what they could. I was stopping with Frank H.[21] and Isaac Chamberlain[22] at that time (Built tent with them) and Frank was one of the detail. He knew most of my things. Things were scattered about the camp in every direction. He found my knapsack, woolen blanket, towel, and empty portfolio. Drawers, stockings, shirts, and tent blankets were all gone. Frank found both of his rubber blankets, but lost his woolen blanket but found another which no one claimed. I have got a rubber blanket in the same way. So with Frank's and Isaac's one, we built a good tent. Cover the ground with cedar boughs and then we spread a woolen blanket. I have got drawers, shirts, and stockings enough now.

We have good living now. Plenty of meat, salt, and fresh beef, pork, stewed beans, and rice, and molasses, and tea and coffee.

There have times when we had not lived so well but Uncle Sam means to use us well when he can.

I haven't so much time to write as I anticipated this morning. So I shall write you again soon and tell Father more about the battle. The roses and magnolia are so wilted that I will not send them this time. You shall hear from me again soon.

From your affectionate son,

Rufus

June 17, 1862
Seven Pines, Va.

Dear Father,

My pencil does not work very well and I think it will be quite as pleasing to you to see a letter from me written with a pen.

If I could spend half an hour with you this morning, as I should be very happy to, I think I could give you a pretty good description of the battle,[23] so far as I saw it, and our position. But without the aid of the lines which I should be able to draw and point out to you, if I was with you, I am afraid it will be rather a difficult task. My will is good enough. You are not more anxious to learn than I am to tell you. I will first make it as plain as possible with words and then perhaps draw a few lines to assist.

We were in line very quickly after the firing commenced. Moved a few rods to the left and halted on the road leading from Williamsburg to Virginia.[24] Here we were near a clump of plantation buildings (a planters house and several slave huts). We halted here some fifteen or twenty minutes. We stood front to the road. Ambulances were bringing past us the dead and wounded. Those not wounded so badly walked in, some assisted by their comrades, others alone using canes. This was a hard sight. I had thought I would never mention it but it is well enough perhaps that I do, for you know such things must be. In our rear was a panic stricken regiment just come in, or rather a part of a regiment for they were badly scattered. Their colonel was trying to rally them again for the fight, but with poor success.

Our next move was to the right of the Williamsburg Stage Road onto one crossing the railroad. We halted again, half way between the Williamsburg Road and the railroad. Here we halted a short time in front of an old building, which for the time, was being used for a hospital. At this place the bullets were coming towards us, but not very thick. They were fighting in the woods in front of us. I saw a regiment of our men pass in the woods in front of us on a charge (I couldn't see the rebs). General Couch led them on but they were repulsed (our men) with great loss.

Soon after, General Couch came up in front of our line. He was sitting on his horse in front of me when a ball struck the ground at his horse's feet. He gave it a look of contempt. Another came, striking a tree directly behind Lieutenant Mayhew and a few inches above his head. He was standing in the rear of us, and it passed as near the head of my right hand man as it did to Mayhew's. He had another narrow escape just previous to that. He fell and was in the act of getting up when a piece of shell passed over him.

Our next move was acrost the railroad. Veering a little to the right some after crossing the railroad from the road which we came up on and formed a line in the woods. Here we soon expected to encounter the enemy. (When I say "we," I don't mean to include our officers, for we never know what they think until they speak.) But we soon made another move.

And now, I have got to take you around a bend which I am afraid is going to be rather troublesome but if I can send you the map,[25] which a lucky hit has thrown in my way, I think I can make it all plain.

I have just received the *Trumpet* June 7th. I am too busy to look at it.

I am now going to take a slip of paper and designate the places and letter them on the map.

The route from D to E was hasty. After forming our line at E, we noticed a change in our officers. General Couch and staff, Colonel Russell, and others looked troubled. The men whispered, "There is trouble. We are cut off. We have got to go to Richmond. Prisoners!" This doubtless would have proved true, had it not been for the timely arrival of General Sumner[26] with his troops. We are at E. Capt. Walker[27] (one of Couch's aides) rides hurriedly up and tells him that a large rebel force is right upon us. "Impossible," says Couch. "They must be our men." I should have told you, before that this took place (some 20 minutes before), an aide sent from Sumner to Couch told him if he could hold his position one-half an hour longer, he would be with him.

Now is the critical moment. The rebels are upon us. Sumner and his troops are in sight. We move back towards D to the bend. It is but a few rods. A regiment of our men are running out of the woods there, closely followed by a large rebel force. I will make a mark where we stood.

Now, Sumner's men are resting a little in our rear. They have had a forced march. Rickett's Battery, belonging to Sumner's command, commenced and coming a little in advance is on the bend with us. (It is the smartest battery in the country.) We have got our position in their rear to support them.

The rebs fire upon our men which are retreating out of the woods. We received a part of their volley. Some of the balls come too high and some too low. But one did harm. That struck one of the Company I in the leg. He had to have it amputated. The right wing of our regiment returned the fire, mistaking the order given to the battery to fire.

Now the battery opens upon them. The rebs are retreating, followed by a such a storm of shot as they never dreamed of. Hundreds must have fallen on that ground. We were called away from there soon after the battery opened but the engagement lasted there until dark. They seemed to be determined to have that battery.

From E to F where we spent the night, I will dot the route. I did not pass a very pleasant [night] there. It was rather cool and we had no blankets. Not a bit do I care now. I am just as comfortable at this present time as I had had forty.

The battle commenced again about sunrise and lasted near us about two hours but we made but little change in our position that day and were not engaged at any time. Our troops occupied the railroad as far as I could see, using it for a breastwork. Most of the fighting was farther on the railroad towards Richmond than I could see. I don't know why we were not engaged. I know we shared the dangers without seeming to help so much as we might. G is a camp which we occupied June 8th. H we occupy now.

Yours Affectionately,

Rufus

[The letter continues on a separate sheet.]

Camp Seven Pines

A first halt where the wounded came in. B second halt where Couch led the charge. Couch in front of our line. A bullet strikes at his horse's feet. Lieutenant Mayhew's escape.————C third halt acrost the railroad. Verge to the right. Form a line in the woods, expect to fight D.

Dear Father,

I had not the room on the other sheet for the closing words so I will improve the rest of this for that purpose.

I have done my best to give you a true idea of all that I saw. I think it will be interesting to you all and the time which it has occupied has been very pleasantly spent.

Dear Mother,

A few words to you. This has been a very fine day and I have enjoyed it much. Yesterday and today have seemed more like autumn (Indian summer) clear and cool. How I love to think of those days at home. I haven't had any work to do today and but little for a number of days.

I have had plenty of good food today. Vegetable soup for dinner. Rice and sugar for supper. I have got your clean clothes on and a clean shirt in my knapsack. A good tent and agreeable companions.

Yours Affectionately,

Rufus

June 20, 1862
Seven Pines, Virginia

Dear Mother,

I don't think of anything special to write this morning, but when I have time it is never more pleasantly occupied than when writing to you. I received your letter containing this sheet of paper, day before yesterday. I have got paper enough now, but want you to send the envelopes with stamps, just as you have. The size is quite right and the quality is much better than I can get here.

You may be at loss to know why I sometimes do not return the same envelopes which you send me. The reason is some of the boys have been out of stamps and envelopes when I have had a spare one. The one I sent you last with a hole in the corner was repaid to me and I have had several gifts from one and another in that line. I don't think of anything that I am in need of more that you can send me, but if there should be, I will let you know.

Since being paid off this time, I have bought some little trifles that it would not pay to send home for. I have lost my needle book which you made me. I was very sorry to part with it, but I had just given my trousers a good mending. So one needle and a little thread will do my sewing for a long while. I don't wear clothes out very fast here. My shirts (the one which you made for me) and which I saved is as good as new. Nothing has provoked me more than the loss of the one which I left in my knapsack, for I think it was likely to be the work of our men of some other regiments as the rebels, although I have got a good one in its stead.

I have just received Henry's letter. The mail arrived a few minutes ago whilst I was eating my dinner. We had stewed beans and they were good.

I have not lost my little jackknife and I wouldn't for one hundred dollars. It is a good knife. I have lost my toothbrush but I don't think it is worthwhile to send one. I can buy one here and it will cost but little more than at home. I have got a pencil which I have just bought but I think I shall not use it any more. I have taken to liking a pen much better and I think you will not object.

If I was really in want of anything that I could not get easily here, I would tell you so and I know you would be glad to send it. I like best to have you send the stamps on the envelopes. I have got two envelopes directed to you now without stamps. Send me two stamps for those and a stamp on all the envelopes you send. The one you sent today comes very acceptable.

I wrote you last Sunday, the fifteenth, and again the seventeenth to Father, and to Ruth yesterday. I have not received a letter from her since the one I sent you.

I have no doubt we are on the eve of a battle, but how soon it will come no one can tell. I shall try when it comes to do my duty, trusting in God for the result.

I have got two rosebuds that I am going to send to Mother. There is nothing peculiar about them but I know she will like to see them. I shall try to send you a magnolia. I know it will not look very pretty when it reaches you.

We are having very fine weather and I am well.
Yours Affectionately,
Rufus

June 21, 1862
Seven Pines, Va.

Dear Brother,

Another pleasant morning has dawned upon us and I have a few leisure moments to write to you. Perhaps more than a few moments, for if we are not detailed for fatigue or picket duty, I shall have most of the day to myself. I have taken quite a notion to writing of late, since I find I can write with a pen.

It is drill time now. I will give you our morning exercises when I come in.

Well, the drill is over and I will now tell you what has taken place this morning up to this time (½ past 8).

The first thing then is our early rise. A new rule which has been in force about a week requires us to be up at ½ past 3 and stand in line of battle until sunrise. This is to prevent an unexpected attack. Yesterday morning and this a part of the time was occupied with battalion drill. The next thing is to wash up and get breakfast. I have lived like a hero since we were paid off. Uncle Sam's fare begun to improve about that time and I buy a little to go with it. My breakfast this morning was a good cup of tea (which I steeped myself), some little English herrings such as you have seen at home, a piece of cheese, and my hard bread.

I have omitted one thing which comes immediately after drill before washing and breakfast which is police duty and means in this case to take some twigs and brush up and carry off the waste which has collected around our tents and hang the blankets out to air.

After breakfast, I light my pipe and take a walk about camp to see what is going on. I have a pear tree—not a very good looking one—but filled with fruit, a few apple, peach, and cherry trees and a few rose bushes to look after. They are all well filled with fruit and the cherries are almost ripe. The cherry trees stand in the front yard of a house which is just in the rear of our camp. They are the old fashion red cherry. I have seen a number of trees filled with cherries like Mother's flesh colored. The trees were much larger but the fruit not more than ¾ the size which those bear. That kind was ripe 3 weeks ago.

Well, as you see, I had written you but a few lines after my morning walk before I had to fall in for the 2nd drill. This commences at ½ past 7 and continues an hour. We have no music of any kind along the lines now, save an old triangle which was picked up on the place here and probably used by the slaves when they had a dance. It is used now instead of a drum to call us together for drill.

Within the last two weeks, there has been a change ordered in our diet. The doctors say it is not good for us to drink so much coffee. We are having tea more instead. I like the change. I had used but very little coffee for several weeks. I had got rather tired of it. So when we had no tea, I drank cola water. We have had a little apple sauce and some potatoes lately. We have dried vegetables which we use for making soups. It is turnip, carrot, and cabbage dried and pressed into cakes. Fresh beef and a little rice is used with it and it makes a good soup.

It is now nearly 4 o'clock. I have had nothing to do since morning but eat, sleep, and write. You can see how much I have done of the letter and that will be enough for you to know, although I will say we had some of the vegetable soup for dinner and after that I had a nap which lasted until about this time. I think I am rather too lazy for home use, but it does very well here. I sleep like a pig nights, but the early rise and the warm weather inclines me to have a nap in the day time.

I have nothing new in regard to the war to write about of the pending battle. There was some cannonading on our right this morning (nothing uncommon). Since then, it has been as still as Sunday.

We are detailed occasionally to work on a fort near us which we have nearly completed and have done a little corduroying.

Sunday morning
June 22nd

I left my letter last night to go and get some boughs to cover the ground in my tent. When we have a good thickness of spruce or cedar boughs under us and a blanket spread over them, we have a good soft bed. We have had inspection this morning and, as it is Sunday, I suppose we shall have no other duty until evening parade.

The weather is as fine as yesterday and I think it is as still here now as it is in High Street. I think you are now about starting for meeting. Oh, how I should like to go with you. I think oftener of the little church and the people that assemble there than I write. Three faces I shouldn't see that were ever so familiar. They have gone to their long home. It is hard to realize. I am glad to hear that you have so good a Sabbath School. I hope it will continue to prosper. I feel if I should ever take part in it again, I should work with greater zeal and strive to be more faithful.

I am glad to hear that the trees are looking so well. What a treat it would be to take a walk with you after meeting to look at them. I hope the white grafts will ripen. You know I always felt a peculiar interest in them. Does that old tree on the west wall (the apple) bear this year? You must not get discouraged about the strawberries. I think that mischievous worm can be easily destroyed. It may be the tan you are putting around them will do it. If not, I think sale, lime, or ashes will do it. And if these should fail, I would try Guano water but I don't think they will trouble you another year.

It is dinner time now, so I will close.

It is beans again today, but they don't come too often.

My health is good.

Yours Affectionately,
Rufus

June 22, 1862
Sunday Afternoon
West Sumner

My dear Brother,

Having a little leisure, I thought I could not do better than to devote a good part of it in writing to you. We are all well and hope this will find you the same. It is a long time since I have heard from you and I feel anxious to hear from you often for you are so near the enemy that I have fears for your safety, although I know that the same Power protects you there as at home and in Him we must put our trust and be resigned to His will, whatever it may be.

I had not forgotten that I was owing you a letter and have thought every Sabbath I would write but the day would pass without my getting time. But I find there is nothing like improving the present moment when you have anything to do.

I saw in my paper last Sunday an account of the battle in which your division was engaged. I did not know until then that you were there and you can judge of my feelings on reading it. I have looked anxiously in every mail for a letter from you or some of our folks, and had anything happened to you, I think that some of the folks would have written. But I long to read a letter once more in your own handwriting. Then I shall feel sure you are safe.

Oh, I shall be so glad when this wicked war is ended and our friends can return to their homes once more. It will be a joyful day. But to some it will make their sorrow the more keen to witness the joy of others.

Were there any in your company killed or wounded and what were your feelings? I suppose that you were all excited and had no fear.

How thankful I am that we live so far from the battlegrounds. I pity those women and children that are driven from their homes and those that are obliged to stay and witness the movements of an army if they are true to the Union. If not, I have no sympathy for them, for they have brought the curse upon themselves.

I heard from Hiram this last week. He was well and thought when they had taken Richmond and hung Jeff Davis the war would end. He said there was talk that the regiment that he belonged to were going to Charlestown, South Carolina. I hope they will not, for they have got good, comfortable quarters now. They live in houses and it is a very beautiful place where they are and I feel quite safe about him. He says that they sometimes see small parties of rebels on the main land which fire at their pickets but they do not fear them any.

In one of his letters he sent me a leaf of a magnolia flower. He says they were the most splendid flower that he ever saw. I think I should like to live out that way.

I am almost sick of living down east.[28] It is too cold and rough winters.

Sometimes I want to go up to Massachusetts so much to see the folks, that I can hardly deny myself the privilege. But I know that I should feel very unpleasant for you and Hiram would not be there. But I hope that it will not be long before you will both be at home. I anticipate a great deal of happiness then. We do not know how to prize friends until we are separated from them and the thought comes that we may never see them again.

I have not heard from the folks since you wrote to me and I do not know how long before that. I suppose that they are as well as usual or I should have heard.

Perhaps you want to know what I am doing and how I get along this summer. I do not do much of anything. I hardly see what I have done at the end of a week. I have two cows to milk and take care of this summer and four children. That is all I do. I am weaning the baby and he is some cross. I suppose that you can hardly realize that I have got a boy that you have never seen that is almost a year old. But so it is. But I hope that in less than another year you will come and see us all.

The children go to school. They are not very forward scholars, but perhaps they will learn faster when they are older. Alice commenced studying arithmetic last winter. She does not write yet, but I think I shall get a writing book this summer. Henry can spell pretty well and reads carefully. He is slow and sure. They send their love to you and want to see you. Little Nelly is a little firebrand. She is old and gritty. She is not so pretty as she was when a baby but her eyes are blacker, if anything. She looks more like Dotty Beal. The baby looks like Henry.

Meranda and her children are all well. I have not seen her for some time, but when I see [her] she always speaks of you and sends her best respects. I believe that I told you that Albert had got to be a second lieutenant. He makes good pay now and I am glad for him. Father's folks are all well as usual. Horace is courting pretty strong. I should not be surprised if he was married this summer or fall.

We have had a great deal of dry weather, so that hay will be rather scarce. But there is a prospect of there being good crops of everything else.

I will now close for you will think I am getting tedious. You must take good care of yourself and keep up good courage for the war will not last always. Write as soon as you have leisure after receiving this, for I am anxious to hear from you.

Give my best respects to Luke Noyes and receive the love of your affectionate sister.
Ruth P. Barrows
P.S. Write what brigade you are in. I have forgotten. I sent your last letter to Hiram. I remembered it was Couch's division, but the brigade I had forgotten.

June 24, 1862
Seven Pines, Va.

Dear Brother,

Frank is writing a few lines home today and has given me an invitation to enclose a few lines with his. I have not an opportunity to write a very long letter, but a few lines will be better than nothing to let you know that I am well.

We are on picket today (Company K) about ½ a mile from our camp. There are pickets ahead of us. We are held here as a reserve for those ahead if need be to fall back upon. We are stationed at a saw mill, quite a pleasant place and duties not at all hard.

We have got a prisoner to guard at a house near by. He is not a soldier but a citizen come back to this place to avoid danger.

We came out here this morning at 11 o'clock and shall probably be relieved tomorrow morning about that time. We had a heavy shower last night commencing about 11 o'clock and some pretty heavy thunder. I suppose all together it was what might be called a tempest. Our tent which I said Chamberlain, Frank, and I occupy kept us as dry as a bone.

It is now nearly 4 o'clock. We have had no rain yet today, but it has looked much like it all the time and I think it will soon. I have picked a few ripe huckleberries today. I know of nothing more to write you for war news. Things are going on about the same with us as usual. I will try to write you again soon.

Yours Affectionately,

Rufus

July 4, 1862
Virginia

Dear Brother,

I hear that we are to have an opportunity to send our letters today and I hasten to improve the opportunity not knowing how much time I may have.

You have no doubt read news through the papers of much fighting[29] here since I last wrote you. The 7th were in the fight a week ago last Wednesday. My last letter to you was dated June 24. We were on picket that day. The fight commenced the next morning about nine o'clock, a little before we were relieved.

The fight began near our old encampment where we lost our knapsacks. We were marched up there as a reserve. About noon we were called to the front. We held a position there until the next morning. I shall never forget the position either, for our regiment laid some four hours flat on our bellies in an open field in front of a piece of wood which was occupied by the rebs. There was no conflict between us and the rebs until after dark, save their sharpshooters tried to pick some of us off. But we lay a little too low for them. There was plenty of shell and some canister passed over our heads and some of it pretty near.

After dark, our colonel gave us orders to withdraw as quietly as possible, all his orders being passed along the line in a whisper. But a regiment can't move without noise. We drew their fire before we had got 20 feet. Two or three good volleys. We laid down to it again, and when they had got through we up and returned it and retreated to the position a little farther on which we wanted to occupy for the night.

We had but two men wounded through the whole time, only one of them very slightly. But Augustus Fullerton,[30] I fear, is fatally wounded.

After gaining our position, we commenced immediately to throw up a breastwork. When we had got it about half done, they came up and gave us another volley. We were better prepared for them this time and gave them so well a directed fire that they soon left.

Since that time there has been a great change in our lines. We are now down on the James River. I think you will get quite as correct an idea of the change which has recently been made in our lines from the papers as I can give you.

I received a letter from you and Father last Sunday and one from you today since I began this letter. I was glad to hear from you.

Billy Howland, I think, is in Washington and in good health. The last I heard from John B.,[31] he had not left the hospital but was well.

I must close now, for it is time to make my cup of tea for supper. My health is good. I shall try to write you a few lines tomorrow if the mail does not leave tonight.

Yours Affectionately,
Rufus

July 11, 1862
Friday
Harrison Landing, Virginia

Dear Brother,

I received yours and Father's letter bearing date July 6th this morning but a few minutes ago. I was very glad to see it and I thank God that my life and health are spared to write to you again. I have not written to you since the fourth, not because we have had a great deal to do much of the time but we made another move Sunday morning which however was but a short distance. But fixing our camp in the woods requires some labor to clear away the dead wood and leaves and pitch our tents substantially as we hope for a few weeks.

Tuesday and Wednesday of this week, I think were the warmest days I ever knew and I did not feel energy enough to attempt to write.

We have got a pretty good company place now, but our Colonel, as I have understood, not feeling quite satisfied with it, went out yesterday to find a better one. But returned better satisfied with this than any he could find. The atmosphere, he says, is not so tainted with the smell of dead soldiers, horses, and mules here as in other locations which, if he had to make a change, he would have had to have taken.

So fierce was the contest for eight days commencing with Wednesday, June 25th, that both armies were obliged to leave many of their dead unburied. As I wrote you in my last, we had a part in the fight[32] on the 25th. Since then the 7th have had no part in any of the battles except our position in the line and the support of our battery, which was not called into action. I think our battles were well fought, although our loss is great. But that of the enemy is much greater. Our retreat was skillfully accomplished. We had a long line to support. You will see by the map which I sent you that we had a front of not less than 15 miles. And whilst our ranks were growing thinner from day to day, they were continually receiving reinforcements until I suppose they outnumbered us nearly three to one. They pushed us hard on our retreat. Either hoping to create a panic or being too full of whiskey to know what was for their best good, they rushed on in great numbers, seemingly regardless of consequences. And our men having choice of position caused them great destruction.

They keep their men full of whiskey all the time while we, when we go into battle, are clear headed and know what we are about. We never draw rations of whiskey except when it is very strong weather or on fatigue duty and then not more than ½ the time. I have never drawn my ration or tasted a drop.

It is very quiet here and we are resting fast. Most all are in good spirits. We believe in God and believe that He has raised up men equal to the work which is to be done.

The greatest inconvenience which we suffer here is for the want of good water. But we are digging wells and hope to have plenty of it soon. We have to go a mile now to get good spring water and on the way, there is a good stream to wash in.

We have seen hard times since the 15th of June, but we have much to thank God, for our lives have been spared. Fortune has favored the 7th Regiment. Although being called a good regiment, we have been placed in responsible positions and where great danger was expected.

I am glad you have concluded not to go to Lynn. I think Father and Mother would feel lonesome with us all gone. And who would help Father get the hay? I am afraid our farm would miss you more than you think.

I got my *Trumpet* last Saturday night and am expecting another soon. I received a paper and letter from Edwin at the same time. I am going to send you a letter which I received from Ruth a short time ago. I wrote her about a week previous to receiving it.

Give my love to Grandpa Samuel and all his folks. I am glad to hear that Grandpa is better. Tell James I think of him every day. If you come across any paper that you think will be interesting, please send it. I don't mean to send it every week, but occasionally. I would not send the *Agriculturist*, for I think you had better keep them.

I must close now, but I think I will write to you again soon.

From your brother,

Rufus

July 18,[33] 1862

Harrison Landing, Virginia

Dear Brother,

I have just finished reading yours and Father's letter which I received by this morning's mail a little after seven o'clock.

I have not written to you so often of late as I used to for the reason that the weather has been very warm and I have not felt quite well all the time. I haven't been sick, but my appetite left me for a few days and I felt but little energy to do anything.

Luke wrote home yesterday, but I concluded to wait until this morning that I might tell you that I had received your letter. Luke is well this morning. My health is good now as ever and yesterday noon I found my appetite had fully returned. We had fried steak for dinner and in addition to that I had a few cookies and a piece of cheese and that was not all. I had a little sauce which I made of green pears and grapes which I found the day before when I was on picket. It was very good. I think Mother would have said so, if she could have seen it. The pears were rather small, but I peeled and cut them, put the grapes in with them, and boiled in a small quantity of water and plenty of sugar.

My money is almost gone but I think we shall be paid off again before many days. I have been thinking for the last few days of sending to you for a box. I have not fully determined to do so yet. Some of our company have sent and I am waiting to see what success they have in getting them through. I think there is a prospect of our staying here another month and if so, there will be time enough to do it. I mentioned it to Luke and he is anxious to send with me as soon as we can feel satisfied that we can do so with safety. I will give you a list of prices of some things here sold by sutlers. Cheese fifty cents per pound, butter seventy-five cents, raisins fifty cents, cookies from two to three cents apiece, figs two cents apiece, oranges and lemons from twelve to twenty cents apiece, and everything else in proportion. I think if I could invest my six dollars at home, it would cover all expenses of transportation and save me nearly fifty percent. I shall make up my mind as quickly as possible and, if I conclude to send, give you all the information I can to direct.

I will tell you now of some things that I should like to have. Oranges, lemons, figs, raisins, dried apples, molasses sugar if it could be sent in a tight can, and some of Mother's ginger snaps. I cannot think of anything else that Mother could cook that would keep until it reached me. This is only a part, but I will make all my wants known if I have concluded to send.

I have received the paper containing the two postage stamps and the one letter with the needles and thread. I shall look for another paper tomorrow morning.

I do not think of any news to write. So I will say a few words about the house we live in. Frank and Isaac Chamberlain continue to be my companions in the house. We have got the best one, I think, in our company, though others have copied our style. In the first place, we raise a platform about two feet from the ground, about seven feet square and four forked sticks for the frame to rest upon. And for the floor, we use red cedar which splits very straight and even. Then a crotched stake at each end for the ridge pole to rest upon and it is ready to cover with our tent blankets. The floor we cover with cedar boughs to make it lay soft and cover them with a rubber blanket. We find it very good to be up from the ground, especially when it rains. We have had several pretty severe tempests since we have been here. I think some of them rather beat anything I ever saw at home.

We have plenty of water now in camp but it is not first rate. There was a while that it was difficult to get enough clean water even to wash my face in without going to the spring and taking it home in a canteen. I am very particular about my person. I have done a great deal of washing since I have been in the army. I have time enough now to wash my clothes and body as often as I like.

I have just put on a new pair of trousers which I drew today. This makes the third pair since I left home. My bill for clothing last year was $28.58. I was entitled to $45.98.

I don't think of anything more to write of things here. I am glad to hear that things are looking so well at home. I think it will be a good plan to break up that piece this fall. I suppose it will pay better than to let it remain in such poor condition.

I will say to Father that I am glad he mentioned the chickens. There is nothing at home that I do not feel interested to know about. I expected to see a few words from Mother this time and I was not disappointed.

I think I will write you again soon.

Yours Truly,

Rufus

July 21, 1862
Harrison Landing, Virginia

Dear Brother,

I am now ready to tell you my wants and they are so many I am afraid I shall have room to write but little else. I will say in the first place that I am feeling first rate this morning.

The weather has been a little cooler since I last wrote you and this morning is one of the finest. I begin to feel that I am having too easy a time in this more pleasant grove, though it was not quite so pleasant when we first came in to it. But many hands make light work and now it is very much improved. It seems to be the opinion of the folks here that we shall not have much of anything to do again before the last of August. Though some of our wise ones here have come to the conclusion that doubtful things are very uncertain. But nevertheless Luke and I have held a council this morning and conclude that it will do to venture the box.

I will now give you a memoranda of the articles which I want and the one which Luke is writing to his folks this morning is like this in the main.

1 doz. Lemons	2 qts. Indian meal
1 doz. Oranges	A few rolls Lozenges (cheek of sass)
1 Drum Figs 5 lbs.	Pickles
3 lbs. Dates	1 Pr. Suspenders
1 lb. Raisins	Tooth Brush & Soap
3 lbs. Dried Apples	Paper & Envelopes
Box of Mustard & Black Pepper	1 lb. Navy Tobacco
Molasses Sugar a few lbs.	Fine Comb (not very fine)
Salt Fish	1 Cotton Handkerchief

Now there may be some things which I have named in my list which it may be very inconvenient for you to get. If so, <u>leave them out</u> as I don't expect you to be governed altogether by my list. I had much rather you would use your own judgment, both in regard to the things which you will send and the quantity. I think oranges and lemons will be hard to get and molasses sugar also. If so, send a few pounds of white instead. The fish I would trim so as to send the best. If you have room for a few potatoes, I will have one good dinner. Send a little bag of meal and what a gracious Johnny I will have! I want a tin plate to bake it in. Tell Mr. Ripley you want a French tin plate that will hold about a quart and I think you will get one that will stand fire. And I want a small tin pail (double tin) that will hold a small quart. We will call it a long tin pail. The plate or pan will not be soldered but pressed into a form. The rim about 1½ inches deep, perhaps two inches, but not very large round.

I am afraid I shall perplex you a great deal. Perhaps you will not know how to send pickles if you have them. Then don't bother with them. I want Mother to send me a few ginger snaps. I think the box will be from four to six days coming to me. So I don't think it will be safe to send any cooked victuals.

I don't think of anything more that I want. I have got a good supply of clothing. Three shirts, two white ones, two pairs of drawers, two pairs of stockings. If I had more, it would be too much left to carry in my knapsack. The needles and thread which you sent me will last me six months. A quire[34] of paper will be sufficient and a half a dozen envelopes. I like the way you send them in your letters best (a few pens). I don't want any medicine of any kind. I don't know how soon I may need some, but I have taken so little since I left home and feel so well now that I don't think it will be worthwhile to send any.

Direct to: Westover Landing, Va.
               Adams Express
               Couch's Division
               7 Mass. Vols., Co. K

Westover is on the James River. Adams Express have opened an office there within a few weeks. I want you to send me a bill of every article. Tell Whitmarsh, or whoever you send to Adams Express, to take a receipt from Adams Express and you send it to me immediately. I think my bill will amount to $5.84 say nothing of the express.

John Bouldra arrived here yesterday morning.

[The letter ends here.]

                    July 26, 1862
                    Harrison Landing, Virginia

Dear Brother,

I received your letter yesterday morning and one from Edwin. I am sorry you have the toothache for more than one reason. It is hard to bear, if not dangerous. I think you had better have it out.

I like long letters. My ink is nearly out and pens rather poor. So I conclude to write this time with my pencil. This is a little sheet that Mother sent me a month ago or more, when I was at Seven Pines.

I have just returned from a pond about ¾ of a mile from our camp where I had a good wash. It is the first time that I have been there. O. M. Cole[35] and I went together. I was happily disappointed in finding so large and nice a pond. It is the first I have seen that deserves the name since I left home. It was an excellent place to try my swimming powers again. But I met with no better success.

I received the two *Trumpets* last Wednesday morning. They were very interesting. I like Thayer's reasoning on the question of God. What it demands. It is the best I have ever seen on that subject.

I don't think of anything new to write. We are living for the present a very quiet and an easy life. We have left war out of our camp. We don't know how soon we may have to go out and face the enemy again. I borrow no trouble on that account. Strength has been given me thus far to do my duty, I believe. I trust the same help will continue with me to the end.

I have just eaten my dinner. We had stewed beans. We have had baked beans twice since we have been here and they were very good. I have a good appetite though not quite so craving as it was a while ago when the weather was cooler and we had more work to do. We are having very fine weather now, though I find it pretty warm when I go out into the open field. It is very pleasant in our camp. Sunshine and shade about equal. I should have written to you yesterday, but I was detailed for fatigue duty. It was very light work but we were employed most of the day, cleaning up leaves and brush about the Colonel's quarters before going to work in the morning.

I had my hair cut and my whiskers trimmed very close all over my face. Many in our company did not know me at first sight. Noah Harding[36] was my barber. He is very particular about his work. I recollect Mother said, when she saw him at Taunton, "What a pretty young man." He is that! I was not acquainted with him then, but I know him now as one of the pleasantest fellows in the company.

I thought when I began that I wouldn't think of enough to fill this sheet but it is full now and I have a few more words to write.

I am afraid the box which I sent home for is agoing to make you a great deal of trouble. I sent for a large quantity of figs, (5 pounds) thinking that plenty of them could be bought for 15 or 20 cents per pound. But I hear now that they are very scarce in town and are worth 20 to 30 cents. What I am writing now will do no good with respect to sending the box for I suppose it will be started before you get this. But I want to tell you as soon as possible that I shall not be disappointed when I open the box, if there is not one-half in it which I wrote for.

I think it will take longer than the time I set to come through. I set it ten days now at least. They come to Fortress Monroe very quick but are a long while on the James River. Some of our boys will have boxes today, if ten days is enough to bring them through. The teamers have not got back from the Landing yet. So I think I shall not be able to tell you the result as I shall have to mail my letter soon.

Luke is well. I can't [see] much, but his bare feet from my tent, but I think he is taking his share of comfort.

I must close now. My health is very good.
Yours truly,
Rufus

August 3, 1862
Harrison Landing, Virginia

Dear Brother,

I received yours of the twenty-seventh and Samuel's last Friday morning. I have delayed writing you a little longer than I should, but I got out of paper and envelopes.

Soon after receiving our mail Friday morning, our company left camp for 24 hours on picket duty. On our return yesterday about noon, we were glad to learn that the paymaster was here ready to pay us off. I have now bought a few sheets of paper and envelopes enough, I think, to last until the box comes. I was glad to see the postage stamps.

Luke received a letter from his folks this morning telling him that our box started Thursday morning. I hope we can soon tell you that it is in our possession, although but one box has been received in our camp yet and to that a very small one and many of them have been on the road three weeks. But I think arrangements have been made within the past week to forward them quicker. I have some hopes of seeing ours by next Saturday night if we remain here.

It seems to be the impression of some of the boys that we shall not remain here much longer. I think we shall not, though I am hardly prepared to give you my reasons for thinking so. No one dares to venture an opinion as to where we shall go.

Perhaps it is necessary to reinforce Pope,[37] or will be soon. If that is the case and troops are to be drawn from here for that purpose before we receive aid from the new enlistments, shall we be strong enough to hold our present position, especially if, as it has been reported, some of England's subjects have provided the Secesh with iron clad gunboats which are already floating in the James River?

I am yet hopeful that our cause will in the end be prosperous. I am far from being discouraged, but I must confess that things are a looking a little dark to me just now. The South are alive in their work, up and doing, and what they do they mean. But the question will come to mind, "What have the North been doing all the time?" I think they have been too slow. I think we have had men enough in the field to have crushed the Rebellion by this time. We have waited too long and moved too slow. The South have taken great advantages of the time we have given them, and I fear they will give us great trouble in return. It is always darkest just before day. So is the old saying. So I will wait a little and think what I may do instead of what might have been done.

Perhaps Father will give me his idea of things when he writes again. I will say in answer to Father's question that it has seemed strange to me that our Colonel has not taken notice of the prices our sutler has charged us for things. But I believe one reason is he is not a high liver himself, consequently thinks that hard bread and salt horse is good enough for us. I think Colonel Davis would have been a better man in that respect.

We have had plenty of potatoes and onions within the last ten days and cabbage once. I can perceive that the change of diet has had a good effect on me. I am glad you sent Dr. Hall's advice. I think much of it. I should like to have that bushel of currants, but I think when the box comes I shall have as much as I can take care of. If we move, the box will find us and I think most of the stuff you send will keep quite a while.

I think your invention, Henry, is a great thing. I think much of it. It would be a good idea to mention it in some of the *Agriculturist Papers*. It is no less useful because it is simple. I love to hear about the trees. I can see every one as you speak of them.

I take great pleasure in talking with Isaac Chamberlain about trees and fruit. He worked at Bryant's Nursery 5 years. He seen us there buying trees. He knows all the different kinds of fruit. I have spent hours talking with him on that subject after we had gone to bed. The red astrachan[38] and sweet bough are not greater favorites with you and I than with him. I have not told him of your invention yet, but shall the first opportunity.

Johnny Bouldra is in our company. He showed me a horse yesterday that he thinks looks almost exactly like ours. All the difference he could see was in the color, which was not quite dark enough, not quite fat enough, and tail not quite long enough. So I think I have got a pretty good idea of him. Not very beautiful, but in harness looks well enough.

Mother has not told me anything about her tomato plants lately nor of any of the flowers. I do not see many now here in the woods.

Tell Samuel I feel greatly obliged to him for his letter. I shall answer soon.

My health is good. It is now meeting time, so I will close.
Yours Truly,
Rufus

August 4, 1862
Harrison Landing, Virginia

Dear Mother,

This morning's mail brought me your letter. I find enclosed the envelope bill of the box and articles. I have just finished my breakfast and, as there is nothing to prevent my writing, I thought it best to improve the earliest opportunity.

Perhaps you will like to know what we had for breakfast, so I will tell you what I eat. Hard bread and apple sauce. We had three kinds of meat, salt and fresh beef and boiled pork. I eat a very small piece of the latter which was lean. I have nothing to say in praise of the sauce. The apples (dried) were sweet to begin with. Boiled in an old iron kettle without being picked over. Badly cooked with bad water. Someone is to blame for all this, or at least a part of it.

Some of the companies have sunk wells 25 feet and have got good water. I think there are as many good working men in our camp as in any other. I have hinted, but my chief object in doing so is to let you know that such is state of things is not of necessity.

I go to a good spring twice a day. It is a long walk, but it is usually about all the exercise I have and I think it does me good. What I have written in relation to the cooking of the apple [sauce] is an exception. Though they use bad water all the time, we do not perceive it in our potato and onion soup or in beans baked or stewed. It is the exception when these dishes are not well cooked.

I will be very careful about eating when the box comes. If I am not a good cook, I am a neat and careful one. I shall cook my apples, both dried and green, in good spring water in such quantities as I shall want for the day. Perhaps you will think in my present circumstances, where luxuries are few, that a good thing would be quickly swallowed. This is not so much the case with me now as when I was at home. A little there is much here and, very naturally, I have fallen into the habit of "mincing" as the boys call it when they notice how long I am at my meals. I find nothing at the sutlers that I am so fond of as molasses cookies. I can get fifteen now for twenty-five cents. I can easily exchange the pickles for something else or sell them if I don't like them. Our sutler sells large quantities of what I call copper pickles.

My white shirts are woolen. If it is so and if I can, I shall send home for some shirts and undershirts in season for winter. I have no fears but the jell will be good.

I have forgotten the language I used when speaking of Luke. I only meant to say that he was lying in his tent with his shoes and stockings off and appeared to be taking great comfort. I could only see his feet from where I was seated when writing. I think he never enjoyed better health than at present and I can say the same of myself.

I must draw my letter to a close now, for I must write to Edwin today. I have owed him a letter a long while. I shall write you often now that I have plenty of paper and envelopes.

Your Affectionate Son,
Rufus

August 10, 1862
Harrison Landing, Virginia

Dear Brother,

I have but little time to write this morning. Our knapsacks are packed for another move. We don't know where we are going. The teams take our knapsacks along for us and we are ordered to take three days rations in our haversacks. We have spent five days out of camp since I last wrote you, but this time we break camp for good.

I hear this morning that Edwin has enlisted. The news did not affect me as I thought it would. I thought such news would make me tremble from head to foot. I have been selfish and feared that I should hear such news of you or Edwin, though I have always thought you would mention it to me if you thought of doing so. You may be drafted, but I hope not. I want you to stay at home with Father and Mother. You can be a patriot there as well as here and as such, I believe, you are and ever will be. I would that Edwin's term of enlistment could be added to mine, that I might serve out both and he remain at home. But he is in God's keeping and there I am not afraid to leave him. He will care for him now and always.

A few boxes arrived here yesterday for our company, but mine has not come. I have no idea when or where I shall see it, though I expect to at some time.

I received a letter from you and Father last Saturday morning whilst out of camp on duty and the *Traveler* this morning. I think the papers and letters which you sent all reach me.

It is very warm weather here now, but most of our marching has been done nights.

In your next letter, I want you to send me a little cayenne pepper. I have tried it and think it does me good but I cannot easily get it here.

My health continues good. I cannot write more now but I will write you again soon.

Yours truly,
Rufus

August 13, 1862
Harrison Landing, Virginia

Dear Brother,

While Luke has been writing to his folks, I have been writing a few lines to Ruth. It is almost eight weeks since I have written to her before today. I have not heard from her since about that time. She had not received my letter when she wrote.

We have been ready to march since I last wrote both of you (day before yesterday) but are not off yet. Don't know where we are going any better now, but expect to know that we are somewhere soon.

I am well, as usual, with the exception of a slight headache. I have a pretty good appetite. Luke and I took dinner together today. We had boiled onions and potatoes. E. M. Bain[39] gave me some dried apples which came in his box. So we topped off our dinner with hard bread and apple sauce. Luke thought it was the best sauce he had seen and I know it was much better than that furnished us by the cooks. Our box has not come yet. I don't expect to see it here.

I am very anxious to hear from home. I don't know for a certainty that Edwin has enlisted, though Mr. John Noyes says in a letter to H. Beebe that he came into Holland's store whilst he was writing for that purpose. I suppose it is too late now, but when he enlisted, if he has done so, he could have had his choice as to what regiment he would join. If he must be a soldier, I should like to have had him with me. I think I could be of great help to him.

I don't think of anything more to write at present but I shall write you often.

Yes, one thing more. I want one of those little Sabbath School Question Books, if you can get it for me without too much trouble. I have forgotten the title of it, but you will know what one I mean when I tell you it was the one I used in my class before I left home. I think it was Scriptural Lessons. Not easy lessons or the Life of Christ.

I think I shall have time to get a good long lesson. If you send it, roll it up in a newspaper.

Yours Affectionately,
Rufus

August 24, 1862
Camp near Yorktown, Virginia

Dear Brother,

My last letter to you was a few lines enclosed with Luke's, which I mailed a short time previous to leaving Harrison Landing. I thought then I should be able to write you again soon, but we have had a long and tedious march.

I left camp Friday morning the fifteenth with a detail of four others from our company to act as guards to the wagon train belonging to our division. Our division did not move until the next day after. Though, we got but little the start of them, we made but four miles the first day. You can have but a small idea of the magnitude of the train which we moved with a part of the time. We were a part of the time moving on the road with 1500 wagons each drawn by from two to six horses or mules. Most of them six mules. The roads were very dry and dusty most of the way. At times, the dust was so thick that I could not see a man marching twenty feet in advance of me.

I was sick when I left camp but I did not know then what was the matter with me. I knew I had got to march but which way or how far was a mystery. But I hoped for the best and my hopes have been fully realized, for I find myself today feeling quite well although my eyes and complexion are yet a little yellow. I have had the jaundice, though not so badly as a great many in our company. It has been a very common complaint with us the last two months. But I did not mistrust that that was my ail until they told me I was looking yellow. My symptoms were slight pain and soreness in lower part of the stomach and bowels and the loss of appetite. I bought a small can of concentrated milk before I left camp and I took this with me and with a little flour which I bought on the way I was able to make a good pot of porridge as often as I felt faint, though I was sure to feel sickness at the stomach any time I ate anything or drank a swallow of water.

I borrowed some cayenne pepper off one of the boys before starting on the march which I used this freely and I think it with very good effect though. It was really like a medicine to me. I have since learned that our doctor uses it quite freely with his medicines with people sick with that complaint.

I must tell you about the milk for I think a great deal of it. It is put up in half pint cans, costs seventy-five cents. It is about as thick as cream, sweetened a very little. I think there is as much virtue in a large spoonful of it as there is in half pint of new milk and it seems to me quite good. I have used it in tea and coffee and should not know it from new milk.

I will now give you our route from Harrison Landing to Hampton or a mile below there. We spent two days and were then ordered back to this place. I am speaking of the wagon train. The troops of our division did not advance beyond this place, but for some reason we were ordered down there. As I have told you, we made but little advance the first day. It was nearly four o'clock in the afternoon before we got started and we halted for the night a little before sunset. It was rather a cool night. I laid down early and slept about 3 hours. I think I was up before 12 o'clock. It was too cold to sleep more that night with what covering I had (a rubber blanket and a thin linen tent blanket).

(My woolen blanket, and everything else I had, was sent off with my knapsack several days before we left camp.) I have just got it again not 10 minutes ago. All safe and sound.

About 3 o'clock, I made a pot of tea and put in a good part of the milk. After drinking it, I felt pretty well and in ½ an hour we were on the move again but made but very little progress until after noon. There were other trains and batteries on the road which had to pass us before we could proceed. Our train was not in motion more than 1½ hours before noon.

There was thousands of acres of corn on the road, large enough to boil, and thousands of ears were boiled and roasted by our men that forenoon. I was hungry about 7 o'clock and ventured to roast an ear and eat it with a good relish. That was not enough. I roasted 3 more and eat them all before noon. I don't think it hurt me at all but I have not eaten so much corn since, nor did I feel really hungry for anything but sour apples until last Friday when I got back here.

Well, I am mixing things up. So I am afraid it will plague you to understand but bear in mind that it is Saturday, the 2nd day of our march. At 12, our train is in motion again. At 3, we are on the Charles City road. At 5, passing Charles City Courthouse. (This is not a city. I don't know how it happens to have the name. It is but a very small village.) Five miles more brings us to a halt for the night. I made a pot of tea and got to bed about 9 o'clock feeling pretty tired and sick but I slept soundly and comfortable until 5 the next morning.

It is now Sunday morning. The teams start off in such a hurry that we don't have time to make tea but 5 or 6 miles brings us to the Chickahominy where we have time enough to breakfast.

It took 2 hours to get our train over the pontoon bridge and we halted another hour after crossing to feed the mules. I improved the opportunity to bathe in the river.

When the train started again, I told Captain Foster[40] (Captain of the guard) that I was sick and got permission to ride a part of the time. This was a great help to me.

At 5 o'clock we halted within ½ a mile of Williamsburg for the night. I sent up to the city and bought a loaf of soft bread for 10 cents. I had chocolate enough in my haversack for one mess. So even with rather a poor appetite, I made a pretty good supper. Went to bed early and had a good night's rest. I only took a cup of tea in the morning and then, with the rest of the detail from our camp, took an early start in advance of the teams into the city. It was full 3 hours before our teams came up and although I did not feel any too well, I enjoyed my visit there very much. It was a fine morning. We found some apples there that were as good as porter[41] ever dared to be, though not quite so large. We shook them from the tree and paid a cent apiece for them. We were only going to pick up some under the tree, when we heard a voice from the back yard warning us away. We found that they were owned by two secesh ladies whose husbands, I suppose, were off to the war. They were willing to sell them. So we shook off as many as we wanted. They were slightly sour and so brittle and soft that they would break in falling to the ground.

It is getting late so I must cut my story short. We passed over the old battleground at Williamsburg at 5 o'clock. That night we passed through Yorktown and late in the evening halted at Big Bethel.

Tuesday about noon brought us to the end of our journey. We stopped there until Thursday noon when we had orders back to this place.

My health was not any better whilst I stopped there. If anything I was worse but I kept up good courage expecting every day to feel better and so one day I happened to. I was careful not to eat anything that I did not like. There was plenty of good things to sell there. I spent most of my money for apples and apple pie. They were both very good. Five of us bought a watermelon, and I ate my share of that. It was a good large one and once I had some oysters raw with plenty of pepper and vinegar. I believe I did not eat a morsel of anything whilst I was there that was not good medicine for my disorder and I took a bath every morning before breakfast.

I have not time now to tell you what I was about yesterday. Only I fished me a good oyster dinner out of the creek. I have not received a letter from anyone since from you a week ago last Friday. But I shall expect one tomorrow.

I long to hear from Edwin. I hear that he belongs to the 33rd Regiment and is at Washington.

I have not got the box yet, but I think if we are to stop here any length of time we shall get it soon.

Mother must not worry because I have been sick. I feel as well today as usual and have a good appetite. The march was rather hard for me, but I think I got well quicker than if I had stayed in camp. The change of air, scenery, diet, and the salt baths, I believe, were all in my favor.

I think I shall write you again very soon.

Yours Truly,

Rufus

August 24, 1862
West Sumner, Maine

Dear Brother,

I received your letter last Thursday and was very glad to hear from you and more. You say that you wish it was not so much of a task for you to write. I know just how it is, for it is hard work for me to set myself to writing. But after I commence, I don't know when to leave off. I have been almost all day writing to Hiram. It will be two weeks Tuesday since I have heard from him. We usually get a letter once a fortnight, but sometimes it is longer. I think he has been highly favored in not having to be in battle. I do not feel so much anxiety on his account as I should if he was at any other place, but I fear that their turn will come yet.

I had a letter from Mother about two weeks ago. They were all well. I should be very glad to have Mother and Father come and see me, but I suppose it is hard times up there. But when the war is ended, I hope to see all my friends.

I feel thankful that your life has been spared and hope and trust that you will live to tell us of the great battles you have been in and of the great victories gained. I hope the North will never leave the field until the Rebellion is entirely crushed but I think that as long as there is slavery there will be a rebellion. I fear that your General McClellan is a slavery man. I think if he had not been, this war would have progressed faster than it has and we should have seen some signs of peace. Do you feel much confidence in him?

I suppose that you want to know how we are and what we are doing. I can't say that we do much. But we are all well and have been ever since Hiram went away. We have aplenty of apples and have had a lot of strawberries and raspberries. Blackberries are going to [be] very plenty. They have just begun to ripen. I have had apple and milk three times this fall.

Whenever I eat them, it reminds me of the good times that we had that fall you were down here. But I hope another fall will see you all here again. I hope that Henry will not be drafted for Father and Mother will be so lonesome if all the children are gone from home.

I do not hear any news of late. I expect that they will be drafting in this town the first of September. Horace would get clear if he was drafted because he lost his toe. We told him last winter that perhaps there would be good come from losing his toe. As it is, he could not leave very well for it is almost impossible to get help on the farm.

As it is getting late, I will draw my letter to a close. You must keep up good courage and look ahead for the good time coming. Be careful of your health. The children send their love to you. You would hardly know them. They have grown so.

Hiram's address is: Company F
                        9th Maine Regiment
                        Port Royal, South Carolina

Receive the love of your affectionate sister,
Ruth P. Barrows
P.S. Write us as often as you can, for I want to hear from you, although
I sometimes feel afraid that you will think that I do not care about you.
I am so negligent about writing but hope you will excuse me.
Ruth

August 27, 1862
Camp near Yorktown, Virginia

Dear Mother,

I feel almost sure there is a letter for me somewhere from you but I
have not received a letter from anyone since I last wrote home. Last eve,
and twice this morning, small parcels of letters have come to our camp.
It is said that our mail is badly mixed up and it will come as fast as it can
be sorted. So I have hopes of receiving letters soon.

I know you will want to learn first of all that I am well. For several
days, my appetite has been very good and I feel as well this morning as
ever and more than that I have the prospect of a leisure day before me.
I think I shall improve a part of the afternoon to go oystering. It is about
a half a mile to the creek where we go. They are not very plenty, but a
half an hour is time enough to get enough for a good supper.

I was at work yesterday on detail with half of our camp near Yorktown
digging down breastworks thrown up by our men last May. Today the
other half of the camp goes and we are at leisure. There was a thousand
or more men at work there yesterday. There is three or four miles of it
to be dug down, so that the enemy may not take the advantage of it,
which we calculated on when they occupied Yorktown. It is not hard
work. We are divided into three reliefs each working a half an hour. So
that gave us one hour's rest to every half hour work.

I had time enough to read, although I had nothing with me but my *Testament*. But that was enough. I love to read the Psalms. I will mention to you
a few that I read with particular interest. The 9th, 15th, 25th, 27th, 28th.

When I returned from work last night, I found Isaac C.,[42] my mess mate,
had been oystering. And the result was enough for a good supper for us
both and as he is at work today, I mean, if possible, to have as good a
supper for him tonight. We stewed them and they seemed to me as good
as any I ever tasted, although we had no butter or milk to put with them
but plenty of black pepper and hard bread for crackers.

I had in mind the other day when I was writing to Henry to tell him of our oystering the day before. We got forty or fifty that day and we eat them raw with pepper and vinegar. We have to wade in about knee deep and feel them off the bottom with our hands. We have a piece of board floating around with us which we place them upon that as fast as we find them.

We have drawn each a loaf of soft bread today. It is baked in ovens which we find here near our camp. They needed little repairing. I think we shall have it right along now as long we stay here. It is not probable that we shall stay here long but we have no idea where we shall go.

I like this place for many reasons. We have excellent water. I have been and got my oysters since I began this page and got them shucked out enough for supper.

The box has not come yet. We shall move once more, I think, before we see it.

I will close now, hoping that this will find my Mother well and happy. From your affectionate son,

Rufus

September 5, 1862
Camp near Chain Bridge, Va.

Dear Brother,

This fine morning finds me in possession of five letters, four papers, one handkerchief and package of pepper, all of which I received by last night's mail. And one thing more which came not by the mail, though it might have had something to do with it: Good health and spirits. This comes of the kind Providence which has ever been so near me.

I received a letter from you last Friday week ago this morning, just as [we] were about leaving Yorktown dated August 24th. Father's of August 19th and yours August 31st came last night. Edwin's August 20 from Lynnfield. I also received one from Ruth and one from Hiram and I am happy to say that neither of my letters reported to me any illness but all seemed in good spirits.

We left our camp near Yorktown on the morning of August 29th and arrived at Yorktown about noon. At five o'clock we went aboard a ferry boat which took us to the steamer *Knickerbocker*. On this boat, we expected to make our trip and felt pleased with our accommodations. But in this we were disappointed. At ten o'clock that night we found ourselves alongside a barque to which we were transferred. Here our accommodations were very poor. Huddled together like sheep, we were towed down the York River, acrost the Chesapeake Bay, up the Potomac to

Alexandria, landing on Monday morning about ten o'clock almost as weary as if we had marched the whole of the way.

That afternoon, we marched three miles from Alexandria towards Fairfax where we halted and threw off our knapsacks expecting to rest for the night. But we had not rested ten minutes, when we were ordered to Fairfax Courthouse. We left our knapsacks, taking only our rubber blankets with us. At twelve o'clock that night we arrived to within three miles of the Courthouse, where we halted for the rest of the night and built fires of rails to warm and dry ourselves for it was very cool and we had marched most of the way through a drenching rain.

Early in the morning we were ordered back to where we left our knapsacks, but not to rest, for at night our Colonel has got to report us near to Chain Bridge. The distance from Alexandria to Fairfax, where we stopped Monday night, and back to this place is not less than four miles. Some have called it the hardest march we have ever had and I don't know but it is considering the disadvantages with which we undertook it. I have never before heard so much complaint of blistered feet and lame legs. Sure, mine never were so lame before, but my feet did not suffer very badly. But we have had a good rest since we came here. Fine weather and a good creek to bathe in and plenty to eat. I never felt better in my life than at this moment.

It will be useless for me to attempt to give you any news concerning the late battles. I am not posted. I have scarcely seen a paper since we left Harrison Landing and camp news is worse than nothing.

I have no idea how long we are to remain here or what will turn up next. I shall write you again soon if I can. Your letter was very interesting. How I long to see my home again at this season. It would be more than joy. I saw Mother last night in my dreams. That is all I can remember.
Yours Truly,
Rufus

September 25, 1862
Camp near Downsville, Md.

Dear Brother,

It is a long while since I have written to you. My last was whilst at Chain Bridge. No doubt you are feeling very anxious about me. I could not write to you before. We have been on the march most of the time since and when I could have written you a few lines my knapsack containing my paper has been a long way in the rear.

We have been marched very hard but have had no fighting though we have narrowly escaped it. The rebels have taken a pretty severe drubbing here in Md. as I think the papers will tell you. I shall not attempt to give you any particulars of our march or the battles this time but if we stop here a few days as I hope to perhaps I will. We have marched through a very pretty country. Yes, more than that, <u>beautiful.</u>

There has been plenty of fruit on the road. I have eaten peaches and apples to my heart's content. And have had plenty of potatoes most of the time. We have had no cooking done for us since we left Chain Bridge. Our rations whilst on the march have been raw pork and hard bread but we have managed to take along with us potatoes and apples enough to go with it.

So I will tell you what I have had for breakfast and supper most of the time whilst on the march, though I had to rise early and work quick for we commenced our marches generally by ½ past 5 in the morning. So the fires were kindled at 4. 3 good sized potatoes put on to boil, though cooking the apples comes first though it took but little longer to make sauce of them than it did to boil the potatoes as they were sour and very mellow. I peeled and sliced them very thin then put the potatoes and coffee on. When they were nearly ½ done, I began to fry my meat. Most of our pork is as good as I ever saw. When I have good luck, I can get such a breakfast as this in 35 minutes and, Henry, if you could see my nice fried pork and white mealy potatoes mashed up on my plate with a little gravy on them and the sauce sweetened a very little, you would say it was good enough for anyone.

I have never lived so well in the army as since we left the Bridge. I cannot tell you of all the good things I have had tonight for I haven't time. But I will in my next.

I have received 2 letters from Edwin since he arrived at Maryland. And but one from you dated September 9th. No papers. We haven't got the box yet and no signs of it at present. I want Mother to send me an undershirt by mail as soon as convenient. I shall want another before a great while and the shirts. I think it will be best to send one at a time by mail, as it seems to me they will come through better. I want a little more cayenne in the next paper and a nutmeg.

My health is good. Luke is well. Is busy today, will probably write tomorrow.

Mother, the shirts you made me last fall were not too large, just right.
Rufus

[The following was enclosed in the same envelope as the letter above.]

Dear Mother,

Your letter (August 19th) reached me just as I had finished my last page. I was glad to see it. Oh, how thankful I feel that I have a Mother to think of me and write to me. I have not forgotten the evening that I spent with you preparing the apples to dry. I love to think of it now. You do not think of me oftener than I think of home. This is the season that wakes up all my home feelings, when the fruit is ripe. I hope to be with you by another fall, though I hardly expect to before my term of enlistment is out, but the time will soon pass away and I hope there will be no need of any of us longer than that.

I wrote on my other sheet for some shirts, but I don't want you to hurry too much about them. I am in need of an undershirt more than anything else at present. If you send them singly, as I think will be best, it will cost you about six stamps to each package.

Please send me a pair of suspenders with the first. If I ever get the box, I can sell the pair in that at full cost. I think I shall write to you several times before you send all the packages, and if there is anything else that I want, I will tell you.

I am glad to hear that Grandpa is so well. I have great hopes that I shall see him again. I have not thought that Father has grown careless of me. I shall expect a good long letter from him next week containing a little of everything.

I want (and I had come near forgetting it for the tenth time when I was writing to you) that you should send me your photographs, Father, Mother, and Henry. You can get them at North Bridgewater, at S. W. S. Howard's, corner of School and Main Street for 8 cents apiece. Just right to send in a letter. Size about one inch square and that is as large as I could carry with me with safely.

I must close now but will try to write again soon.

From your Affectionate Son,
Rufus

October 6, 1862
Camp near Downsville

Dear Father,

Your letter of September 28th reached me this morning. I have had a letter from home every week, though the mail has not come so regularly of late as usual. But I have been very negligent of late about writing home. I wrote home September 5th from Chain Bridge and not again until a week ago last Saturday to Henry. That was my first opportunity after writing from Chain Bridge. When I last wrote to Henry and Mother, I thought I should have written again twice before this time. But General Couch thought we should be the better for having two drills a day. Then I have traveled some miles for potatoes and apples, thinking that I would have a good time today and write tomorrow. Then washing clothes, guard duty, cooking as we have had to do until within a few days, and a review by the President. All these things have occupied much of my time for a few days past.

I have not been very well. I think I have eaten too many apples which gave me the diarrhea. I am better today and think I shall soon be entirely well. I took two of Soule's Pills as I thought my stomach was a little out of order and they helped me. Thomas Sherman[43] gave them to me and I told him I would make them good to him again. He thinks they are a very good pill and I have no doubt they are as good as any. So if you will, send me a box of them. Luke will take half of them or you may keep a part of them to try and then we shall probably have enough. Thomas thinks they are better than Ayer's because they do not gripe. Perhaps Mother will like them better.

We are having very pleasant weather and it gives me great pleasure to hear about the fine lot of fruit that we are having this year. You don't write too much of things about home. Of yourselves, the house, and the barn and of everything about home, I love to hear. I must write you a short letter this time because I am afraid the mail will leave very soon.

I heard this morning, with deep regret, that another member of our company has gone to his long home, Frank Hutchinson. I was not prepared to hear it. I thought, when he left us, he would recover.

I have not got any papers since I left Chain Bridge. When you send another, put in a roll of peppermint lozenges. You will find good ones at Nat Dyer's, if you happen to go that way.

I am out of money. I don't know how long before we shall be paid off again. Please send me two dollars of the postage stamp currency if convenient.

I must close now while there is a chance to send this today.

Yours Affectionately,

Rufus

P.S. Tell Samuel his turn will come soon.

October 15, 1862
Camp near Downsville, Maryland

Dear Brother,

The long looked for box has finally come. We opened it yesterday morning. I was happily disappointed to find so much in it that was not spoiled, especially after removing the cover and finding such a heap of rotten apples. There was not a particle of sound potato or apple. I did not expect there would be.

Of course, you know everything eatible must be more or less damaged. The cheese was badly heated but not moldy. I don't really dislike it and yet I can get along with very little of it. We have sold half of it at eleven cents per pound. Probably shall sell the rest of it. Some like it first rate.

The fish is what Father would call "done fish." It is as red as salmon and not so bad. The air has improved it very much. The raisins and dates I must put down worthless, though we have picked them over a little, and found a few good ones. The raisins look as well as ever, but they got wet with the apple juice and soured. The jell in my pail is very good, what there is left of it. About two-thirds of it leaked out.

It is very much better than that in the box. The pan and pail are just what I wanted. Tobacco a little moldy, but not hurt much. Lozenges, rather moist, but eatible, handkerchief, comb, brush, soap and suspenders all dry and good as new. Nutmegs, pepper both kinds, and mustard not damaged. White sugar, a little moist, but not hurt. Tea as good as when you put it up, and I am glad it is. Pickles came through in good shape and I think they are very good. Holland Noyes sent us some writing paper, envelopes and stamps. The envelopes and stamps were good. Paper worthless. Perhaps, I have forgotten to mention some things that were good, but nothing of any amount.

I am writing with the pencil which Charlie sent me. It is a good one, but it is better to know that Charlie thinks of me.

Now for something else. Since I last wrote you, I have been quite unwell with diarrhea and cold. Yesterday, was my first well day and this morning my breakfast was eaten with good appetite. I had soft bread and butter and a slice of fried steak which was very tender and good. I have received many kindnesses from members of our company and some from other companies. Willard Lincoln, Company A, gave me some medicine which helped me very much. And day before yesterday, I took two of Ayer's pills which he gave me which did me good.

I went to the doctor twice whilst I was sick. He excused me from one drill the first day and gave a dose of salts. The next day he put me on duty, though my duties have been light all through. Major Harlow came to see me whilst I was sick and enquired how long I had been sick and what the matter was with me. He also wanted to know if there was anything I wanted? I told him straw to put in my tent. He was not slow to understand that I was without money. He lent me 75 cents. I could have had more, if I had wanted it.

I feel perfectly well now and have got a good appetite. Jacob Harding and I sleep together now and with our straw and blankets, we make a good warm bed in our tent. And I think that is one of the most essential things, to sleep warm.

I have not received my undershirt yet, though I have received your letter stating that you mailed it the day before, and two papers at the same time commencing a new story (late ones). There is a number in the rear yet. Our mail is very irregular yet.

You did not say anything about the photographs in your letter. Perhaps you forgot it. I hope you will send them. S. W. S. Howard, North Bridgewater, takes them about an inch square for 8 cents.

I don't know how much longer we shall stay here. It may be a month. But I don't think it best to risk sending the boots at present. There would no harm in your getting up a pair and, if it should look favorable to send them by mail, you will have them ready. Perhaps there may be some other way. Take your time for it, for my shoes are good at present, and I have got my name on the list for another pair Weascots Calf. I think [it] is best with a large heel, not too high, bottoms about the same as you sent last winter.

I must close now, hoping to hear from you soon. You have got a long distance to walk this winter, but pretty good pay.

Yours Truly,

Rufus

October 21, 1862
Camp near Cherry Run, Maryland

Dear Father,

I have had a good mail this morning: 3 letters—yours October 19th, Henry's October 12th, and one from Edwin which I will send to you, and a *Freeman* September 6th containing the cayenne.

It is a cold, stormy morning, a northeaster, too cold to write a long letter but we have got a good fire of rails in front of our tent and plenty of straw inside. So I think I can keep comfortable writing a little while.

My undershirt and suspenders came this morning and I am very much pleased with them. I want to know next time you write what they cost, not that I have any idea of selling, but I want to know how high priced goods I am wearing on my back.

I put on my new frock coat which I drew this morning. It is quite a pretty one. Dark blue and pretty fine. 9 bright buttons in front. Buttons up high in the neck and sets well. Our clothing is coming a little at a time, but I think we shall get it all soon.

I received the money today. So I believe I have received all the things which you have sent. I think Henry had better not send the boots at present. I will give him seasonable warning. I have just got a pair of new shoes. Good ones. You may send the shirts along now as soon as convenient.

I am afraid Mother is working too hard this fall. 50 pounds of apples is a great many to dry. The 3 lines from Mother in Henry's letter are worth much to me. I hope I shall see Mother's photograph soon. Ed tells

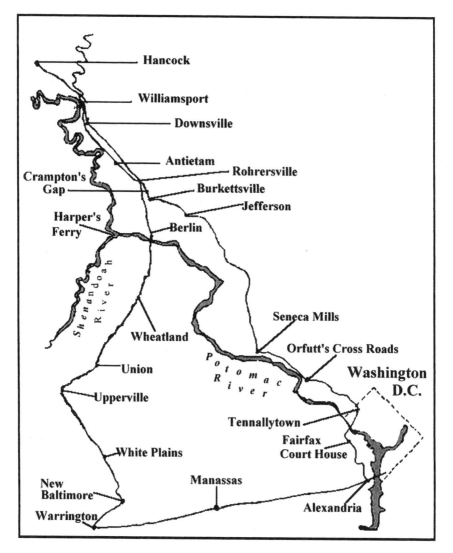

Route of the Seventh Regiment, September 5, 1862–November 16, 1862.

me he has got it. Eat all the apples you can. You must not worry about me now, for I am well.

Rufus

October 24, 1862
Friday
Camp near Cherry Run, Maryland

Dear Mother,

I am going to write to you this time. Sometimes it is to Father and sometimes to Henry that I feel most like writing to. But this time it is to Mother.

I suppose it makes but little difference so long as you hear from me. I suppose you are feeling rather anxious about me as you know I have been sick. I am well now, have a good appetite, and am gaining flesh though I got somewhat reduced during my sickness. A week ago I only weighed 122½. This morning I find I have gained a pound.

It has been some time since I have written home. I think my last letter was soon after we got the box. I did not think it would be so long, but there has been much to prevent. The last letter which I received from you was a week ago last Thursday night, from Father, containing the pictures and the two papers containing the nutmegs. I was on guard that night. It was raining quite hard and too dark to see to read a word. I felt great curiosity to know what had come in my letter. So I opened it and felt very carefully, thinking that it might possibly contain the $2.00 which I sent for. I was satisfied that the pictures were in it, but how many I did not know. It was a long night for I wanted to see Father, Mother, and Henry. My disappointment was great when I found Mother's was not there. I began to think, "Could it be possible that I could have lost it in the dark?" I cannot think so, for I was very careful but I think I shall see it in my next letter. And I hope that will come this afternoon and be as good as Father's and Henry's. They are perfect, both of them. And yet Father's seems to me to have a likeness to him which is greater than I ever saw in a picture before.

I have not received the undershirt or the money yet. It is a little singular as I have received letters and papers which you have mailed since. But others are troubled in the same way.

Last Sunday eve (the last mail we have had) I received two papers, one journal, and one *Freeman*. I found the lozenges and nutmegs. The lozenges were just what I wanted.

We left camp near Downsville last Monday noon. Are now about twenty miles from that place. Handcock and Clear Spring are the nearest settlements to us now. Handcock is about ten from us, and Clear Spring seven miles. Both quite smart places.

I would not send any more shirts until I can tell you I have got the first one. I wear my old woolen shirt now under the white. I don't see but it is about as good as ever only some smaller, but it keeps me very comfortable. We are expecting to be new clothed throughout by Uncle Sam very soon. Some of it came today. I got a pair of shoes that I am very much pleased with. I have booked my name for a new cap, overcoat, frock coat, blouse, trousers, shoes, and two pairs of stockings. I am going to keep warm this winter.

The folks, where we are now, give us lots of straw to put in our tents. Luke, Jacob, and I sleep together. We manage to get some little luxury to eat almost every day. I have had butter by me for the last two weeks. I sometimes swap of my rations of coffee at the houses in the neighborhood for apple pie, bread or potatoes. I found a spool of black thread which I swapped off a few mornings since for a breakfast of soft bread and cider, apple sauce, and coffee with milk in it. I think I am very ingenious in those matters.

I must close now. Hoping to hear from you again soon.
From Your Affectionate Son,
Rufus

November 2, 1862
Camp near Berling, Maryland

Dear Mother,

I received your letter last evening with a great deal of pleasure and two papers and the Supporter. I am glad you sent that. I believe it is a good thing.

I don't know how much time I shall have to write this morning. We may stop here today and may be off in less than an hour.

We have had some hard marching for the last week but I have stood it well. Since I last wrote home, we have spent another day at our old camp at Downsville. It was there (last Thursday eve) that I received a letter from Henry containing your picture. You don't know how glad I was to see it. It is a good one, as natural as either of the others and I prize them more than anything else you have sent.

I am sorry you are feeling so much anxiety for me. I wish you could know how well I am feeling this morning. I wish I could know that you was feeling as hopeful this morning as I do that we shall meet again. That the happy day, though it may yet look far off, will surely come in God's time.

We are having the finest weather now and I feel in such good spirits with enough of everything to make me comfortable.

The more I think of it, I will give Henry credit for the last dollar which he sent me. The money which you have sent me has done me a great deal of good. I can think of [more] to write but I hear orders to pack up. So I must close.

Yours Truly,

Rufus

November 14, 1862
Camp near New Baltimore, Maryland

Dear Mother,

Luke says he hardly knows what to write and that is about my case. So I tell him we will write a home letter without trying to tell much news.

I received your letter of November second day before yesterday and just now one from Father and Henry full of good news.

My second long shirt came with Mother's letter day before yesterday. So I have now got both the long ones and the undershirt which you bought for me. They are all good. Nobody but Mother could have sent me such good ones, so soft and warm. You say you don't know which to send, another bought one or one that you can make for me. I don't think this will reach you in season to help you decide. But if it should, I should hardly know what to say. For either will be as good as possible. So I want to leave it all with Mother. We have got plenty of clothing now.

Have had our share of snow and rain but the weather has been very fine for the last three days. I don't call myself quite well yet. My legs are a little weak and my appetite not very good. But if you will promise not to feel too much anxiety for me, I think I will soon tell you that I am as well as ever.

The doctor is very kind to me now, and I assure you I have friends here that will not see me suffer. We are encamped in the woods on the side of a hill. We came here last Sunday. I don't know how long we shall stop here. Luke and I built our tent together as usual. Have got a good tight one. Plenty of dry oak leaves and two good rubber blankets and each have a new thick woolen blanket. Luke has done most all of the work for us both since we have been here. He is very kind to me.

I think I feel better tonight than I have for some time. At any rate, I feel very cheerful. I won't write any more now for Luke is going to the office with his and will take mine. So good night to Mother and all the loved ones at home.

Rufus
P.S. Send me another dollar and a pair of mittens. I will write again soon.

November 17, 1862
Carver Hospital
Washington, D.C.

Dear Brother,

I find myself here very unexpectedly through the kindness of the doctor and some other friends which I had in my regiment. I have time to write you only a few lines this morning as I want this to reach you the earliest moment.

I left camp early Sunday morning for this place taking cars at Warrington and came through by way of Manassas Junction, Fairfax, and Alexandria. Arrived here yesterday about noon.

I had a hard time of it coming through but I haven't time to give you an account of it now. I am not worse than I have been, except the fatigue of the journey. I find myself now in very comfortable quarters. I think I shall gain strength here very fast.

I want you to send me a little money as soon as possible.

Direct your letters now to Carver Hospital, Washington, D.C. Say nothing of Company or Regiment.

I will write you again soon.
Rufus

November 22, 1862
Carver Hospital
Washington, D.C.

Dear Mother,

When I wrote to Henry last Tuesday morning, I thought I should have written home again before this time, but to tell the truth I have felt so little like it that I have been putting it off from day to day hoping to feel better.

I am not dangerously sick, of that I feel very confident, but I am very weak and my appetite most of the time very poor. I feel my weakness mostly in my legs though I have not near my natural strength anywhere. I have no pains in my legs, body, or head to speak of. Diarrhea (though not very bad at present), weakness, and loss of appetite (no cold to speak of) seems to be the sum of my ails. Though I have no doubt but the diarrhea that I have had upon me now something over two months is the chief cause of my weakness. A part of the time it has been pretty bad.

[The letter continues on the same page.]

Sunday Morning
November 23
Dear Mother,

Darkness overtook me last night before I could finish my letter and I have too much yet to write to think of finishing before the mail leaves this morning. So I will write what I can and then continue to write more, hoping to have another ready to mail for you tomorrow morning.

I am feeling a little better this morning. My appetite was a little better than usual. Three small potatoes, two spoonfuls of rice pudding, and a very small piece of bread and butter was all I wanted. I could have had a cup of coffee with milk and sugar but I preferred cold water. Shall have tea for dinner and supper.

I must close now or I shall miss this morning's mail. It may be several days before I can write to Luke. So I should like to have his folks tell him where I am so that he can send me whatever may have gone to the regiment for me.

Yours Affectionately,
Rufus

November 23, 1862
Carver Hospital
Washington, D.C.

Dear Mother,

It is getting rather late in the afternoon, but I shall try to write you a few lines. I have so much to write I hardly know where to begin but I suppose something concerning my feelings will be most pleasing to you. I cannot tell you that I can perceive much difference in my feelings from what there has been for the last few days. That weakness which makes it so disagreeable for me to move and the continual faintness at the stomach which seems to say more food but when I begin to eat it says, "No, I do not want it."

Now there are sometimes exceptions to this. Last Friday noon we had salt fish and potatoes for dinner. We had nothing to put with it or on it. It was fish and potato. I did not feel very hungry when I went to the table but thought it would taste good. And surely it did and I ate a very hearty dinner and I felt better for it all the afternoon. This is one thing that makes me think, if I could have just what I wanted to eat, it would be better for me than medicine.

[The letter continues on the same sheet.

November 24th
Wednesday
Dear Mother,

I received a letter from Henry yesterday containing the money and another one this afternoon. I was very glad to see the money as I was out and had washing out to the amount of thirty-three cents and I was sadly in need of the barber.

I cannot tell you that I am any better yet. I am not of the same opinion I was, when I was writing to you last Sunday, in regard to my diet. I have since learned that it matters but little what I eat. I have to have a sick spell after it. The doctor is giving me iodine, 30 drops per day, and a mixture of quinine three teaspoonfuls and three white powders. Magnesia, I think.

You don't know, Mother, how good it seems to me to get here. I am in good quarters now, have a good bed that I can lie down upon when I please, though it will compare very poorly with the comforts of home. I should like to be at home with you a while. I think I should get well a great deal faster, but I think it will be very doubtful.

I will now say a few words about my diet and by that time it will be too dark to write. Twice a day I have broiled steak and baked potato, if the cooks or nurses don't forget it. Baked rice pudding, two spoonsful or less when I don't have the steak. Always as much toasted bread and butter as I want, but I want but very little. I roast two sour apples on the stove almost every day. They relish as well as anything.

I must stop now. I think I shall write oftener. It is not so hard for me today as I thought.
Yours Affectionately,
Rufus

November 28, 1862
Carver Hospital
Washington, D.C.

Dear Father,

I have just received your letter of Tuesday the 25th containing the money. The undershirt did not come today. I shall expect it tomorrow. I cannot tell you yet that I am yet any better and I am not worse. My weakness continues about the same and appetite very poor. Diarrhea sometimes very bad. Then again almost well.

Mr. Tufts has just left me. He has seen the doctor of my ward and he says that I shall have an examination in a few days and wants I should let him know the result as soon after as possible.

Saturday morning,
November 29th

You have done a big thing in the hog line this year. I hope I shall be at home with a good appetite to help you eat some of him but I have great doubts about it.

This is getting to be a more comfortable place than it was when I first came here. Ten or twelve noisy fellows have been sent to their regiments and we have two new nurses in exchange for two very poor ones which took their leave yesterday morning. Things are much more comfortable here now. I must not write much more this morning as the mail will leave soon.

I think I shall write to Luke today to send my description papers.
Yours Truly,
Rufus

December 5, 1862
Carver Hospital
Washington, D.C.

Dear Mother,

Your letters of Nov. 28th and 30th are received and I feel very sorry now that I have not answered them before. I have not been quite so well for the last four or five days is the reason why I have not. My diarrhea has been worse and that gave me some pain in the back and weakened my knees somewhat. But my diarrhea has left me almost entirely today and I think it is altogether the best feeling day I have had since I have been in the hospital.

I felt a better appetite for my dinner today than usual. It was the most I have eaten at one time for a long while. Two small potatoes, a piece of fried sausage about one and one-half inches in length, and two baked apples. Somehow I feel today that I am really on the mending hand. My courage is good and has been all the time. My quarters are good. Much more comfortable than when I first came here. I have a good, comfortable bed. Plenty of company. I have one acquaintance with me from Company I. He came with me.

I received your dispatch yesterday but was too thoughtless to answer

it. I cannot get a furlough at present. I shall write you again this afternoon. The mail will leave soon, so I must close. Send me a little sage in
the next paper.
Yours Affectionately,
Rufus

December 7, 1862
Carver Hospital
Washington, D.C.

Dear Brother,

We are having a regular New England day. Wind northwest, pretty
sharp air, and almost snow enough for sleighing. This weather, I feel, is
good for me. I find I am gaining strength though not very fast and appetite also improving a little. Diarrhea pretty bad yesterday, but not much
today. The doctor is giving me pills now to stop it.

I think you was a little too sanguine that I was going to get the furlough. I felt very doubtful about it, so was but very little disappointed,
also though home is as dear to me as ever and much I should like to see
it.

I was examined last Tuesday by two doctors. They decided that I was
not entitled to a furlough as I had not been in the hospital but two weeks
and was no worse than when I entered. But there is one consolation. I
don't think they will send me back to my regiment until I am quite well.

And now I think of it, I don't want you to come to see me, unless I
get a great deal sicker than at the present. It will be too expensive, and
another thing I find in spite of all I can say, you are boiling over with
anxiety for me. Of what use is it? It will do no good and troubles me very
much. I know I was too negligent about writing to you, and you know
that is apt to be the case when I am well. Now I have given you the
outlines of a scolding and I feel better and I hope you will too.

I should like to have my boots pretty soon and I think there will be
no trouble in sending them by express. You might send them in a small
box, but the trouble is, I don't know what to have sent with them, though
I can think of a few things that I should like to have that I think would
do me good now. Cranberry sauce, pretty sour, is one thing. A pound of
loaf sugar is another. I think that is good for diarrhea. A few oranges, if
you can get them. I don't care if they are not very sweet. If you think it
will do to risk me with a few cakes and pies, a pound of butter, and a
chick, and a lump of pudding, you may send them. I don't feel that I
could make great use of any of these things at present, except the cranberry and oranges, but I have a good cool place in a back room to keep

a box, but I shall have to get some better of my diarrhea and a little better appetite before I could use much of it. Mother must do as she thinks best about sending it. She can tell best how long such things will keep. I wouldn't send many apples, only a few kinds I have never seen, as I can buy them pretty cheap here and a few pears if they will keep. I wouldn't send for anything to eat at present but I want the sauce and the oranges and even now you need not be in a very great hurry about sending it.

The next time I write I will tell you about my journey here from Warington and what kind of a hospital we have got. I will stop now. So good evening.

Yours truly,
Rufus

December 11, 1862
Thursday
Carver Hospital
Washington, D.C.

Dear Father,

I received your letter and the dollar from Henry yesterday. I think my not writing you so often as I should has caused you a great deal of anxiety and trouble. But it is hard work to begin. I put it off from one day to another thinking to feel more like it and, when I am writing, I think I will write a little every day.

I am not any worse than my last letter represents to you. I think I am gaining slowly. I think you received a letter from me last night which answers the questions contained in the dispatch. But I will say now that I didn't think at the time of my examination nor do I now think that it will be possible for me to get my discharge or a furlough at present. But I want to come home bad enough. I think I would get well a great deal faster if I could.

I have written to Luke for my description papers. I expect I should have to have that at any rate before I could get home. I suppose he will send it as soon as he can. I can then get paid off here for four months. That would give me funds enough. About strength of body, I don't know how that would be but I think I could do it if they would let me try.

[The letter continues.]

Friday morning
December 12th

I thought when I left off writing last night I should have time to write quite a letter this morning but I find if I send by this morning's mail, I shall only have time enough to tell you that I am quite as well as usual and appetite for breakfast is a little better than usual.

Yours Truly,

Rufus

December 13, 1862

Carver Hospital

Washington, D.C.

Dear Brother,

I have got a large sheet of paper before me, larger I think, than I shall be able to fill this afternoon. I was presented with a few sheets of it yesterday morning by some ladies who came in to see how we were getting along. They also gave me a little jell which was the nicest thing which I ever saw of that kind. But it didn't suit my taste the best. I don't know what kind it was, though I know there was wine in it. They told me so and the color was almost white.

I feel that I am getting better though very slowly. My diarrhea is much better today and my appetite a little better. But I don't feel much stronger yet. But I will venture that part of it when I get entirely over my diarrhea.

I will now say to Father that I have just received his and Mother's letter. I have been before the Board for examination for a furlough or a discharge. What more could I do? They wouldn't grant either. I don't know of any more that I could do. Mr. Tufts has been to see me again today and I think he is a little hopeful that he can yet do something towards getting me home. I think I have now written all the particulars under that head.

I have received the writing paper and envelopes. I have not a sore throat, nor am I unwell in any way except as I have told you. But I wanted it for a drink, thinking that it would be better than clear cold water for my diarrhea. I have never had any extra postage to pay.

I received a letter from Luke yesterday. He thinks my description list will be along soon. I received two dollars from him. Money which was due to me in the company.

I don't think of anything more to write this time. So I will stop for this time.

Yours Truly,

Rufus

December 16, 1862
Carver Hospital
Washington, D.C.

Dear Brother,

I am hoping to receive a letter from home today. An hour will tell the story as it now nearly two P.M. and the mail arrives at three. If not today, I have not doubt I shall tomorrow.

I am as weak yet as that old rat that father killed twenty years ago on the cellar stairs at the old Arnold House, but I am almost well of my diarrhea. I don't know but what I haven't had anything pass me but once today and that was very slight. My appetite is about the same. Sometimes pretty good, but oftener very poor.

I have just received your letter with the three dollars. I am glad you have been to see the doctor, for I find that I have been very imprudent. I have eaten of almost everything since I have been in the hospital. It is but a day or two since I have succeeded in finding a place where I could get porridge. At this place I can get it without money by going after it. And so I could custard, if eggs could be had, but they are not in the market.

I wouldn't send any more money at present. I will write you when I want more.

My courage is good yet and I think if I am careful (and I mean to be) that it will not be long before I can tell you that I am entirely well.
Yours Affectionately,
Rufus

December 17, 1862
Carver Hospital
Washington, D.C.

Dear Brother,

I write you a few lines this morning to tell you that I am to leave here in a few hours for Philadelphia. I am pleased with the idea. Everyone says that it is a better place than this. There are three going with me from this ward.

I think the prospect of my getting home will be much greater there. I have no time to write more this morning as the mail will leave very soon.
Yours Truly,
Rufus

December 19, 1862
U. S. General Hospital, Ward N
West Philadelphia

Dear Brother,

I left the hospital at Washington on the morning of the 17th as I wrote you in my last I thought I should and arrived here yesterday about noon. I had a much easier time coming here than I expected. I had to ride all night, but the cars were easy. I rested well last night and feel better today than I have for a long while. Yesterday, my diarrhea was pretty bad but all right again today. I am not any stronger yet, but my appetite is a little better today.

I have already seen enough of this place to know that it is a thousand times better than the place I left. Here a man in every stage of sickness can and will have everything that heart can wish. Everything is kept as clean and neat as a parlor and we don't have to go out of doors for anything.

The doctor will fix my diet tomorrow. I don't know yet what it will be. I have had to go the full diet table today, as it is called. Tomorrow, it will be one-half diet. We had this morning bread and butter and boiled mackerel. It was No. 1 and so was the bread and butter. Coffee with milk and sugar for breakfast, water for dinner, and tea for supper. For dinner today, we had cod fish and potatoes and round turnips. The nurse gave me a pint of milk. I drank that and eat nothing but turnip. It was as good as sweet potato.

This is the largest hospital in the city. I should like to have my boots as soon as convenient and that is all that I can think of that I do want. I have got a better bed in this hospital, a very nice one. They have given me a woolen wrapper (loose coat) and a very large, wide towel.

Truly I feel that my wants, if not now, will soon be all supplied. I can't write everything this time, so I might as well stop now.
Yours Truly,
Rufus
Direct your letters,

U.S.A. General Hospital
Ward N
West Philadelphia

Everything you have sent to Carver Hospital, I shall get without any trouble. Don't send the boots until I write again.
Rufus

December 26, 1862
Philadelphia

To Rufus Robbins
Dear Sir and Brother:

Mrs. Thomas and I visited your son this afternoon. He is No. 80 of Ward N in the West Philadelphia Hospital, situated about 4 miles from my residence.

He has a good bed in a large, cheerful, well-warmed and well-ventilated building, bountifully supplied with provisions, and with nurses who strive to do their best. I know nothing of the skill of the attendant physician, but presume he has the confidence of the authorities in charge.

There is (I am proud to say) a grand overflowing of the bounty of the ladies of our city, in furnishing all conceivable extras for the sick and wounded heroes of the Republic. Anything that can be had with love or money is furnished by a kindness that knows no exceptions.

Yesterday, there was a very liberal Christmas dinner furnished to all the men by voluntary contributions and all the wards of the immense hospital, accommodating about three thousand, are beautifully decorated with evergreen, woven in many fanciful figures and shapes, and interspersed with mottoes and flags.

But all this is of small service to your son. I consider him a very sick man. Honesty requires me to say this to you without reservation. He has long been troubled with diarrhea that has become chronic.

I do not swear that he is beyond the reach of cure even in the hospital, but I have insisted that he shall have tapioca, sago, and other nourishing articles fitted to his case—and he has promised me that he will do so.

One of the Surgeon's orderlies (a soldier friend of mine) will have a special eye to Rufus and if the sick man lacks anything at the hospital, I will gladly see that it is furnished him, including some wholesome, genuine Spanish wine, a fine tonic for convalescents.

It is my desire that he should come to my house on a "Pass" as soon as he is able. I am sure it would do him good.

He has not yet received his "description list." It will be written for, again and again, until we succeed. And then, if he is not greatly better by that time, I will make an appeal to Dr. Hayes to have him discharged. We cannot reach this end without the "description list" referred to.

Rufus bade me say to you that he has a strong constitution, and that he is determined to get well! I am sure our visit gave him good courage.

I will go to see him again, and shall be hearing from him every few days. There are so many hospitals that I cannot go very often to anyone of them. Having much correspondence, I write hastily and am
Truly Yours,
Abel C. Thomas
218 Lombard St.
Philadelphia

NOTES

1. Samuel H. Foster, 25, Corporal, Company K.
2. David P. Robinson, 36, Private, Company K.
3. James M. Penniman, 18, Corporal, Company K.
4. Candle wax has dripped on the letter and burned two small holes in it.
5. Albert Lufkin, 26, Private, Company K.
6. Isaac F. Hill, 27, Sergeant, Company K.
7. John R. Bouldra, 18, Private, Company K. Enlisted January 20, 1862. Discharged 1864 as prisoner of war.
8. The first part of this letter, most probably to Edwin, is missing.
9. One gill equals four ounces.
10. David A. Russell, Colonel, Brigadier General U.S.V. November 29, 1862.
11. Charles Raymond, Lieutenant Colonel, Resigned October 24, 1862.
12. Charles H. Knott (or Nott), 22, Private, Company K.
13. Baking soda.
14. Probably Benjamin F. Hutchinson.
15. Edward D. Hutchinson, 21, Musician, Company K, discharged March 17, 1862, disability.
16. This note, written on a small, separate piece of paper, was enclosed with the longer letter.
17. Andrew S. Lawton, 20, Private, Company A, killed by a projectile from Fort Magruder, May 6, 1862.
18. Frank Erskin, 18, Private, Company K.
19. Brigadier General Fitz John Porter, Commander of the Fifth Corps.
20. Brigadier General Silas Casey, commander of the Second Division of the Fourth Corps.
21. Frank Hutchinson.
22. Isaac Chamberlain, 36, Private, Company K.
23. The Battle of Seven Pines May 31, 1862.
24. It seems that Rufus means "to that portion of Virginia not on the peninsula."

25. This map has been lost.

26. Brigadier General Edwin V. Sumner, Commander of the Second Corps.

27. The spelling of this name is not clear.

28. That is, in Maine.

29. June 25, the Battle of Nine Mile Road. Cf. Appendix II: Letter from Captain George Reed, commander of Company K, published in the *Abington Standard*, September 6, 1862.

30. Augustine Fullerton, 18, Private, Company K. Fullerton did not die from these wounds and was discharged on June 27, 1864, at the expiration of service. Cf. Appendix II, Captain George Reed's Letter to the *Abington Standard*.

31. Most probably John Bouldra.

32. Battle of Nine Mile Road.

33. The date written on this letter is "July 28, 1862," but this is probably an error in the light of Rufus' references in this and the next (July 21) letter to the "box."

34. Twenty-four sheets of paper, ¹⁄₂₀ of a ream.

35. Orman M. Cole, 27, Private, Company K.

36. Noah Harding, 25, Private, Company K.

37. General John Pope.

38. A kind of apple.

39. Edward M. Bain, 27, Sergeant, Company K.

40. Ward L. Foster, 37, Captain, Company K.

41. A kind of yellow apple.

42. Isaac Chamberlain.

43. Thomas B. Sherman, 27, Corporal, Company K.

LETTERS FROM 1863

February 16, 1863
Philadelphia, Pennsylvania

My dear Mrs. Robbins,

Before Rufus died I promised him that if he did not live to see any of his folks I would write to his dear Mother and tell her what he wanted said to her. Afterward, his father and brother came and received those parting words from his own lips. But I still felt as if I too would like to communicate with you and tell you something of your dear son's last hours, but I have been prevented from time to time until a much longer time has elapsed than I would have wished, for his was a peculiarly happy death bed and I love to think, talk, or write about it. His faith was clear, strong, and unwavering.

He told me over and over again, he had no fears. He would like to see his Mother, but if it was the Lord's will, he was quite willing to go. He spoke of death always more as a journey he was about to take to a new and desirable home, rather than a dreaded change. One day, before he said anything about me writing to you, he told me of a very beautiful Psalm which had opened itself to you, and what you had written him about it. He said he could not remember exactly where it was (for he was very weak and his memory failed him sometimes), but he had read it very often while down on the peninsula and had found great comfort in it. He said there was something in it about "God covering him, and he must trust in Him, and He would give His angels charge over him, so that no evil should befall him."

AMERICAN TELEGRAPH COMPANY.

TERMS AND CONDITIONS ON WHICH MESSAGES ARE RECEIVED BY THIS COMPANY FOR TRANSMISSION.

The public are notified that, in order to guard against mistakes in the transmission of messages, every message of importance ought to be repeated by being sent back from the station at which it is to be received to the station from which it is originally sent. Half the usual price for transmission will be charged for repeating the message, and while this Company will, as heretofore, use every precaution to ensure correctness, it will not be responsible for mistakes or delays in the transmission or delivery of repeated messages beyond five hundred times the amount paid for sending the message, nor will it be responsible for mistakes or delays in the transmission of unrepeated messages, from whatever cause they may arise, nor for the delays arising from interruptions in the workings of its telegraphs, nor for any mistakes or omission of any other Company over whose lines a message is to be sent to reach the place of destination. All messages will hereafter be received by this Company for transmission subject to the above conditions.

Received at Washington — Fri Jany 2nd 1863 at 7 o'clock, ____ minutes.

By telegraph from Philadelphia To Rupby Babbing
Washington

Rupby is failing very fast.

Anxious to see you.

Sig. Abel C Thomas

9½ pd 75 pay 50 Dely

I told him it was the 91st Psalm and repeated a part of it to him which seemed to give him great satisfaction. He said, "After reading that I never felt afraid of any dangers by day or by night, for I knew it was all in God's hand and He would do all right." He said God had been very good to bring him this far on his way. He hoped to live to get home to see his dear mother. He thought she would feel so bad to have him die among strangers, but if it was ordered differently he was willing, and he hoped she would have strength given her to bear it.

At last, he suddenly grew much worse, and we knew he could not live a great while.

Mr. Thomas telegraphed for his father on Friday, but we thought it best not to tell him lest something should prevent his father's coming and so he be disappointed. But to prepare his mind for it, I said to him the next day, "Rufus, Mr. Thomas and I think your father has a mind to come on to see you. His last letter sounded like it; we would not wonder to see him almost any time."

"Oh," said he, "I wish he would, either he or my brother. They could not both leave I suppose, but I should like to see one of them. Yesterday, I was so bad I thought I could not live and I had a mind to telegraph to them, but I feel better today."

"Last night," said he, "I dreamt I was at home and I was out under the trees and they looked so beautiful. When I got awake it was toward morning, and I longed so to be there to walk under the trees and look up into the sky. Just then I opened my eyes and right down through the window the beautiful moon and one bright star was shining for me. I could not keep the tears back when I thought how good God is. It was just as if He had said, 'You cannot come out to see them but they shall come to you.' "

After some little silence he said, "Mrs. Thomas, if I do not live to see any of my folks, I want you to write to my Mother, and tell her not to grieve for me. I feel that it is not hard to die, and I am willing to go if it is the Lord's will. I have everything I want, everybody is kind to me, and I have nothing left to desire except that she will believe that it is all right and not grieve for me. I feel that I was never very wicked. I think I always wanted to do what was right, but tell my Mother that since I went into the army, I have thought more of religious things than I ever thought before. I have read my Bible more and I feel that a new light has been given to me. I feel sure that all men are brothers and that God is the father of us all. And into his hand I am willing to consign myself. Tell her, I have no doubts about the future. It is all bright to me, and no fear of dying, for I feel that God will make it easy for me."

So he kept on talking for a long time, all in the same strain of perfect trust and composure, and again and again he hoped his mother would not fret about him.

I have tried to tell you as near as I can, his exact words and can only add, "May I die the death of the righteous, may my last end be like his."

His father and brother will tell you further particulars of how he was situated and the kind attentions he received from everyone around him. Of course, it was not home, but I do assure you he was made as comfortable as he could possibly be under the circumstances. This he said himself repeatedly. The nurse who attended him—Mr. Loomis—is one of the best I ever saw. I have seen him a number of times since and for the sake of his kindness to Rufus, I have sent to him many nice things for the men under his charge—things that were sent to me for sick and wounded soldiers. I feel that in his hands they will be faithfully distributed.

I hope you have received Rufus' effects before this time. I went out to the hospital two or three times, also to the New England Association's Rooms, and as far as I can ascertain they were taken away by the agent of that Association. Indeed, one of the gentlemen told me that he got the portfolio and papers and gave Mr. Hall (the undertaker) the order to get the clothes. If you have not received them yet, you had better write at once to them to send them on. The longer these things are neglected, the more difficult it is to adjust them.

If there is anything else you would like to know or any things I have not made plain to you, if you will let me know, I will be glad to write it to you.

I too am a Mother. I too have given back the children that were kindly lent me for a season. And with all a woman's sympathy for your sorrow, I must still commend you to the only true source of consolation. "Shall we take the good from His hands and not accept the evil also." Trust, as Rufus did, and He will give you peace.

Remember me most kindly to Mr. Robbins and Henry. We feel an interest in them and shall not soon forget them.

I am yours in sympathy,
Mrs. L. Thomas

Esteemed Friends:

Mrs. Thomas has so fully, and I think so fitly, expressed the thoughts and feelings appropriate to the occasion, that I have nothing to add, except an abundance of my hearty sympathy, accompanied by earnest prayer that your religious experiences may be serene and blessed to the end. We are all in the hands of the Good Father, and his merciful overrulings are an Eternal Rock.

With best regards,
Truly yours,
Abel C. Thomas

Rufus Robbins, Jr., Private, Seventh Regiment Massachusetts Volunteers, age thirty-four years and seven months, died January 7, 1863. He is buried in his hometown of South Abington (now Whitman), Massachusetts.

APPENDIX I: CHRONOLOGY OF THE SEVENTH REGIMENT, JULY 15, 1861– NOVEMBER 16, 1862

The following chronology is taken from Rufus' letters and from Nelson V. Hutchinson's, *History of the Seventh Massachusetts Volunteer Infantry in the War of the Rebellion of the Southern States Against Constitutional Authority* (Taunton, Massachusetts: The Regimental Association, 1890), passim.

In July 1861 when it arrived in Washington, D.C., the Massachusetts Seventh Regiment of Volunteers was assigned to the Third Brigade, First Division, of the Fourth Corps of the Army of the Potomac. By December 1862, the regiment had been reassigned to the Sixth Corps, Third Division, Second Brigade.

July 15, 1861

Arrived in Washington and set up camp on Kalorama Heights on "the left side of Rock Creek, a babbling, noisy brook, whose banks were fringed with growth of woods and briers, blackberry bushes and brambles." Camp Kalorama (or Camp Old Colony) is on a hill and occupies 10 to 15 acres surrounded by a forest. Rufus' company (Company K) is located on the west side of the hill.

August 6, 1861

Moved four–five miles from Kalorama Heights to Camp Brightwood on a hill with low land all around and located "at the junction of Seventh and Fourteenth Streets, some five miles from the center of Washington." Spent the winter at Camp Brightwood.

March 11, 1862

Marched from Washington across the Potomac about fifteen miles to Prospect Hill, Va. which was about seven miles from Chain Bridge. This movement was undertaken as part of the Bull Run (Manassas) campaign.

March 14, 1862

Left Prospect Hill and returned to within a mile of Chain Bridge, spent the night there, and then returned to Camp Brightwood by a different route through Georgetown and Washington.

March 24, 1862

Boarded steamer *Daniel Webster* and sailed to Fortress Monroe, Va.

March 29, 1862

Disembarked, passed through Fortress Monroe (did not stop there), marched seven to twelve miles and went into camp at Camp W. F. Smith, Va. Stopped there about one week.

April 4, 1862

Marched eight miles and camped.

April 5, 1862

Marched ten miles and camped near Warwick Court House, Va., at Camp Winfield Scott and engaged in the siege of Yorktown.

April 14, 1862

Left Warwick Court House and marched five miles toward Yorktown. Camped within two miles of the Confederate lines.

April 20, 1862

Lightly engaged.

April 23, 1862	Returned to Warwick Court House.
May 4, 1862	Marched eight miles toward Williamsburg and camped for the night.
May 5, 1862	First battle: marched on to the field of Williamsburg at 2:30 P.M. and was subjected to a very severe artillery fire. In the evening, Company K was detailed as skirmishers, advanced under Captain Reed, with a detachment of General Davidson's Brigade, and occupied Fort Magruder at daylight.
May 10, 1862	Marched seven miles and camped near Roper's Church.
May 13, 1862	Marched thirteen miles to New Kent Court House.
May 16, 1862	Made an armed reconnaissance and succeeded in driving the rebel cavalry back toward the Chickahominy, camping at Baltimore Cross Roads.
May 17, 1862	Made a reconnaissance of six miles and camped three miles from Bottom's Bridge.
May 18, 1862	Pickets and the Eighth Pennsylvania Cavalry took possession of the Richmond and West Point Railroad to within about one mile of the bridge crossing the Chickahominy River.
May 19, 1862	Marched one mile and camped on the bank of the river near the railroad.
May 20, 1862	Company C had a very brisk skirmish before Bottom's Bridge.
May 21, 1862	Company F and Company A had a very lively skirmish and succeeded in driving away the rebels and crossing the river (two wounded, one prisoner).
May 24, 1862	Marched five miles toward Richmond.
May 25, 1862	Marched three miles and camped near Fair Oaks.

May 31, 1862	The Battle of Fair Oaks. Supported a battery of heavy artillery. (Four wounded).
June 2, 1862	Marched to Golding's Farm two miles to right front.
June 7, 1862	Marched to Savage Station.
June 25, 1862	Battle of Nine Mile Road. (Sixteen killed or wounded).
June 27, 1862	Marched eight miles toward Malvern Hill and camped for the night on the Charles-City Road.
June 28, 1862	Marched five miles and camped.
June 29, 1862	Skirmish with enemy cavalry. Marched ten miles toward the James River.
June 30, 1862	Marched two miles and camped near Turkey Island Bend.
July 1, 1862	Marched one mile to woods near Malvern Hill and went on picket.
July 2, 1862	Marched nine miles and camped near Harrison's Landing.
July 3, 1862	Marched three miles out on the front lines and camped.
August 5, 1862	Reconnaissance to Turkey Island Bend, got lost, returned to camp.
August 8, 1862	Reconnaissance to Haxall's Station, also marched over Malvern Hill.
August 16, 1862	Broke camp, marched sixteen miles down the peninsula, and camped near Charles City Court House.
August 17, 1862	Marched twenty-five miles, crossed Chickahominy, rested on bank for the night.
August 18, 1862	Marched eighteen miles through Williamsburg, camped five miles beyond the city.
August 20, 1862	Marched eight miles, passing through Yorktown, camped two miles from town on Big Bethel Road.

August 29, 1862   Marched to Yorktown. Company K boarded a "barque" that was towed down the York River, across the Chesapeake Bay, up the Potomac to Alexandria.

August 31, 1862   Arrived at Alexandria.

September 1, 1862   Disembarked, marched fifteen miles toward Fairfax Court House, then ordered back to the fortifications of Washington, Pope having received a disastrous defeat at Bull Run. Returned to within four miles of Chain Bridge, formed line of battle, and camped.

September 5, 1862   Crossed Chain Bridge, marched through Tenallytown, Md., about nine miles.

September 6, 1862   Marched to Orfutt's Cross Roads, Md., and rested two days.

September 9, 1862   Marched eight miles and bivouacked near Seneca Mills.

September 10, 1862   Marched twenty-five miles over the mountains, through Jefferson.

September 14, 1862   Marched through Burkettsville and South Mountain Gap (or Crampton Pass) into Pleasant Valley.

September 17, 1862   Marched eight miles up South Mountain through Rohrersville.

September 18, 1862   Marched through battlefield of Antietam. While passing through Turner's Gap, Companies H and K rejoined the regiment. Companies H and K had passed over Crampton's Gap. Arriving at the battlefield, the 7th formed a line of battle behind Porter's Fifth Corps, rested for a few hours, then crossed Antietam River and was placed upon the skirmish line. There was active skirmishing all along the line, but the 7th was not severely engaged.

September 19, 1862   Massed for a grand rush on Lee's lines, but the Confederates had retreated during the night.

September 20, 1862	Engaged in driving back Stuart's cavalry across the river at Williamsport.
September 23, 1862	Marched two miles to Downsville and camped.
October 18, 1862	Marched twenty-eight miles toward Hancock, Md.
October 20, 1862	Arrived at Hancock, Md.
October 21, 1862	Marched back to Cherry Run.
October 27, 1862	Marched through Clear Springs and bivouacked near Williamsport.
October 29, 1862	Marched to Downsville.
October 31, 1862	Marched fourteen miles to Rohersville.
November 1, 1862	Marched ten miles and bivouacked near Berlin.
November 3, 1862	Marched ten miles, crossing the Potomac into Virginia, and camped near Wheatland.
November 4, 1862	Marched fifteen miles and camped near Union Village.
November 5, 1862	Marched and camped near Upperville.
November 6, 1862	Marched fifteen miles and camped at White Plains.
November 9, 1862	Marched five miles and camped on Hog Mountain, near New Baltimore, Va.
November 16, 1862	Rufus leaves the Seventh and is brought by train from Warrington, through Manassas Junction, Fairfax, and Alexandria, to Carver Hospital in Washington.
December 17, 1862	Rufus leaves Washington by train for U.S. General Hospital in West Philadelphia.
December 19, 1862	Rufus arrives at U.S. General Hospital in West Philadelphia.

APPENDIX II: CAPTAIN GEORGE REED'S LETTER TO THE *ABINGTON STANDARD*

On Wednesday, June 25, early in the morning, a smart firing commenced on our right from Hooker's pickets. It soon increased, and in a little while the heavy boom of cannon broke upon our ears, which showed it was something more serious than mere picket skirmishing. I had hardly reached camp when I received orders to have my company in readiness to march at a moment's notice. Cartridges were issued, haversacks filled, canteens replenished, and shortly the order came to "Fall in," and in a very few moments the Seventh were marching with full ranks in the direction of the firing. We proceeded to the front of our lines, stacked arms, and waited some three hours, while the firing sensibly slackened.

Gens. Couch, Kearny,[1] Hooker,[2] Keyes,[3] Palmer,[4] Grover,[5] and others were in consultation on our left, and our brigade[6] finally received orders to advance. We proceeded at the double-quick some two miles, and were posted in front of De Russy's battery as a support. The batteries were firing shell very rapidly, and we had been in position but a few moments when the casing of one of the shells hit Lieut. Bullock of Fall River on the left hip, cutting his sword in two, and inflicting an awful and mortal wound. We then moved about a hundred yards to the right, and were ordered to advance, which we did, passing over dead horses, broken gun-carriages, and cut-up roads, to the extreme front of the line. We were posted across an open field, some eight hundred yards from thick woods where the rebels were stationed, with the right and left of our regiment under cover of a swamp.

My company being in the centre of the regiment, we were in a very exposed position, and soon were made aware of the presence of sharp-shooters by the whistling of bullets in very uncomfortable proximity to our ears. Major Harlow was selected by them as a mark, but though they shot all around him, they did not succeed in hitting him. We were ordered to lie down when we took our position, and this made it extremely difficult to hit us. But one rebel in a large oak fired very accurately, and, selecting Capt. Bliss of Company F as his mark, sent a ball crashing through the brain of John White, who was lying by the captain's side. The rebel did not exult long in his deed, as one of our skirmishers who had been watching for him, shot him as he exposed himself to fire, and he came rushing down into the fork of the tree ere the report of his rifle had ceased to echo in the surrounding woods.

At this time word was passed down the line for our men to lie close as possible, as the rebels were moving artillery to the front. In a few minutes they opened upon us with a sharp fire of shell, which was exceedingly well directed, and in good range, the shell bursting over in front and in rear of us, and it seemed as if half of the regiment would be disabled, but, singular to relate, not a man of our regiment was injured, while the Second Rhode Island, which lay right in our rear, lost a good many. They then commenced a terrible fire of grape and canister, which swept over us in a fearful manner some fifteen minutes, cutting shrubs as clean as with a scythe, and striking all around us without injuring a man. At dusk their firing ceased, and their artillery limbered up and retired. We seized the opportunity given us in the darkness to eat a few hard bread (or, as the men say, reduce a few squares), as we had eaten nothing since morning, and were getting faint and exhausted from our uncomfortable position.

The enemy had been driven about a mile, and we were an advance picket with orders to hold the position. As the evening advanced, it became evident that we should have great odds to encounter, as we could hear regiment after regiment march up in front of us, hear the word of command of the officers to halt, right dress, order arms, and even heard old Magruder order one Capt. Nolen to have their dead near the old oak-tree removed for burial, our skirmisher having piled them up there to some purpose.

About nine in the evening, Adjt. Packard came along the line with orders from the colonel to have the men in readiness to move in good order, and in perfect silence, a short distance to the rear. The men were formed in line, faced by the rear rank, and were moving silently away, when Company C got into some disorder, and the colonel halted the line. Some of Company K halted before I heard the order, while the rest of the company were some two rods in advance. I had just gone to the left to move them up into line, when a most severe and galling fire of musketry was opened within two hundred yards of our line from, I should think, a whole brigade. The suddenness of the attack, and the men being out of their accustomed places, threw them into some confusion, and some of the men who were in the advance faced about and fired right into our faces. The Second Rhode Island upon our right also commenced firing, without waiting to see whether they were firing upon friend or foe. Company K was in the centre of this converging fire, and never before was it my fortune to stand where the bullets flew so thick and fat as they did for some ten minutes on this eventful night. The night was very dark, and nothing could look so pretty, and at the same time so fearful, as the sheet of fire which blazed from the unseen foe in our front. Company K soon got into order, and returned the fire with interest, and nothing was heard for a time but the short, sharp commands of the officers, and the rapid crack of the rifles of the combatants.

In the height of the fire, Private Augustine Fullerton—a braver and a better soldier I have not got in my company—came up to me, and said, "Captain, I am shot badly."—"Where?" I asked him. "Right through here," he said, placing his hand upon his right breast, and the poor boy's voice quivered with emotion as he thought of his home and friends. I sent him to the rear in charge of Private J. E. Josselyn, and he had hardly started, when Private Sylvester Edmund of Scituate came up with, "Captain, they have hit me right here in the shoulder." I sent him to the rear also. These two with Private T. H. Cook who had accidentally shot himself in the foot in the afternoon, were all the casualties I had in my company.

In a short time we had the satisfaction of finding the fire of the enemy slackening, and soon it had ceased. Our men were then ordered to go to work digging rifle-pits, and though weak and exhausted, they set to work with a right good will, and in the hardest digging ever seen. They had worked about three hours when another fierce attack was made by the rebels, but the men laid down their shovels, grasped their rifles without the slightest confusion, and poured a steady and well-directed fire into the flash of the enemy's rifles till they retired. The men then fell to work again, and labored until about three o'clock A.M., the colonel moving along the lines, and encouraging the troops, exhorting them, telling them their salvation depended upon their labors.

We were indeed in a fearful position, having been ordered to hold it at all hazards,—and Col. Russell was not the man to draw back without an order,—while the rebels could bring heavy odds against us. The Rhode Island regiment[7] had been withdrawn, and the New York regiment[8] on our left was completely demoralized, their colonel being intemperate, their lieutenant-colonel being too timid to take command, and most of their officers having left, together with several hundred of the men. We had certainly a brigade to contend with, and probably a larger force was being concentrated on the rebel side. Daylight was looked for with deep anxiety, but we had determined to give a good account of the Seventh, and defend our position to the last. Just before daylight we had an order to fall back to the rifle-pits, a little more than a mile in our rear, and the men were quietly withdrawn.

In the whole affair the bearing of Company K was very gratifying to me, and I think it was owing to the coolness and example of Lieuts. Mayhew and Gurney, who rendered me valuable assistance, as indeed they have on all occasions when we have been called upon to encounter the enemy.

We now took our position in Casey's rifle-pits, and remained there until noon, or very near that time, when we returned to camp, and ate for the first time that day. It had been an exceedingly hard spell for us, as my company had been on picket-duty the night previous, so we had no sleep for two nights, with scarcely a mouthful to eat for over twenty-four hours, and at work all night—the second night—after a very fatiguing march during the day. We had hardly reached camp when a tremendous cannonading broke out on our extreme right, and continued without intermission until nine in the evening. We were ordered to be ready to march at any moment, but were not ordered out during the afternoon.

The next morning, Friday, the cannonading was resumed with great fury, and soon we had orders to fall in and march, but, instead of moving to the right, we marched to the rear, past Savage Station, nearly to the Chickahominy, and then set our faces towards the James River. We rested after a very long and fatiguing march, 'mid the dust and heat of a sultry day, through the camp of Peck's division on the extreme left of our line.

In the morning we were routed out at four, and ordered to fall in as soon as we had made our coffee, but before the order could be carried out, Company K was detailed for duty, and had to leave without breakfast. We were marched to White-Oak-Swamp Creek, and went to work to repair the road, and build a bridge across the creek. The men having had no breakfast, and nearly beaten out by the duties of the last few days, were employed some two hours in carrying huge logs and laying them across the stream.

When our regiment came up, we were ordered to fall in, and proceeded on our march. We were now on a new route in the enemy's country, and leading the advance, a position which, while one of honor, is by no means one of ease. We marched a few miles, halted, and learned we were to remain there twenty-four hours as pickets. Our line was formed in an open piece of woods with a large field of wheat in our front. We stacked arms, masked them with green boughs, posted sentries, and lay down to obtain some rest. We could have no fires near the front, and the men who wanted coffee had to proceed some distance to the rear to make it. A battery of six-pound guns was placed at the fence between the wood and the wheat-field, and masked so that the most acute scout could not have told, at a distance of a hundred yards, whether it was any thing but underbrush. We had to be on the watch all night for fear of an attack, but the day dawned without any thing of moment occurring.

The forenoon passed off very quietly, the men employing the time, as a general thing, in trying to sleep. Just after one P.M., I was lying near our stack of arms, almost asleep, when I was suddenly aroused by the tramp of horses and the yell of rebel cavalry right in our lines. Our men were lying in all shapes, without their equipments, but in an incredibly short time we were in line, and eager for the fight.

It was a surprise to us, as they had driven in our cavalry scouts, and came in so mixed up with them, that our sentries dared not fire for fear of killing our own men. The rebs rushed up to the wood, and wheeled into line, but before they formed, we poured such a fire into them that they broke in confusion, with the loss of their major commanding, two captains, and nine men killed, and some twenty-five prisoners. As they were skedaddling down the road, our battery opened on them, overturning horses and men to their evident consternation. They supposed they were attacking a small cavalry picket, and, with their five companies of cavalry, rushed confidently on to a regiment of Massachusetts infantry. We took sabres of the United-States pattern, stolen by Floyd, Sharp's carbine rifles, double-barrelled gun, and some valuable horses. Indeed, their major, though mortally wounded, thought more about his horse than any thing else, for he said he had paid two hundred dollars for him only a few days before.

In the afternoon we were relieved by the Sixth Maine, and received orders to cross White-Oak Swamp in advance, and in the night. This was regarded as rather tough, as we had no sleep the night previous, to speak of, had been exposed to a heavy rain, and had not got our blankets dry, which made knapsacks hang rather heavy. We had been on short allowance of food, had scarcely any chance to make coffee,—that sheet-anchor of the soldier,—and were nearly worn out by fatigue and exposure.

Speaking of food, the officers are sometimes placed in very unpleasant circumstance with regard to rations. Not drawing any thing from Government, and the brigade commissary being miles in the rear, on protracted marches they frequently find themselves blessed with a good appetite, and nothing to eat. As this only happens when the men are nearly out, it becomes a grave question of ways and means as to the manner of supplying our internal economy. Lieut. Gurney and myself started on this march with half a hard bread between us, and with no knowledge as to how or when we should obtain more. However, orders must be obeyed, and we started in good spirits for our long and dangerous march.

We reached the edge of the swamp at dark, when every man had orders to cap his piece, carry it at the shoulder, not to fire without orders, not to light a match, or suffer his dipper to rattle, to preserve the most perfect silence, and to keep closed up at all hazards. We then plunged into the recesses of the swamp, and so dark was it that I could not see the man before me, although my hand was on his knapsack. For eight long hours we were in this horrible hole, wading streams, stumbling over fallen trees, halting whenever we approached a more than ordinarily dangerous place, until the ground had been felt over before the main body of the regiment proceeded on their way. During one of these halts, I fell asleep standing at the head of my company, and did not wake until the leading file nearly stumbled over me. We had a battery with us of six rifled guns, two Parrotts, two three-inch rifles, and two brass twelve-pounders. Once we were halted, and the artillery ordered to the front, I concluded we were in for it, but at three A.M. we reached the James River, and the welcome words, "Break ranks," greeted our ears. At five A.M. we were aroused, and with out any breakfast, put in motion over an exceedingly dusty road at a very quick pace, and some of the men grumbled, as they had no supper the night before.

Think of it, you who live at home and think the soldier is more than paid for his services. Think of those who have endured such privations and hardships amid the swamps of the Old Dominion, and if any poor fellow gets his discharge from the service, do not pursue him with im-putations of cowardice until you have been through a tithe of what he has. You can have no idea of what is sacrificed and endured by the vol-unteer who has left home and friends to fight his and your enemy, and restore the stars and stripes to their old position as the flag of a united and happy people.

But to return. We were marched two or three miles, halted, and waited two hours in the hot sun for further orders. We then marched into a large wheat-field where the golden grain had just been harvested, and lay in huge stacks for acres and acres. Cherry-trees loaded with their tempt-ing fruit were scattered around, and an orchard of apple-trees, with ap-ples nearly ripe, was discovered by our boys. After we had stacked arms and been dismissed, away rushed the men, some for water, some for the fruit, some for straw, and some soon spied a field of potatoes, which were uprooted, and for a little while we revelled in all the luxuries of the season. Six hours after our entrance, there was a contrast in the appearance of the place to what it was when we arrived. The whole of Porter's division had entered the same field, and between their boys and ours every thing was stripped. The huge stacks of wheat had disappeared, fruit trees were despoiled, the potatoes were all dug, and the men were sighing for new fields to conquer.

In the afternoon the enemy attacked our left, and soon a furious cannonading was in progress. The *Galena* and *Monitor* were lying within a half-mile of us, and in a few minutes after the firing commenced, a signal-officer mounted the chimney of a large house in the field where we lay, and signaled to the boats. A thundering roar soon announced that the terrible gunboats had opened upon the rebel hordes. Their 155-pound shell flew with an unearthly scream over our heads, and we could hear them burst some two miles to the front, to the great terror of the rebels, and the corresponding joy of our forces. We were not ordered out that afternoon, but lay there watching the ceaseless stream of baggage-wagons and troops which continued to pour in till far into the night. The battle had ceased at dark, but once in a while the deep roar of a gun was heard, with an occasional report from a musket or rifle. Finally all was hushed save the continuous rattle of our baggage-train.

Tuesday morning all was quiet until ten o'clock, when the ball again opened. We were soon called into line, and after standing a half-hour stacked arms, and were dismissed with orders to commanders of companies to keep their men ready for a call. In about an hour it came, and we moved once more for the field of battle. Choked with dust, the perspiration streaming down their faces, the men soon presented an uncouth and strange appearance, but they toiled on, lightening their way with jokes and sarcasms upon the appearance of the various regiments, or such general officers as they passed. We met the wounded by score, some in ambulances, some on stretchers, and some on foot wending their way to the rear.

When we reached the battle-field, a grand spectacle was spread out before us. Imagine a high ridge of land where we stood, falling off gradually to a stream of water some half mile to the front, then rising as gradually on the other side of the stream to a thick wood where the rebels were posted. The length of this opening was three miles, and its width one mile. In this amphitheatre, line after line of our batteries could be seen with their supports of infantry extending for miles. Some two hundred pieces of artillery were thus disposed in various commanding positions from right to left, as far as the eye could discern.

We entered upon the left centre, halted, formed line, and stacked arms, and the men given a chance to rest. While we were watching the scene, a puff of smoke, followed by the screaming of a shell, from the edge of the wood opposite, showed that the rebels were commencing fire again.

In a few moments battery after battery on our side opened in reply, and the air was filled with shells, hissing and screaming, some bursting in mid-air, others falling among the dense masses of the enemy before they exploded, and still others plunging far over the wood, scattering their shower of fragments harmlessly around. In the midst of this terrific fire, an aid rode up to Col. Russell with, "Is this the Massachusetts Seventh?"—"Yes," said the colonel. "You are ordered to report to Gen. Hancock on extreme right, as the enemy are concentrating troops there, and he must hold his position."—"Fall in," was the word, and we were again on the march, traversing the field of battle from left to right, through woods and wheat-fields and over creeks, till at dark we reached our position. Two companies were detailed for picket-duty, when there was found to be a misunderstanding of the line by the regiment posted on our left, and on the line being re-organized by Major Harlow of the Seventh, it threw my company out, and we returned to the regiment, getting lost in the thick woods, and floundering around in the dark for an hour before we found it. The men had permission to lie down with equipments on, ready to start at a moment's notice.

In the middle of the night we were aroused, and I was ordered to have my company fall in silently and rapidly, and to move forward when the left of the regiment started. The first sound that struck my ear was the rumble of artillery in every direction, mingled with the roll of baggage-wagons, and the indescribable sound produced by the tread of many thousand men. I knew at once some very important movement was in progress. The men were soon in line, and we commenced our march, but it was difficult to move the regiment in a thick wood, with a dark night and no path, and it required all our attention not to get strayed from the main body. After groping among roots, brambles, and fallen trees, slipping into holes, and falling over prostrate timber, we emerged from the pathless wood, upon the main road, and joined the living stream that was flowing to the rear. Innumerable baggage-wagons mixed up with the artillery blocked the road for miles, while regiment after regiment passed, some at double-quick, others at rout-step.

While we were halted, awaiting orders, the colonel had the quarter-master issue what rations he had on hand. Six hard-bread were given to each man, with the caution to be saving of them, as there was no knowing when we could obtain any more. After waiting for an hour, we received our orders. The colonel sent for the officers, and said our regiment had been detailed as the extreme rear-guard, that it was a position of great danger and responsibility, and he relied on their efforts to encourage the men, and hold the enemy in check, that they had better communicate the fact to the men, so that they could act understandingly. This was done, our pieces were loaded, and officers and men resigned themselves to the almost certain fact of death or a prison, which seemed inevitable under the circumstances.

Thus we remained for an hour or more watching the different regiments as they filed past, and commenting on the terrified appearance of the great majority of the wagoners, as with oaths and execrations, and frantic lashing of the mules, they urged their heavily loaded teams over the muddy road. They had been passing for eight hours when our men were ordered to fall in, and we proceeded at the double-quick over a road where deep mud was the best travelling, crowding by the enormous number of wagons that filled the way, until half of the men fell behind from sheer exhaustion. We at length reached our designated position, and formed in divisions on a large hill near the James River, covered with splendid wheat all ready for the harvest. We remained an hour or more at this place, but the rebels not appearing, the word was again "Forward." The men wallowed through the wheat,—or what was the wheat-field, for after the passage of an army over such a place it would take a shrewd man to guess or determine what green thing had ever grown there,— and rushed with their dippers to dip up the mingled clay and rain-water which ran down the gullies, and quench their raging thirst. I drank it repeatedly, and never water tasted sweeter, though it was liquid mud. After an exhausting march we reached James River at noon on Wednesday, July 2, 1862, making eight days of hardship, exposure, and fatigue, that will challenge comparison with any campaign of this most unhappy war. The men were thoroughly worn out. It had been the battle, march, and picket, for eight days, with scarcely any food, insufficient water, no rest, and harassed in mind and body. Friends were missing on every side, no one knowing whether they were numbered with the slain or held as prisoners by the enemy. Gloom and depression pervaded every countenance as we formed our line and stacked arms in a magnificent wheat-field on the bank of the river, and then came the welcome order to "break ranks." The field, soaked by the heavy rain, trodden, by thousands of men and animals, and cut up by the artillery and wagons, was a deep bed of mud, but officers and men spread their blankets, and were soon wrapped in slumber, dreaming of their own happy firesides, the war and its attendant horrors forgotten.

NOTES

Originally published in the *Abington Standard* at Abington, Massachusetts, September 6, 1862, this letter is taken from the reprinted version in Nelson V. Hutchinson's, *History of the Seventh Massachusetts Volunteer Infantry in the War of the Rebellion of the Southern States Against*

Constitutional Authority (Taunton, Massachusetts: The Regimental Association, 1890).

1. Brigadier General Philip Kearny, Commander of the Third Division of the Third Corps.

2. Brigadier General Joseph Hooker, Commander of the Second Division of the Third Corps.

3. Brigadier General Erasmus D. Keyes, Commander of the Fourth Corps.

4. Brigadier General Innis N. Palmer, Commander of the Third Brigade of the First Division of the Fourth Corps.

5. Brigadier General Cuvier Grover, Commander of the First Brigade of the Second Division of the Third Corps.

6. Third Brigade of the First Division of the Fourth Corps.

7. The Second Rhode Island Regiment.

8. The Thirty-sixth New York Regiment.

INDEX